6 YELLOW BALLOONS

An MK's China Story

Rosalie Hall Hunt

ROSALIE HALL HUNT

Cover Photo: Courtesy Alan Luan
Dagoba — Yuan Dynasty (1280-1368 AD). Ancient Street (aka Small Pier Street), Zhenjiang, China, two blocks from Baptist Mission Compound. The characters: Zhao (Jaw) Byan: Great Dagoba.

Cover Design: Eric J. Hudiburg, justusproductions.org

ISBN 978-1-940645-95-7

Greenville, South Carolina

PUBLISHED IN THE UNITED STATES OF AMERICA

Endorsements for *6 Yellow Balloons*

We have all read the history of Baptist missions through the words of Rosalie Hunt. Now, we have the incredible privilege of reading Rosalie's own story. Once you read the story of "The Man on the Steps," your life will be changed forever, as mine was years ago when she told me this story. Seeing it in print has made an indelible imprint on my heart. I encourage every believer to read this incredible account of a family commitment to the mission of God.

David George, President
Woman's Missionary Union Foundation, SBC

Rich in family history and adorned with the memories and perspective that can only come from one who has lived as a third-culture kid, comes this riveting story from the pen of Rosalie Hunt. Rosalie grew up as an MK (missionary kid) during some of the most formative years of mission history in China. Her experience and reputation as a writer-storyteller are on full display in this informative, poignant, vibrant book. Read it, but be forewarned: You, too, may hear that compelling voice that has spoken down through the ages: "Whom shall I send, and who will go for us?"

Gordon Fort, MK from Rhodesia
Former Missionary to Botswana
Former Vice President of Overseas Operations, IMB
Special Ambassador for the President, IMB

"MK" was Rosalie's first title, and she proudly continues being a "missionary kid." She is an MK who treasured yellow balloons full of American air while growing up in Old China. She has soared through many lands as a missionary, writer, and interpreter of missions. When she comes down to earth, she refills her heart with heritage of a family that always loved and served Jesus. Rosalie Hall Hunt continues to treasure the relics of her family, while she tracks her beloved Chinese people through time and space. I thank her and salute her for sharing a breath of joyful memory with Christian readers.

Catherine Allen, Baptist historian and advocate for women in mission
President Emeritus, Woman's Department of Baptist World Alliance

The first book I ever read by Rosalie Hall Hunt was *Bless God and Take Courage: The Judson History and Legacy*. I was hooked. I became a "groupie," reading everything Rosalie wrote. Her exceptional gift of storytelling makes history come alive and ignites in the reader a desire for missions praying and involvement.

Ruby Fulbright, Missionary, 1974-1986, Zambia, Africa
Executive Director Emeritus, North Carolina WMU
Former Vice President, North American Baptist Women's Union

Rosalie Hall Hunt's books have inspired and affected our current ministry in New York City. Her insight and excitement are contagious, and each page of this book makes you want to read what happens next. *6 Yellow Balloons* honors the amazing stories of those who came before and makes me excited for the next phases of God's work in our new global situation.

Taylor Field, Send Relief Missionary, NAMB
Founder/Director, Graffiti, New York City Homeless Ministries
Author of Relentless: The Path of Holding On

Missionary children in a foreign culture learn early in life to be sensitive to the world about them. They develop vivid and detailed memories of life, family dynamics, and relationships. They remember the feelings, emotions, and scenes as well as the personal, cultural, and historical crises they encounter daily. Rosalie Hall Hunt has beautifully described all of these things — from her arrival in China as a child, and extending throughout her life. Her descriptions are as though each experience happened just yesterday. Reading this book, you will get to know an MK who grew up on the mission field and became wholly integrated into her new culture and became a truly healthy "third-culture person."

Sam James, Missionary to Vietnam
President, Vietnam Baptist Theological Seminary
IMB Regional Director, East Asia
Vice President, Europe, The Middle East and North Africa
Vice President, Leadership Development

Rosalie has previously captivated our hearts with beautiful mission stories of others. Now we sit at her feet, eager to hear her very own story. God blessed Rosalie's family with a purpose worthy of their lives. That single-minded purpose took them around the world to proclaim the love of Christ. As you read Rosalie's words, remember: His grace is still meant to be shared. May the example of these faithful servants help you find your place in His plans.

Sandy Wisdom-Martin, Executive Director-Treasurer
Woman's Missionary Union, SBC

Time stands still when you are with Rosalie Hall Hunt. I could listen to her stories for hours and still leave wanting a few more nuggets. Now we have the privilege of seeing behind the scenes of her storied life as Rosalie tackles possibly her greatest challenge to date: sifting through decades of life through photos, letters, personal experiences — and lots and lots of memories.

Jennifer Rash, President and Editor-in-Chief
The Alabama Baptist Media

Dedication

To the Children of Missionaries
MKs (missionary kids) who share a unique and lasting bond

TABLE OF CONTENTS

Foreword

Every day was a new adventure! That is how I felt growing up as an MK (missionary kid). Reading 6 *Yellow Balloons: An MK's China Story* made me laugh, cry and be homesick for the country I grew up in. It was wonderful! The common thread throughout this book is missions — and what it looks like preparing, going and coming to and from the mission field as they ministered in His name. You will love this mission story as you walk through the journey of an MK!

Rosalie Hall Hunt's story and mine have so many similarities, although in different parts of the world. Traveling on ships across the oceans, packing footlockers, barrels of clothes and supplies for four years were all a part of our lives. Reading of preparing for school years through the Calvert Course curriculum brought back memories of the way I, too, went to school for the first seven grades. What a great education!

The food and smells that I love came flooding back to me as I read of the markets where food was prepared. You will be transported to her country where customs, languages, foods and people are so different — but where Jesus was shared with so many, even a leper. The love of Jesus is so evident as seen through this missionary kid's eyes. What a privilege I had, growing up on the mission field. The legacy — the urgent need to tell others about Jesus — is a part of who MKs are.

Kaye Miller
Former national president,
Woman's Missionary Union,
and an MK from Thailand

ACKNOWLEDGMENTS

No less than several thousand times in the writing of *6 Yellow Balloons: An MK's China Story* did I wish I could ask Mama and Dad this question or that, or check with Aunt Grace about what had happened when. Their letters, however, were a gold mine and a new look into their hearts and hopes when I opened and read them more than thirty years after their deaths.

I am truly thankful for the good records kept by the International Mission Board, and even more grateful for archivist Kyndal Owens, who is highly knowledgeable about IMB holdings and superbly capable in locating needed information. Her extensive knowledge of missions work in China is impressive. Large sections of history relating to missions in China in the early part of the twentieth century has likewise been made accessible to me through the research of Baptist historian Catherine Allen. Dr. Allen has written extensively about Baptist missions in China and has graciously shared helpful information and insight.

Material in the archives of national Woman's Missionary Union has provided a valuable source of information related not only to women's work in China but also Baptist missions in Asia in general. In addition, I want to express thanks to a treasured Chinese friend of many years, Esther Wu (Wu Lo Ping Ren), whose missions roots span four generations, and whose knowledge of missions endeavors is extensive. I am especially grateful for Aiteh Zhang, my dear friend since our childhood days in Chinkiang — for her encouragement and insight, as well as her memories of her family and other Chinese pastor friends.

As with previous books, special appreciation goes to our grandson Eric Hudiburg, who prepared and edited pictures and is responsible for the cover design of *6 Yellow Balloons*. Thankfully, our daughter Alice rescued me no less than several hundred times from computer technology disaster through the whole process. Another indispensable part of the whole process is a truly capable and indispensable editor, Ella Robinson. She is more than a skillful crutch. She is a friend.

PREFACE

6 Yellow Balloons: An MK's China Story set out to be a brief look at family "once upon a time" tales — or so I thought when I decided to write an account of our family's years in China, stretching back a century ago. Not so. Mama used to love to quote Mad Bad Bobby Burns (Robert Burns, the Bard of Scotland) who so famously said, "The best laid schemes o' mice an' men gang aft agley." After getting about halfway through the first part of this account, I realized just how "gang aft agley," for the telling of the family China story was way more complicated than I originally envisioned.

Some lessons learned became starkly apparent in a hurry. Lesson One: More than a century and a quarter of history, world change, wars and rumors of wars, natural disasters and man-made ones as well, doesn't translate into a few simple chapters. Lesson Two: It is infinitely easier to write about missions heroes in the third person than first person accounts of someone you know all too well. It became traumatic in a hurry. Nevertheless, once started, somehow I was unable to stop. I felt compelled. Some of the time it was like persistently scratching at a sore spot that prefers to be left alone. Other times, the memories just flowed, as did the tears. Oftentimes the tears were caused by laughter over some crazy coincidence of colliding circumstances, other moments by a sorrow that had been buried deep but began to hurt when it was resurrected. Of one thing I am sure: I love the privilege of being an MK (missionary kid). It has been an adventure.

I sorted thousands of pictures, a task that had been conveniently put on the back burner for forty years. Next came the thousands of letters — a few dating back to the Civil War and its effects on South Carolina, many from the 1920s to 1930s, and a liberal portion written during World War II. Hundreds of letters written between 1962 and our retirement in 1996 needed to be collated and examined.

The insights I have personally gained through this journey were totally unexpected. Some have been shocking, others embarrassing, and still others, funny. It has been a special revelation of contributions my parents made, of lives they touched and blessed along their journeys, and a totally fresh appreciation of the profound blessing of having Grace Wells as my "aunt next door" and Harold and Alice Hall as my father and mother. What a privilege I have had — one totally undeserved but thereby even more appreciated. I hope their lives and dedication will also be a blessing to you.

Read on and discover how six yellow balloons provided a touchstone of the familiar for a young eight-year-old thrust in the midst of all things new.

6 YELLOW BALLOONS

An MK's China Story

A beggar in China

ONE

THE MAN ON THE STEPS

You wonder what a normal, average, well-fed nine-year-old child could possibly know about despair. By the age of nine, I had already done a lot of reading and could probably have given you a pretty decent definition of the word. But that Christmas morning in Central China, I recognized the hollow, hopeless, haunting look of utter despair in the eyes of a beggar.

Christmas in China. It was wonderful. Sad. Exciting. Incredibly lonely. Maybe Christmas becomes the most difficult season to handle when you are 10,000 miles from all that is familiar. No Christmas lights, no Ho Ho Hos from Santa Clauses on nearly every street corner. In (Chinkiang) Zhenjiang, China, there was not a jolly old Saint Nicholas to be had, no shops lighted up with decorations, no Christmas carols singing or silver bells ringing in the crisp winter air. I was nine years old, and my only hold on anything familiar was our immediate family: Mama, Daddy,

Art and Aunt Grace next door. Art was three years my senior and a bit disdainful of pesky little sisters — but then, we were the only two "foreign" children, living in our city of over a quarter million, so we had learned to live in generally amicable tolerance of each other. I could even admit to occasionally having a good time with my twelve-year-old brother.

It was 1947, and Mama worked hard to make it seem like an American Christmas. We had a lovely live tree and, wonder of wonders, during the Japanese occupation from 1938 to 1940, Mama and Daddy had managed to seal off a room in our (Yangchow) Yangzhou house by removing the door and plastering it over. Into this secret room they put some family mementos before we were forced to leave China. I was only three then, and had no memory of the secret room, just what Daddy and Mama had told me about it. But that little room miraculously survived World War II undetected, and we returned following the war and found the family treasures — including Christmas tree ornaments — patiently waiting for us. Now those ornaments adorned our spruce tree.

Planning ahead was a habit of Mama's, and she had tucked away Christmas presents for several years in the shipment that traveled to China on the SS *General Gordon*. The main items on Mama's list: a treasure trove of books. Arthur and I shared a love of reading — a love that lasted a lifetime for both of us. (Art ended up collecting first editions and rare books, and I ended up writing books — although mine were never rare!) Aunt Grace, Mama's oldest sister, had come to China in 1923, six years ahead of Mama, and she was a splendid part of our lives — especially so at Christmas. And Aunt Grace knitted; she could knit just about anything, and we knew we would find special surprises under the tree personally handcrafted by our talented aunt.

I felt quite grown up this year. After all, I was nine now, and I could be tough and suck it up and enjoy Christmas even on the other side of the world from my wonderful grandparents and cousins, and my special friend Gail who had lived across the street. The Christmas Eve service was held this year at our church just down the hill and a short block away. The familiar old carols sounded just as beautiful when sung in Chinese, and we walked briskly home in the freezing weather, excited about Christmas in the morning.

Sure enough, Art and I woke up early, anxious to finish with breakfast and quickly get to those stockings hanging invitingly on the mantel. Most importantly, all the presents under the tree beckoned to us to open them. Wanting to look appropriately festive on Christmas morning, I decked out in a little red wool skirt with a green sweater Aunt Grace had knitted that fall. Just right for Christmas — red and green. Arthur and I were impatient for breakfast to be over and get to the important business at hand. Normally, eating was at the top of my priority list (I was a sturdy child) but not *this* morning. However, just as we finished eating the last satisfying bite of breakfast biscuit, we heard a knock on our front porch door. We lived in one of the two mission houses built back in the 1880s. Being on the side of a mountain and with a surrounding wall to protect from marauding bandits, we nearly always knew in advance when someone was coming. Our district was called Yin Shan Men ("Silver Mountain Gate"), and most of the foreign legations were in this area. Not expecting morning guests, we were surprised to hear the knock. Who might it be? I spoke up, "I'll go see who it is," thinking I could make short work of this interruption of our important Christmas morning tradition.

We had a large screened-in porch with cement steps leading up to the door. Situated on the side of what was known as Yin Shan ("Silver Mountain"), it required good muscles to quickly climb our cobbled driveway and then come up two flights of steps. To my surprise, I didn't see anyone standing at the door. Then, looking down, I saw him. The man kneeling on the steps was looking up at me. The first thing I noticed were his hands — gnarled and twisted — with most of the fingers just mere stumps. He had those hands lifted in supplication. Looking at his face, I saw that part of his nose was gone, and part of each ear was missing. Those feet. No shoes and just stumps of toes. It was cold on the side of our mountain, and the wind could be cutting — even on a mild day. This was no mild day. I guess he could read the expression of anguish on my face as I looked into his eyes. In an instant, I realized that this man was not only a beggar (we saw many of those in post-World War II China) but a leper as well. What chance did this poor man have? And how on earth could he have had the strength to crawl all the way up the cobbled drive and then climb up two flights of steps?

Even a child could interpret the expression in the old leper's eyes. It was a look of hopelessness, of despair. Looking earnestly into my face, the leper moved his cupped hands up beseechingly and said, *"Chíng gáy wō myàn bāw chr bah; wóe ùh sžle"* (Please give me some bread. I am starving). I looked into those pleading eyes and did what anyone with a thread of compassion would have done. *"Dúng eē shyàh"* (Wait a minute). I spoke quickly and headed to the kitchen — Christmas tree, stocking and presents far from my mind. Gathering up two hands full of bread and biscuits, I returned to the steps — only to find that the beggar had not moved. He still had those leprous hands uplifted. I took the bread and biscuits and carefully placed them in his hands. He was shaking so badly that two of the biscuits fell on the steps — he glanced up at me, then down at the crumbles and spoke quite matter-of-factly, *"Wóe bùh néng dzàu tah, wō ùh sžle"* (I can't waste any. I'm starving). The leper took those stumps of fingers and picked up every little crumb from the gritty steps. And I stood there weeping, a nine-year-old child, and God spoke to my heart in that searing moment. Without hesitation, I responded, vowing, *God, someday let me come back to China and tell people like this that* You *are the bread of life.*

With what felt like a bleeding heart, I watched the leper as he quickly ate some of the bread, put the rest in his pockets, and slowly, haltingly made his way down those steps, over the cobblestones and down to the gate. As I watched him painstakingly make his way out the entrance, I realized that I did not even know the leper's name. I never saw him again, but he changed my life. And as I grew into a bit of deeper understanding of God's Word, I recalled the words of Jesus when He said, "Inasmuch as you have done it unto one of the least of these My brethren, you have done it unto Me." Nonetheless, all I could think that extraordinary Christmas morning was, *Oh God, I wish I had done more.*

Stockings and presents and Christmas candy faded away in my heart as

I slowly walked back inside to join the family. I was still a little nine-year-old child, far from what was comfortable and familiar in my life. But now there was a profound difference. I had experienced a Christmas guest that redirected the trajectory of the rest of my life. *Lord, let me someday come back and tell people like this that You are the bread of life.* And, thank God, He let me do just that.

Ah, but the story didn't begin here — it began long years earlier, on a farm in South Carolina and in rural northeastern Oklahoma. And much of it sounded like "once upon a time" stories.

*High school graduate Alice with her
mother, Ann Judson Wells, 1918*

TWO

SUNBEAMS AND STORY TIME

I wish I could have known Mama when she was a little girl. There are so many family stories that make me want to be "in the moment" and experience life at the dawning of the twentieth century and understand what life must have been like for her. Of course, Mother told me countless stories, and her sisters and parents added to the tales, but I wish I knew more. Then recently I had the pleasant surprise of obtaining a copy of her earliest correspondence, dating back to 1922, with the (then) Foreign Mission Board and learning bits and pieces that were new to me. It was rather like someone handing me a fresh new portrait of my mother, Alice Mellichamp Wells, who was born in 1901 in Sumter, South Carolina — the third of five children, each one born a neat stair-step two years apart.

Alice couldn't wait to be a Sunbeam! The morning after her sixth birthday, the great day arrived. Alice was old enough now to join big sisters

Grace and Rhett at Sunbeam Band, and she insisted on wearing the new flower-sprigged dress her Mamma had just finished sewing for her. Best of all, Alice's Aunt Edith, who lived with them — tall, stately, gentle Edith — was the Sunbeam Band leader at Bethel Church. Her sister Grace was already ten, and Rhett had just had her eighth birthday last week. Younger than Alice by two years was their sole brother, four-year-old Henry Herbert. The family's baby was Mamie, affectionately known as "Dumps," although no one was quite sure how the black-haired little imp of a two-year-old had acquired that unusual endearment of a nickname.

The Wells clan had been part of the fabric of Bethel Church for at least five generations. Alice's great-great-great-grandfather Richard Wells and his wife, Mary Haynsworth Wells, were charter members of Bethel at its founding in 1780. The historic church predated the Revolutionary War in which Richard had been a drummer in Captain Matthew Singleton's regiment, serving with Francis Marion, the famed Swamp Fox of Revolutionary lore.

Alice couldn't remember a time when she *wasn't* in Sunday School and church and always at protracted meetings in the middle of summer. This was the first time, however, that *she* could be a Sunbeam, and it felt wonderful. Faraway places with strange-sounding names held an endless fascination for the little blue-eyed girl. Those blue eyes were riveted on Aunt Edith that afternoon at Sunbeams as her aunt told the story of a little boy, Adamu, in East Africa, who had not heard the good news about Jesus. Like each of her siblings, Alice dearly loved stories, but this one took on special significance for a softhearted young six-year-old. She was struck in that moment with a penetrating thought that planted a tiny seed in her tender sensibilities. Someone needed to tell Adamu. That first impression was indelibly printed on her heart, and never withered over the remainder of her long and adventurous life.

Following her first afternoon in Sunbeams, Alice couldn't wait to get back to the family farm to tell Grandmà about it. Henry Wells' mother, Eliza Mary Mellichamp Wells, had lived with them ever since the untimely death of her husband, Richard, in 1895, when he was just forty-five years old. None of the five grandchildren had been born at the time, so Grandpà was simply the familiar and imposing portrait that always hung over the mantel. Now Mamma and Daddy could tell good stories, but the best and most intriguing were stories told by Grandmà. She was full of tales about the Wells and the Mellichamps, dating back to the 1690s, when the first of the family, mostly French Huguenot and English settlers, arrived in Charleston Harbor. Alice adored her grandmother and was secretly proud of having Grandmà's maiden name as her own *middle* name. Alice and her siblings eagerly soaked in engrossing accounts of family lore.

Born in 1848, Grandmà could clearly remember her growing-up days on James Island, just off the coast of Charleston. She vividly recalled the circumstances surrounding the first shot of the Civil War, when a young cadet from The Citadel in Charleston, Ensign George Haynsworth, fired on Fort Sumter from across the bow of the *Star of the West*. Eliza Mary's family was forced to flee their home on James Island to live with relatives in Charleston, where they felt safer. No sooner had they moved in with an uncle, however, than a catastrophic fire destroyed much of the city, including their new residence. Quickly they moved again, this time to Sumter to stay with relatives. Eliza Mary's father, Edward Henry, was away at war, an engineer with the Confederacy. When recounting that story, Grandmà always explained to her eager young listeners that the young cadet who fired that first shot of the war was actually their distant cousin, one of the myriad of Wells relatives sprinkled across the state. South Carolina was full of old family names related to the Wells clan: Haynsworths, Furmans, Perdriaus, Fogles, Michaus, Cuttinos, and on the list went.

On that particular afternoon following Sunbeams, young Alice's mind wasn't on illustrious South Carolina forbears, but rather on children half a world away in Africa — children who did not know about God's love. "Grandmà," she spoke eagerly, "I wish I could go tell Adamu that God loves him, too." Grandmà smiled in her gentle way and reached out for Alice's small hands, taking them in her own warm ones, and assuring her, "My child, you just pray each day that God guides you to tell about His love, and one day you may do that very thing — tell *many* little boys and girls that

God loves them, too." Ever after, the memory of that moment at Grandmà's knees never faded, and her insightful prediction became a reality.

Most of Alice's earliest recollections were built around home in the Privateer area near Sumter. Her father, Henry, had built the place on land long held by the family. About the time she became a teenager, however, Henry Wells built a larger house at nearby Tindal. It was also built on a section of the original Wells land — and, thereafter, the Tindal place was called the Wells farm. Alice realized that her daddy was known as a farmer — for after all, he owned the place. Nonetheless, his real genius was mechanics. Henry Herbert Wells could both design and build almost anything. He was one of the first in South Carolina to can vegetables, and with that skill he conducted quite a thriving business from their back porch at Tindal.

Alice's great-grandfather, Henry Haynsworth Wells, had accrued a lot of land in the 1800s. He built Mt. Hope in 1848, and when they were small, the Wells children loved to visit the old plantation house standing proudly at the end of a row of majestic cedars. They spent many an afternoon exploring the grounds of Mt. Hope. In the house itself, the rooms seemed to strangely echo, rooms that had seen a lot of living for several generations of Wells. By this time, only Great Aunt Cal (Carolina Edith), Daddy's aunt, lived there. She had a companion to keep her company, and the two elderly spinsters just rattled around in the cavernous rooms originally constructed to house a large and industrious family. Aunt Cal had been born before the Civil War began, and in the eyes of the Wells children was herself a rather stern piece of family history, one harking back to a long-gone day. Then Aunt Cal decided to move to a smaller house on the property — and the year Alice was six, Mt. Hope burned to the ground. How the fire started ever remained a mystery, but that took nothing away from the romance of roaming around the plantation grounds and wondering what life had been like in bygone days.

The children had another great aunt, Cal's sister Matt, who lived with the family at Tindal. Great Aunt Matt was all that was gentle and loving, and the children adored her. In their close-knit family, however, it was

Henry Herbert and Ann Wells who had the greatest influence on Alice's life. Mamma, as Alice called her, had come from Orangeburg long years ago to be a companion for Aunt Cal at Mt. Hope. Young Henry Wells had quickly come to appreciate the gentle and quiet Ann Judson Fogle, and they married in 1896.

Anyone familiar with Baptist history and heritage immediately recognized the origins of Ann Judson Fogle Wells' rather unusual combination of given names. Born in 1866, Ann's firmly Baptist parents named her for America's first woman missionary — the renowned Ann Hasseltine Judson — who was known as Woman of the Century in nineteenth-century America. Ann Judson Fogle was a restful person to be around, with her gentle, serene nature. That said, her intelligence and depth of faith ran deep and bore abundant fruit in the lives of her five children, producing one minister and two international missionaries. A fourth daughter became a schoolteacher and longtime Sunbeam Band director, and the fifth remained at home to care for the older family members while still managing to give an astounding number of dollars to missions, especially to the Lottie Moon Christmas offering.

Ann poured herself into her brood of five and learned to read each of her little ones and understand their particular needs and skills. She detected early on an endearing trait in her middle child. From an early age, Alice showed an unusual sensitivity toward the needs and wishes of others, and, with a maturity beyond her years, would happily share her toys with her siblings and quickly go to their aid if they needed help. Ann encouraged this selflessness she discerned in her little girl and, indeed, Alice grew into a woman who, to a remarkable degree, instinctively put the needs of others before her own.

Most people in the Sumter area automatically assumed the whole Wells family had been Baptists from colonial days. However, the children discovered that every one of the last four generations of Wells sons had married Episcopalian women, each of whom ended up becoming a faithful and dedicated Baptist. Alice loved to meander with her sisters through the Wells family cemetery, located not far from their house.

They would wander among the headstones, reading aloud the names of each of those ancestors, beginning with Great-Great-Great-Grandmother Mary Hesse Haynsworth. Her family, many generations Episcopalian, had emigrated from Switzerland. Mary and Richard Wells had been joined in marriage by the renowned Richard Furman, Mary's brother-in-law and the leading Baptist statesman in South Carolina. Then Great-Great-Grandfather Edward married beautiful Esther Perdriau, an Episcopalian from low-country Beaufort. Next, their son, Great-Grandfather Henry Haynsworth of Mt. Hope, married Ann Michau from Williamsburg, yet another Episcopalian. And, of course, there was Richard Wells, their own Grandpà, whose picture hung above the mantel. He had married young Eliza Mary from James Island, where her Uncle Stiles Mellichamp had been the Episcopalian rector. Also in the family, though, was Eliza's father's older brother, Uncle Thomas, who was a Baptist minister, and he performed their wedding ceremony.

Grandmà loved telling the children stories from the war years. Those had been harrowing times and remained vivid in her memory. She even showed the children a letter she had received from a cousin forty years ago, during the war. Cousin Mary Agnes lived not far away on the outskirts of Columbia. Agnes wrote about General Sherman marching through their county, destroying as he went, and his troops setting fire to Columbia. Cousin Mary Agnes and her family hid for three entire days; Sherman missed their place by half a mile. And the irony was, this happened less than two months before peace was signed. Grandmà's tales made those ancestors and bygone days come alive in the minds of her grandchildren.

Their own Grandpà Richard had run away to enlist in the army when he was but sixteen. Although wounded two times, he managed to live through several battles as well as survive typhoid fever. Richard was last wounded in Virginia when he was serving with General Lee in the final months of the war. Grandpà managed to make his way home about a month after the surrender at Appomattox Courthouse. Four of the five Wells sons fought in the war. James Edward, one of the children's great uncles, died early in the conflict, but Henry, the eldest son, had lived until just a week before the final surrender. Henry was mortally wounded at the Battle of Petersburg. Alice's eyes always filled with tears when Grandmà spoke of this uncle who shared their own daddy's name.

Alice particularly enjoyed hearing Grandmà tell of her own childhood on James Island and the carefree days prior to war. She would chuckle a bit when someone teased her about being a staunch Episcopalian until marrying into the fiercely Baptist Wells family. "Ah," she would remind them, "but you must remember, my sixth great-grandfather was William Screven, and he was the founder of the first Baptist church in the South — right down there in Charleston. I'm thinking," she would add, "that the Wells clan can't top *that* for Baptist credentials!"

Grandmà never seemed to tire of talking about years gone by. Like nearly everyone living in those post-war years, Grandmà's life had been marked by tragedy. Her beloved father, Edward Henry, died in a northern prison camp just two months after the war ended. She was only a tender sixteen when the news reached them. "Miss Mamie," as everyone outside the immediate family called her, had a prized possession, her last gift from her father. She loved to tell the account of how her treasured melodeon came to her on a Christmas morning. Each of the grandchildren, as they learned to play the piano, would be privileged to sit on the little round stool and play a melody on the priceless melodeon. Grandmà recounted that at the time of her thirteenth birthday in December 1861, just when she was missing her father so dreadfully at Christmastime, a notice arrived that there was a package waiting for her at the train depot. A family retainer quickly went to the station to pick up the mystery package and soon returned, bearing on his shoulders a rather heavy-looking oblong box. Eliza Mary had no idea what her papa might have sent. The label said Boston. How could that be? Boston was far north, and they were in the middle of a war. Nonetheless, the box had somehow managed to arrive in Sumter. Carefully opening the crate, Eliza Mary's eyes widened in wonder to discover inside a beautifully crafted melodeon with clever legs that folded down, and a special little indented circle to hold her lamp while she played. She was in raptures. With this prize on which to practice, the accomplished young musician soon became organist at their church. Now, a generation later, young Alice loved to run her fingers over the ivory keys and try to pump harmonious sounds from the little organ. That melodeon was many years later passed down to Alice's own daughter, Grandma's only great-granddaughter. To this day, she also loves to touch those keys and coax out melodies that ring with the echoes of the 1800s.

During those school years, Alice not only loved Sunbeams, she loved all her classes at their small country school, and Sunday School at Bethel every week. When she was ten, she made public one Sunday morning at Bethel Church that she had asked Christ to be her Savior. Knowing the Wells family as they did, the church community realized full well that this child, like her older siblings, clearly knew her own heart. She was gladly received for baptism. The church family also understood that at least two of the Wells girls were hoping to become missionaries. Of course, "being a foreign missionary" was frequently heard from the children and youth who had been in Miss Edith Wells' Sunbeam Band. In the case of the Wells girls, however, it became reality.

It was neither easy nor convenient for the five siblings to get to high school in Sumter, for there was no such thing as public transportation. Nonetheless, education was a priority with the family, and their parents saw to it that each child received a high school education. Each one, in turn, graduated from Sumter High School with high marks. Grace went off to Winthrop College with the goal of preparing for a life spent in mission service overseas. That same year, Alice, four years younger, started high school. She, too, had been openly talking about going as a missionary ever since she had turned seven. Rhett, the second daughter, more quiet and introspective than the others, shied away from leaving home, but ended up teaching at the local school for years and becoming a pillar of Bethel Church and the strength of its missionary society.

Grace graduated from Winthrop in 1918, and Alice entered the college that fall. Grace headed to Louisville, Kentucky, and the Woman's Training School at Southern Seminary in September. Matriculating at Winthrop, Alice learned to her delight that there were actually seven other young women at the college who cherished the same career dreams as she. Amazingly, from that single class, three of those students, all Baptists, ended up going to China as missionaries and remaining friends for the rest of their lives. (Martha Franks and Olive Lawton had wonderful missions stories of their own to relate.) Alice thrived on Latin and English, devouring literature and thoroughly enjoying diagramming sentences, much to the amusement of many of her less-interested classmates. However, always in her mind was that single motivating goal — missions service. How it was going to happen she didn't know. She simply accepted that this was God's call on her life.

Alice badly wanted to go straight from college to seminary, but money was proving a problem. There was too little of it. Alice had been attending college mostly on scholarship money, and Mamma and Daddy now had her brother Henry at Furman, and "Dumps" (Mamie) was going to start Winthrop that fall. There was no money for seminary right now. Alice's mind and heart were also dealing with a personal matter at the same time. Like most of her contemporaries, she had dreams of a loving husband and children but had to come to grips with the fact that if she set her focus on a missions career, those dreams of marriage and family might have to vanish. The struggle in her heart was very real, but her final decision never wavered. She was going to answer this call. If a husband appeared, that would be wonderful. If not, she was determined to go alone. Graduation arrived, and, degree in hand, Alice faced her situation. There was no money for seminary right now, but she was determined to find a way to make it happen.

Alice Mellichamp Wells at 25

THREE

THE *SS EMPRESS OF ASIA*

From as early as I can remember, Mama had an endearing way of gnawing at her lower lip when deep in thought. This particular morning, just one month after graduating from Winthrop, she absentmindedly gnawed at her lower lip as she filled out a Student Volunteer Form for the Foreign Mission Board. Grace, now in her final year at the Woman's Training School, had written to let her know that the Board liked for those contemplating mission service to establish contact with them. Alice realized she still needed seminary training, but her intentions had been set on this goal of mission service for nearly fifteen years. The Board's form, spread on the desk before her, asked: When ready to sail? She answered as honestly as she knew how, explaining her lack of funds for seminary just now, but that she was planning to start her training the following year — meaning she could be ready to sail in 1925.

Her next step was to find a job and save money for seminary. Holly Hill High School felt fortunate to be able to hire the recent Winthrop graduate to be their English and Latin instructor. The first day or so, the young fellows in Miss Wells' classes observed the petite young woman with the fresh young face, bright blue eyes, and softly curling brown hair and quickly decided she was going to be a timid and undemanding instructor. They soon discovered the error of their thinking, for she expected nothing but a student's best and had a latent talent for eliciting just that from them. More than one hulking young man discovered that even something as dull as diagramming a sentence could be interesting when pretty Miss Wells smiled and told you what a nice job you were doing with your work. Her students adored their young teacher. Even though her heart was set on her ultimate aim for foreign mission service, Alice, nonetheless, planted herself firmly in the present — focusing on teaching at the high school and working with the young people at Holly Hill Church. The Royal Ambassadors idolized their pretty young leader; she always made missions work around the world seem so immediate. Both male and female in the Holly Hill BYPU (Baptist Young People's Union) were thrilled to have her as their advisor. However, the best days of all for her were those when she received letters from Grace. Her oldest sister was already on her way to China and the fulfillment of her call, and Alice longed to join her as soon as possible. The two sisters had shared this special bond for years.

Alice next taught for a year in Bishopville, again immersing herself in the work of the local church and carefully saving all the money she could for seminary expenses. The school understood that likely she would not be with them long, for she had been clear about her objectives. Nonetheless, when the time came, everyone hated to see her go; they had fallen in love with the dedicated and capable young schoolmarm. Having faithfully saved most of her salary by boarding with a local family, finally Alice had nearly enough money to attend seminary in Louisville. And then, additional help arrived. South Carolina WMU, wanting to invest in a promising young life who felt such a clear call, gave her a scholarship so she could attend the Woman's Training School. When she opened the letter and read the good news, her first thought was, *I'm nearer to China! This scholarship means nearer still!*

Seminary was especially meaningful to Alice, because all her course work was in some way geared toward her ultimate goal of serving overseas. She loved the atmosphere of "House Beautiful," as everyone called the building that housed the young women. Miss Carrie Littlejohn and then Miss Janie Bose were directors during her years, and their gracious supervision created a wonderful learning atmosphere. Some of her richest memories in later years were tied to special gatherings in the Fannie E. Heck Chapel. Miss Heck had died when in her fifties, but her incredible spirit and vision lingered on in the ambiance of the training school. Alice's classmates all shared many common goals, each one with some personal commitment to God's call, although most of them were not planning for overseas service. Alice was gratified with the academic standards maintained by the young women at WTS. They invariably ranked at the top of their seminary classes, although most did not concentrate on being vocal in class. In that day, feminine reticence was much admired.

Many a young seminarian ended up meeting her future husband while at Southern Baptist Theological Seminary, and Alice could have well done the same. However, she was careful to learn about the background of the various young ministerial students who frequently showed an interest in getting to know her better. If the young man did not share her same goal of mission service overseas, she kindly but firmly did not allow a relationship to develop. There was one young seminarian in particular who neither quickly nor easily took "no" for an answer. He was an outstanding student, and all the professors predicted a bright future for him in the pulpit. Nonetheless, he felt no sense of call to missions, and, therefore, Alice kindly, gently, and persistently refused to allow their relationship to become serious. He was most personable, and sometimes in the still of the night she would question whether she was doing the right thing. Yet, always in the fresh light of a new dawn, she would renew her resolve and remain committed to her call, even if it meant going to China alone. Several of Alice's friends questioned her judgment, but those who knew her best understood the strength of her commitment.

Although a bachelor's degree in Christian education and missions could be attained in two years, Alice felt the need of even deeper training available in a third year of coursework that would result in a master's degree. Her two-year scholarship was nearing the end, and then Providence stepped in once again. Dr. Gaines S. Dobbins, renowned professor, later to be called the Father of Christian Education among Baptists, recognized unusual potential in Miss Wells. (Dobbins later served as seminary president and remained active in teaching at various seminaries until nearly ninety.) She had flourished in his classes, and he discerned an unusual depth of mind in the dedicated young student. Alice was both surprised and thrilled to receive a request from Dr. Dobbins to serve as his fellow and complete an important third year of training. Since she was in contact with the Foreign Mission Board, she wrote to tell of this additional possibility for further study. Dr. T.B. Ray, board president, answered immediately, advising her to take advantage of this unique opportunity.

It was a year rich in learning, and graduation felt like another milestone reached. But then, achieving her long-awaited goal hit still another snag. The Foreign Mission Board was not appointing new missionaries because of lack of money. Alice was on the horns of a dilemma. She had the necessary training, had filled out all the necessary appointment applications and had met all the requirements. This time it was lack of funds on the part of the *Board*. Typical for Alice, she swallowed her disappointment and went to work, this time as Baptist Student Union Director at Florida State College for Women (now Florida State University in Tallahassee). Their board of directors understood that Miss Wells was a candidate for foreign missions but wanted her to come as director and serve as long as she could. Also typical for Alice, in addition to actively leading students in missions activities, she was leader of the Young Woman's Auxiliary (now Baptist Young Women) and the RA leader (Royal Ambassadors). By this time, she felt happily familiar with that age group.

Financial conditions in America were the major obstacle blocking the path for Alice, and she spent a good bit of time praying for patience. Every letter from Grace was a new prod and a reminder of where Alice's heart had already gone. Grace finished language school in Nanking and began working in the provincial capital of Jiangsu Province, Chinkiang (now Zhenjiang).

Every detail in Grace's letters — first language school ups and downs, and then beginning work in women's evangelism and teaching — made Alice just that much more eager to get there. She worked hard to make each day count and not simply wish away the present while longing for the future.

On June 1, 1929, a hot summer morning in Tallahassee, Alice went to her post office box, hoping for a letter from Grace and the family, for Grace had just returned to South Carolina on furlough. Six years had been a long time, and she was eager to get a personal account of life in China. Upon reaching the post office, she found no letters from Sumter. Instead, there was an envelope postmarked Richmond, Virginia. Unusual, since the last word she had from Richmond was that there was no money to appoint new missionaries. Consequently, her heart skipped a beat, wondering what this letter might be. Then, her heartbeat began to accelerate in earnest as she read the message. Dr. Ray stated that he knew she was very aware of present conditions, with the board unable to appoint new missionaries just now. However, he wrote, "an emergency had arisen at Shanghai College, making it necessary for our Board to send out two young women this summer who will teach English in that institution. It would be a marvelous opening for witnessing for the gospel." By this point, Alice was nearly trembling with excitement, as she read on:

"I write to ask whether, if the Board should decide that it could appoint you to this work you would be willing to sail early in August. … we are appointing only an occasional missionary where an emergency arises. I think the opportunity presented you in Shanghai is a very great one. Of course, it will be very delightful for you to be in the same mission where your sister is, the Central China Mission. Please write me at once and let me know whether you could consider appointment with a view to being sent out on the date above mentioned."

Would she consider it? Absolutely — here was the answer to the prayers first uttered by a little seven-year-old on the farm in Sumter, South

Carolina. With great excitement and shaking fingers, she sat at her desk and composed a quick note to the family to let them know the wonderful news. And then she sent a Western Union telegram to Dr. Ray: "Letter just received. Am ready for appointment. Letter follows. Alice M Wells." She followed the telegram with a letter to Dr. Ray, addressing needed issues in more detail and concluding by saying, "I am too happy and excited just yet to say all I mean, but I have not failed to realize and appreciate the truly great opportunity offered by this opening." By return mail, Ray responded that the Board would meet the following week and her name would be offered for appointment.

Alice left Tallahassee the next week and returned to Sumter to begin packing and preparing. Spending a few last weeks with her beloved parents loomed large in her thoughts. Theirs was the huge sacrifice, with two of their daughters half a world away and their only son in seminary and likely to be serving far from home as well. She would have a personal touch at home in knowing how to prepare for the field since Grace was on furlough and they could have a few weeks together. In a few weeks, Dr. Ray wrote that the Board would meet on July 16 to officially appoint her, but she must not wait for that, because her passport must be issued at once. That required a trip to Charleston to appear before the district court clerk. By this time, Alice was a bundle of anticipation and mixed emotions — the surprise and joy of actually going to China at last, mixed with the pain of goodbyes to dear ones, for the Wells were a close-knit family.

She learned from Dr. Ray that her traveling companion would be Juanita Byrd of Mt. Olive, Mississippi, who would be the other emergency English teacher at Shanghai University. The next two months were a whirl in Alice's memory as she got her passport, packed, prepared, said painful goodbyes, and boarded the train to head for a new life of adventures. Even the itinerary to the West Coast was exciting to a young teacher who had spent all her life in the South. First stop was Louisville and a day's visit with her beloved brother, H.H., as she called him. Henry Herbert was a seminary student at Louisville and happily took a day away from classes. Then she went to visit friends from her seminary days and say more goodbyes. She was thrilled to find that her first principal, Miss Carrie Littlejohn, had not yet left WTS, and the new principal, Mrs. Bose, (another friend of Alice's) invited her to lunch. Several former classmates joined the luncheon party and gave Alice a royal sendoff. Later in the afternoon, she enjoyed a special visit with Dr. and Mrs. Dobbins, who felt a personal investment in the life of this promising young fledgling missionary.

Goodbyes again, and then she took the Mountaineer Rail to Chicago, where she met Juanita Byrd for the first time. (They became lifelong friends, and Juanita was in Alice's wedding four years later.) Writing a long letter home as the train made its way across the width of America, Alice described her impressions of all the sights and experiences. The two young women reached Vancouver in time to have a day exploring that Canadian city before boarding the steamer, the *SS Empress of Asia,* glistening white in the sparkling waters of the Pacific. Alice was so excited that it was difficult to absorb the significance of this moment — she was actually sailing to China. This had been some twenty-one years in the making, and as she stood at the rail, watching the coast of America grow ever smaller in the distance, it was as if her heart stood on tiptoe so it could peer into the future waiting for her on a distant shore.

*Alice Wells (right) and shipmate Juanita
Byrd boarding the* SS Empress of Asia, *1929*

FOUR

SHANGHAI

When Mama stepped on the *SS Empress of Asia,* it was rather like walking into the next part of her life. She and Juanita were both too excited to get much sleep that first night aboard, not to mention the motions of sleeping on a moving bed, which took even more nights of adjustment. They had a tiny cabin that they shared with a third young missionary, Rachel Newton, who was returning to her field of Chefoo (Yantai) after a furlough. Young Rachel was an old China hand, so she was really a boon for the two new appointees. Her grandfather had been a missionary in Africa, and her parents were now serving in Tsingtao (Qingdao), China. She told her cabin mates about her father's very "missionary" name — William Carey Newton — and shared cultural bits and pieces about living in China, giving them a bit of orientation to their new home as they sailed.

During the voyage, Alice wrote a sort of journal to family in Sumter, intending to mail the lengthy letter from Kobe when the ship docked there. She began with writing about the three of them, explaining, "We three are together so much that the other missionaries onboard started calling us 'The Baptist Triplets.'" Then, Alice continued to fill the letter with delightful accounts of unique experiences like this one written after about ten days out at sea: "Tonight some of us went up to the bow of the ship — at the very point — and watched moonlight glistening on the ocean."

Right on schedule, the *Empress* docked at Shanghai Harbor on August 23. Alice wrote at 11 p.m. that night, giving vivid details of her first day in the long-awaited land of her dreams. To all those at home, she penned, "The trip has been happy and pleasant, but just sort of a dream. Now, I'm *really* here, and I must get down to earth once more." She went on, her excitement bubbling over onto the paper: "If only you could have been in that waving crowd on the dock, Grace, as we had planned. But I'm glad for you that you can be at home this year, and I'm glad for you folks to have her." Quite a crowd had gathered to meet the new missionaries, and Alice wrote in detail, knowing that Grace would especially be interested in who was there. Grace would particularly appreciate that Mary Phillips, her co-worker in Chinkiang, had made the trip to Shanghai to welcome Grace's younger sister. Alice was touched by the gesture, for Grace had written glowingly about Mary.

As she wrote that first night, Alice told them, "The college folks could not have been nicer," and she named each one. Upon arriving on the campus of the university, still more missionaries came to welcome the new teachers. Mary Phillips wanted to take her to Chinkiang for a quick visit before school started on September 9. Of course, Alice was thrilled to go to Grace's home in China and to send to Sumter a fresh report about Chinkiang for Grace.

Wonderful … exhilarating … confusing … contradictory … early perceptions of China were bouncing around in Alice's head those first impressionable weeks, sometimes colliding and contradicting each other. Her first months in China were so full of work, new experiences, a new culture, and a new language that it was difficult for a novice missionary to absorb. She had a full class-load of freshmen coming from all sorts of English-learning backgrounds, and that alone kept her on her toes. She was amazed at the courtesy and politeness that seemed innate in Chinese students. To a person, they showed the greatest respect for teachers, and to a student, they adored the pretty Miss Wells who was so patient with them. Alice was sponsor of one of the Christian fellowship groups, and those students were able to know her even better and would cling to her every word. Teaching English to students for whom it was a second language was an enormous challenge in itself, to say nothing of all the other "new" things in her life.

The campus was a beautiful one, with lovely shade trees and a real collegiate atmosphere. Alice lived on campus in the women's building, with an upstairs room that had a wonderful view of the Whangpoo River that flowed by very close to campus. She could look out her bedroom window and see the ocean steamers from all over the world heading into port in Shanghai. She loved seeing the sails passing by and watching the quaint Chinese junks — so different from small American vessels — as they drifted along. There was never much free time, however, with so many papers to grade. Her first Double Ten celebration was a nice break in routine, as China commemorated the national day of the Republic of China. The Double Ten celebration marked the end of the Ching (Qing) Dynasty and the establishment of the republic.

By the end of her first semester in late January, Alice felt like she had been inundated with papers. She wrote home, "Really, I've never been so sick of anything of the kind as I've been of papers for a week or more. Some days I'd just decide that I was no good to anybody. Well, my reports are now in the Dean's office, and for a little while I'll have a rest from that part of my schedule." Alice loved the students far more than she loved grading endless piles of essays and exams. Now she was anticipating spending Chinese New Year, the country's largest celebration of the year, in Chinkiang.

The school's administration talked of letting the new missionaries have some time to study the Chinese language, but that plan was largely tabled as even more course work came the way of Alice and Juanita, with more and more students matriculating. Alice felt keenly about language study, believing she could not adequately share the message of God's love without a knowledge of the heart language of those with whom she worked. She felt like she was on the horns of a dilemma, being in a country with such crying need of the message of salvation, but feeling she had neither the time nor the tools to do just that. Alice looked on every student contact as an avenue of ministry but felt conflicted about being so limited in ways to share the message.

Her favorite times every week were the Sunday School class she taught and the fellowship groups she led. Those were the means by which she could really get to know her students and their particular needs and hopes. Some of them stood out in her mind, occasionally because one was more vocal, or possibly demanding, than the others. Mostly though, Alice could discern special potential in a student and would accordingly look for a way to encourage that individual to discover new avenues of growth. Some students simply impressed her with their personalities or evident potential. One such freshman was a young student from Canton, Miss Tang Ywè Míng (Tong in Cantonese). In Chinese, the last name is given first. Miss Tong captured Alice's attention during the first week of classes, originally because of her excellent command of English, and soon because of her uniform kindness and thoughtfulness to her classmates. Miss Tong was also in Alice's fellowship class, and the second week of school she was elected president of the group.

Miss Tong was eager to learn all she could about the English language, and about Miss Wells' country of America. The majority of students, including Miss Tong, wanted to also have an English name. Alice asked if she had a preference for a particular name, and the petite young student responded that she would like it to have something to do with the meaning of her Chinese name. Being totally unfamiliar with the language, Alice asked what her name meant in English. Miss Tong indicated that the two characters, *Ywè Míng,* meant "the light of the moon," and then, with an arrested look on her face, she exclaimed, "I know! I could be called Moonshine!" Her teacher managed to swallow her grin and gently suggest, "How about — Moon*beam*?" Moonbeam's face lighted up, and she responded, "That sounds even prettier!" Alice smiled and spoke, "Let me explain just why. You see, in English, *moonshine* means illegal liquor!" — whereupon the newly dubbed Moonbeam burst into laughter and profusely thanked her new teacher for guiding her on the right path. From then on, Miss Tong was known all over campus as Moonbeam. (In later years, she became a prominent pastor's wife in California and represented China at the fiftieth anniversary Jubilee celebration of Woman's Missionary Union in Richmond, Virginia, in 1938. Matthew Tong, her brother, was the leading Baptist pastor in Canton for many years, including after churches were allowed to reopen under Communist control in the 1980s.)

Alice's first birthday in China was bittersweet. She was thrilled to be in the country to which God had called her, yet she was discovering that holidays and special anniversaries were some of the loneliest times for missionaries, being so many thousands of miles away from the known and familiar. Grace had written about this, but Alice realized that one just about had to *experience* that hollow feeling for themselves in order to really grasp such loneliness. One such lonely day was her first birthday in China. However, Juanita; Hannah Plowden, a fellow South Carolinian whom she had known for years; and Elizabeth (Libby) Knabe of the American Board, were a tight band of young English teachers who provided companionship and authentic friendship for one another. The other three had planned long and hard and surprised Alice with a tea party on her special day. It brought her to happy tears, and she was overwhelmed with gifts and attention and kindness. The surprise was an amazing balm to her lonely spirit. However, the most unexpected moment of the special day came in the evening mail — a letter from Grace, saying that she was due to arrive back in Shanghai on September 5. Alice felt like she had opened the biggest present of the day.

Lying in her bed that night, Alice's mind once again drifted to the thought that so often came when she considered her age and circumstances. Those fond dreams she had cherished since girlhood, a loving husband and children to nurture and care for, seemed further away with each passing month. A milestone like a birthday made her even more keenly aware of the passage of time. This was her twenty-ninth birthday, and soon she would genuinely be "on the shelf" at thirty. As usual, she wept a bit — but prayed a lot and drifted off to sleep on the thought of God's loving provision and His great faithfulness to her.

Her first summer vacation in China was a treat for Alice. Through the years, missionaries had learned the hard way that they must take a summer break in order to prevent a breakdown. The heat, poverty, language challenges, the daily living and striving in a culture utterly different from their own broke many a missionary. Therefore, everyone who could arrange to do so headed for a change of scenery and a cooler climate for several weeks. Favorite spots were Tsingtao, on the coast, and Kuling, in the mountains. Grace had told her so much about Tsingtao, and experiencing it for herself was in no way disappointing. She and Juanita took a boat up the coast to the city that had been under German control years before. It was a beautiful area with German "flavor" and excellent roads and facilities.

The weather held for the most part, and hiking, swimming and lots of time for reading were refreshing to the soul. Alice particularly enjoyed experiencing a worship service conducted in English in a beautiful German church; she just sat and drank in the ambiance and the experience of once more singing the great old hymns in English. She later wrote home, describing what she saw as they sailed out of Tsingtao harbor. (This is the same harbor from which Lottie Moon sailed her last trip home in 1912.) Her letter pictured the moment:

> "I want to tell you of one of the most beautiful things I've ever seen. As we slowly sailed away from Tsingtao, the sun was setting, and I can't describe the scene — but in addition to the beautiful, wonderful colors of the sunset, there were the purple hills behind it, and little sail boats between us and the sunset."

All too soon it was back to classes and her second year of teaching. Alice grinned to herself to think of the difference just one year could make.

Now, on top of the excitement of a fresh new beginning, she was exhilarated at the thought of Grace coming within weeks — and those weeks felt like at least a month. The evening finally arrived, and a grand crowd of missionaries and Chinese friends gathered at the harbor to greet the *SS Taiyo Maru* as it slowly and smoothly entered the harbor. More than one of those standing on the wharf shed tears, watching the joy of the two sisters who were reunited in the land each had labeled "home." Alice and Grace had words tumbling all over each other as they shared the joy of reunion and family. Grace spent several days at the campus before heading to her Chinkiang home, and every moment Alice was not teaching, the two were sharing stories and memories. Grace had brought special treats from home for her sister, and Alice nearly collapsed in tears when Grace lifted out of her trunk two cans of Wells Canning Co. vegetables. On top was the big "A," indicating this was homegrown asparagus. She was actually going to be able to eat something grown in the family garden 10,000 miles away. Before Grace left, Alice received mail from Sumter, and the two sisters had the joy of sharing family mail together. Alice wrote home to say: "And we could read your letters together, Mamma. It's too good to be true! But it is true anyway."

In letters home, Alice shared the little everyday bits of news about college life in a distant land, and when she described teaching in a building that was not heated, even in cold, damp weather, she commented, "Three straight hours in unheated classrooms are about all my feet can take!" Final exams were, of all things, to begin the day after Christmas, but Grace could come be with her and even help grade the endless stacks of exams. Then the two went to Chinkiang for the long Chinese New Year, which lasted for most of the month of January, treasured time for the siblings to be together and share their missions experience.

The time with Grace included a trip to the capital city, Nanking, just about an hour from Chinkiang. Since Grace had gone to language school there, she was right at home. Alice was enthralled with the history of the city, walking on the ancient, thick Ming Dynasty city wall, visiting the tombs of several Ming emperors, and walking up the some 400 steps leading to the new Sun Yat Sen mausoleum, which held the body of the founder of the Republic of China who had died in 1925. The mausoleum had just been completed in 1929 and was an imposing sight for a country girl from South Carolina.

Alice loved her students, loved all the challenge and atmosphere, but only tolerated all the grading of papers. They were the bane of her existence. However, there was never time to be bored and always the excitement of letters from home — and not just letters, but occasional visits from Grace when she came to Shanghai for meetings and doctor appointments. In September, Grace wrote of the news coming from Yangchow. That station had long been needing reinforcements, especially hoping for an evangelistic missionary. There were women who were teachers, and a woman doctor, but Dr. D.F. Stamps, newly transferred from North China, was the only evangelist in a sprawling ancient city with multitudes who had never heard. Furthermore, the Foreign Mission Board was not appointing any new missionaries — everyone was still in the throes of the deadly Depression. However, Grace wrote, they had just received the news that a young man, a recent graduate of Southwestern Seminary, was coming to Yangchow and was being financed by seminary friends who supported his missions call. Little did young Miss Wells realize this development would have any significance for her personally, or that her life was about to change once more in a totally unimagined way. Providence was at work again.

Shipmates Juanita, Rachel and Alice

Harold Hall on board the SS President Jefferson, *1931*

FIVE

STARTING IN INDIAN TERRITORY

Meantime, back in the United States, events were taking place in Indian Territory that would have a direct impact on the life of the English professor at Shanghai University. The blending of the story of a young woman from South Carolina and a young man from Indian Territory, Oklahoma, is the reason I have a story to tell. Without the meeting of those two, in a land half a world away, this tale wouldn't be a true story.

Not a day has passed in the twenty years since Dad died that I don't have a question I wish he could answer for me. During my growing-up years, Mama was much more likely than Dad to tell stories from her childhood, so now I have an unquenched curiosity about so many experiences in his early years. Furthermore, it seems that South Carolinians, more so than Oklahomans, tend to study and pass on information about their ancestry. Digging through old letters and family records from Oklahoma has been an eye-opener, revealing the incredible path that led Dad to China nearly

100 years ago. As I read his correspondence with the Foreign Mission Board (now International Mission Board), I found more surprises.

Tucked into the far northern corner of Georgia, and just about twenty miles from South Carolina *and* North Carolina, lay the hamlet of Burton, named for Jeremiah Burton, owner of the post office, proprietor of the general store, and sometime bailiff in the town. That is in the past tense for a reason. In the early part of the twentieth century, Burton was flooded and is now known as beautiful Lake Burton. Exploring the family history, I found all sorts of intriguing tidbits. My paternal grandmother was named Georgia for the state in which she was born, and her father, Jacob Silas, was Jeremiah's son. Her mother, Nancy Carnes, must have been one strong (and adventurous) woman. She had a checkered ancestry, including a father who went by his mother's surname because his mother refused to marry *his* father. Nancy also had a fascinating mixture of ancestries, with more than one Cherokee in her lineage. As a child, I was captivated to learn that I was part Native American and equally surprised to have Grandmother tell me, "We don't talk about those things." I immediately wanted to know, "Why don't we?" I smile now to think of how things have changed in this millennium. Nowadays, who *wouldn't* want an ever-so-great-grandmother with the beautiful name Mahalla Uneqahiwiya, whose father was Totsu'hwa Tsalagi Ugvwiyuhi (Chief Red Bird)?

According to family records, Jacob Silas and Nancy married when she was eighteen and he just seventeen. Nancy gave birth to nine children, with Grandmother Georgia Anna being the youngest daughter. The Burton-Hall record book reveals the puzzling inconsistencies in Grandmother's father's character. Jacob was purported to be an excellent preacher; he was ordained in Georgia in 1880 and later licensed in Indian Territory after the family moved. While he and Nancy were living in Georgia, Jacob lost a leg. Different family members give some pretty disparate reasons for this loss. Aunt Opal declared it was caused by cancer. Uncle Don said Jacob was wounded in the Civil War, but Jacob's brother Virgil said, "No, it was something else." Virgil's version was later authenticated by another of their brothers. It seems that Jacob was seeing another woman, whose husband soon discovered his perfidy and forthwith shot the preacher in the leg. Of course, Nancy found out and proceeded to tell Jacob that if he didn't move the family away from there, she was leaving him. Whereupon, the whole family moved, lock, stock, and barrel — headed west in a covered wagon.

Half a century later, Grandmother Georgia told her grandchildren about traveling west by covered wagon and described some of her adventures along the way. Her youngest brother Gus (who grew up to be an outstanding pastor in Birmingham, Alabama) was born in that covered wagon as they were traveling along the banks of the White River in Arkansas. For some unexplained reason, Jacob, Nancy, and the children returned to Georgia the following year and remained there four more years, likely due to some need in the family. Nonetheless, New Year's Day of 1886 found them headed back west, this time to Indian Territory in northeastern Oklahoma.

Years later, Georgia's brother Virgil, ten years her senior, married Effie Hall. The two families had first become acquainted in Arkansas, and, subsequently, both moved to Indian Territory. Then, at age nineteen, Georgia Burton married Aunt Effie's brother Arthur Orville Hall, a young schoolteacher five years her senior. I have vivid memories of Grandmother Georgia (Georgie—everyone called her). She always seemed to my child's eyes to look a bit sad, and in later years, as I learned some of her story, I could understand that sorrow. The young couple wanted a large family, but it was not to be. Grandmother gave birth to six children but only two lived. Her first child, a boy, was too large to be born and died during delivery. Grandmother herself nearly died of what was then called childbed fever. But in 1901 she gave birth to a healthy little girl, Mellie, and all the kith and kin rejoiced. Grandmother prayed for a son, and child number three *was* a son, but he was premature and died shortly after taking his first breath. Brokenhearted, Georgia prayed on. She then gave birth to twin girls who were born two months premature; they too did not live long. Georgia was a woman of unshaken faith, however, and again she prayed. Years later, she related her story: "I prayed God to please give me a son, and like Hannah [in the Bible], I would give him back to the Lord." God honored that prayer, and in 1905, tiny Harold Edward Hall was born, healthy and kicking and vigorously exercising his strong lungs. He was born in Spavinaw, in the heart of Indian Territory. (Oklahoma became a state when Harold was two years old.)

I have clear memories of Grandfather Hall. He *never* got in a hurry, no matter how hard Grandmother tried to speed things up. He farmed and taught school during the months that farm children could be spared to attend classes. Harold and Mellie's first teacher was their father. Parents in farming areas were delighted that their offspring could have a male instructor. That meant firm discipline. In the case of Arthur Orville Hall, it meant infinite patience. He went to nearby Tahlequah, attended a two-year college, took the exam, and received an official teacher's certificate. Teachers tended to move every two or three years, so Harold moved repeatedly during those growing up years, living in Peggs, Locust Grove, and Yonkers, all in northeast Oklahoma.

Georgia had come from a strong Baptist background, and Arthur's parents were Baptists — although one generation back, much of the family was Catholic. In fact, three aunts were nuns. Harold could never remember a time as a child when they were not in church. His mother always smiled when she told the children that she had grown up in churches where, "When you were happy, you shouted," and on occasion, Mellie and Harold heard her do just that.

When he was fourteen years old, Harold felt the stirring of God's spirit on his heart and made a profession of faith. It became a pivotal moment in his life. His father was teaching part-time, farming part-time, and serving as rural mail carrier to support the family. Harold graduated from high school in Locust Grove, and that summer he first felt God dealing with him about becoming a preacher. His mother had been very clear all through his childhood about how she had bargained with God, that if He would give her a son, she would give him back. Harold listened, and thought, and held his own counsel. Acutely aware of the tugging of God on his heart *personally,* Harold was yet reluctant to make that commitment. His sharp mind loved the idea of law, and he felt a keen interest in becoming a lawyer.

Whatever direction he followed, however, college would be a necessity. No one in the family had ever completed college.

Lack of determination had never been a problem for the young high school graduate, and Harold found a way to attend Oklahoma Baptist University. His parents supported his decision, helping all they could, and Georgia continuing to secretly pray for God to call her son to the ministry. Harold entered OBU the fall of 1924, determined to be a lawyer; however, God turned his determination around in quick order, convicting him of his true calling. In the first month of his college career, Harold surrendered to preach. Never one to sit around and wait, once Harold made that commitment, he never doubted, and he never looked back. God provided, and Harold was able to do some preaching and even pastor a part-time church his last year in college.

Money was not easy to come by in the 1920s in Oklahoma, and many years later Dad told me of an experience that gave him a renewed sense of God's blessings and favor. He was on campus that weekend and had just five dollars in his pocket to cover all of his expenses for the coming week. Walking across campus, he encountered a classmate walking slowly and kicking the gravel on the road as he looked down. Sensing the young man was disturbed, Dad asked him, "What's the problem?" His classmate sighed and shook his head, "I just don't know what I'm going to do. I do not have a penny in my pocket, and I have to somehow get through this coming week before I can get any." On impulse, Dad reached into his pocket and pulled out the lone five-dollar bill and thrust it into his classmate's hands. The student's face lighted up, and he blurted out, "Are you *sure?*" Dad assured him that yes, this is what he wanted to do, and the young man went on his way rejoicing. Dad went on his way wondering what he would for food that weekend. Providence led the way. Going to his post box, he pulled out a letter from a relative he had not heard from in many months, and in it, wonder of wonders, was a crisp five-dollar bill. Now Harold went on his own way rejoicing.

Georgia and Arthur were thrilled with the direction of their son's life and encouraged him in his studies. However, Harold then told them about the rest of his call, and his clear impression that God not only wanted him to preach, He wanted him to preach in China. His mother was stunned. When she could summon the words, she spoke to him in a broken voice, "Son, I promised God that if He gave me a son, I would give him back." Harold recalled that she took a deep breath and added, "But I never asked Him to call you to preach so far away!" It took that stalwart woman a lot of praying and a good number of tears to come to grips with the reality of her son's commitment. Nevertheless, such was the depth of her faith that ever after she was a bulwark of encouragement for her one and only son.

Harold had enjoyed studying Latin and Spanish in college, and he always excelled in class. He entered Southwestern Baptist Theological Seminary in 1928, eyes set firmly on the goal of mission service, and not just anywhere — he felt led to China. He particularly enjoyed studying Greek and Hebrew, and hoped that this ability with languages would one day carry over into the study of Chinese. There was a nucleus of outstanding young ministers in Harold's classes, some of whom became lifelong friends and denominational leaders and missionaries. In that number were Kernie Keagan, who became Southwide director of Baptist Student Unions; Orvil Reid, who became a missionary to Mexico; and Baker James Cauthen, who became president of the Foreign Mission Board. A close friend, Frank Patterson, was later elected director of the Baptist Spanish Publishing House. All three seminary years, Harold traveled on weekends to Oklahoma and pastored two half-time churches. During that time, he baptized some eighty-five people and saw both churches become full-time. Those were years of the Great Depression, and the chances of going to China were appearing slim to none. Because there were no funds, the Foreign Mission Board had stopped appointing new missionaries. However, nothing daunted, Harold told his friends that God called him to go to China *without* money. He would have to exercise faith.

God called. He would go. To Harold, it was that simple. He sat down one evening with his cadre of friends and told them, "I want to go to China on faith. I *know* I am called to do this, and I must answer this call." The friends discussed the situation among themselves, resolving to do something about it. However, times were lean for everyone. These were seminarians with no discretionary money, and they were going to school on faith and a shoestring. Loyal to a man, however, they felt prompted by God to support their friend. Frank Patterson agreed to be treasurer for the group, and four of them pledged to give ten dollars a month to support Harold. Missionaries in China were living on $70 a month. The friends would do their part to make it possible for Harold to be true to his call. Contacting friends, pastors, and churches in Oklahoma, Harold was able to pull together enough support to guarantee a small set amount to come each month. The people of First Baptist Church, Ada, Oklahoma, were faithful supporters, and Ada's WMU committed to send money to the fund each month. They never failed.

Harold was elated. Upon graduating in 1931, he spent the summer preaching in Oklahoma and working toward the goal of mission service in China. Now, to get money for his steamer ticket to Shanghai. Even though it was during the heart of the Great Depression, churches in the state banded together and made up the $185 needed for his ticket. He then sold his faithful and sturdy old Chevrolet that had been like a friend to him throughout the seminary years as he traveled to his weekend preaching duties, and with other gifts from friends and family, he had enough to make a beginning in a new land. Never doubting that God would provide, he sailed with high hopes.

One of Harold's special friends at OBU, and later in seminary, was Herbert Pierce, the son of missionaries in Yangchow (Yangzhou), China. Dad had been earnestly praying about where he would go in China, fully intending that wherever it was, he would work in full cooperation with the missionaries in that place. His friend Herbert explained that, at that time, there were seven women in the city of Yangchow but no men. Harold told his friend, "That looks like a Macedonian call to me!" He wrote to the mission in Yangchow, telling them he would soon be on his way. Herbert's mother and his sister, Ethel, a missionary doctor at the Baptist Hospital, both lived in Yangchow, although his father had died many years ago in a tragic boat accident on the Yangtze River.

Harold left America knowing that it would be years before he could see family and friends again. He also realized, at least in theory, that it was going to be terribly lonely. Although there had been opportunities to marry, he simply recognized that he had not met the right girl. Harold was a handsome young man, with dark hair, bronzed complexion, and a winning smile. Many a young woman at Southwestern had looked in his direction more than once, but he was intent upon his goal: China. Nevertheless, just as in every area of his life, Harold had a deep faith in the Providence of God and trusted Him to direct his life. Just before leaving, Harold returned to Yonkers, Oklahoma, where his parents were then living. The goodbyes were bittersweet for Georgia Hall. Her son was her pride and a joy, but he was going half a world away. Georgia swallowed her grief and sent him on his way with one last fierce hug.

Harold crossed the continent by rail for the first of many times. His ship was to sail from Seattle, Washington — 1,500 miles from Yonkers, Oklahoma. So it was that on September 5, 1931, after years of preparation, Harold stepped onto the deck of the *SS President Jefferson* and was on his way to the task for which God had called him.

Alice Wells on her engagement day, 1933

SIX

FIRST MEETING

Alice looked forward to having final exams over and the dreaded, tall stack of test papers checked and re-checked. Then she could enjoy the long Chinese New Year holiday with Grace in Chinkiang. A break was doubly welcome right then, because so much change and uncertainty was in the very atmosphere of Shanghai. China and Japan had been at enmity in varying degrees and in many parts of China for several years already, and tensions were coming to a boiling point. The threat of war in Shanghai was all too real. The huge, sprawling metropolis was already overburdened with thousands of refugees from devastating floods in other parts of the nation. Now, ominous evidence of Japanese encroachment was too obvious to ignore, with Japanese battleships and aircraft carriers gathering in Shanghai harbor.

University leadership went into emergency session and decided that, with danger so imminent, students should not return for the spring

59

semester. Consequently, hundreds of students completed their exams and quickly headed home to the many provinces of China. They also decided, since they had been talking for the past two years about providing language school for their English professors, this seemed the perfect time: Classes would not be meeting, and Peking was far safer than Shanghai right now. Accordingly, Alice headed to Chinkiang and quality time with her sister before beginning language study in Peking the first of March.

Meanwhile, Yangchow's newest missionary had arrived on the field October 1, and quickly established himself as an important part of the mission family. Harold Hall was warmly welcomed by the Yangchow mission station. Yangchow and Chinkiang worked as a unit for mission planning, and the combined stations rejoiced over a fresh new addition. Grace was impressed by young Mr. Hall's determination and positive attitude about all that was new and unfamiliar. Harold explained to the group at their first station meeting that being able to come to China was the culmination of his goal in answer to a clear call. The homes for all Yangchow mission-aries were on the hospital compound, and Yangchow Station provided the young man with an empty room above the hospital clinic that could serve as a tidy little apartment. Drew and Elizabeth Stamps invited him to their home for his evening meal each day. Seven-year-old George Stamps and four-year-old Winston ("Winkie," to one and all) quickly latched on to their new "Uncle Harold" and made him part of the family.

Clearly, the first priority for the fledgling missionary was learning the language. Harold's preciously guarded monthly stipend could not possibly stretch to cover official language school, so he did the next best thing. Ethel Pierce, the MK-become-physician, was a big help. She introduced him to an elderly scholar who (although not knowing a word of English, spoke and wrote beautiful classical Chinese) became Harold's teacher. The venerable teacher taught in phrases and was amazed at his student's quick grasp and his musical ear that heard and echoed the all-important tones of Mandarin. Harold did not have a clear understanding of the standard approach in studying Chinese, nor did he realize that the usual evange-listic missionary who began studying the challenging language would feel delighted to be able to preach in Mandarin after a year and a half of intensive study. Harold's grasp and skill were so obvious to both his teacher and his fellow missionaries that they encouraged him to start using it regularly. Harold did not realize how quickly he was progressing, so when Dr. Pierce came after Harold's two months of study and asked him to lead the mid-week prayer meeting for the hospital staff, Harold said, "I can't do that! I don't have enough vocabulary!" Ethel Pierce smiled and asked, "Aren't you already memorizing Scripture passages?" When he acknowledged that this was true, she suggested, "All right, just take a verse a night and teach it to the staff. They can be learning Scripture along with you!"

Dr. Pierce's method worked incredibly well, and Harold began leading prayer meeting each week. At the end of his first six months, he preached his first sermon in Chinese at the Nan Men Wai (Outside South Gate) Baptist School, where one of the older missionary women was hoping to start a chapel. Harold wrote to his supporting friends after that first sermon, "Miracle of miracles, ten men professed their faith in Christ, five of them from one clan." Thus, it was that after just half a year on the field, Harold began a preaching mission and brought messages in Mandarin every week. It did wonders for his progress in the language. Elderly Pastor Jiang, of the main Syi Liang Jye (West Porch Street) Church, asked him to preach there once a week as well. Small wonder that his language acquisition was so astounding. (Until the day he died, Dad's Chinese remained absolutely colloquial, and Chinese friends often said, "If we didn't see him, and just heard him speak, we would think it was a fellow Chinese talking with us.")

Harold was happy with so many opportunities and content in knowing he was where he was supposed to be — but at the same time, he was lonely. He often wrote his sister, Mellie, and expressed his feelings but did not speak openly about his loneliness. Such was the depth of his faith that he knew that the God who could get him to China in the midst of a worldwide Depression could also help him with this loneliness.

Christmas arrived, and, strangely, that most wonderful season of the year was often the loneliest for missionaries half a world away from home and dear ones. Alice, who had such a tender heart, often felt a bit guilty because she *did* have family in China with her. The warlike atmosphere in Shanghai, with all the uncertainty and the temporary closing of the college, made it a special blessing to be able to be with Grace in Chinkiang. She just knew it was going to be a time of rest and refreshing before heading to Peking and the long-desired language study. Grace lived with the Marriotts, seasoned China hands who had worked in Chinkiang more than twenty years. They were truly like family to Grace, and Alice was received in like fashion. Libby Knabe, Alice's fellow teacher and close friend, also came to Chinkiang for a couple of weeks and both teachers were grateful for the family atmosphere and relief from the tensions of imminent war surrounding Shanghai.

Dr. Stamps came to Chinkiang for a brief meeting and informed Grace, the Marriotts, and their two visitors that he came with orders from his wife, Elizabeth, that "the goose is dead, and I'm going to lecture you if you don't bring the Chinkiang guests home with you." Libby had never visited the fabled ancient walled city of Yangchow, and Alice looked forward to visiting again with the missionaries there. Accordingly, on January 20, the three young missionary women traveled to Yangchow with their host, Dr. Stamps. He mentioned on the way that their new missionary, Harold Hall, took his meals with them, and he was quite sure Harold would look forward to meeting them. (Alice's only daughter — me — found the account of that meeting and the subsequent months in her "bride's book" many years later.) Alice had heard much about this new missionary from Pa Marriott and was interested in finally meeting him. When it came time for lunch, Elizabeth Stamps conveniently placed them next to each other at the table and conversation flowed easily and naturally. And again that evening, Harold returned, but was taking such a cold that he soon had to go back to his room. Alice later wrote in her bride's book: "I couldn't help but think of him in that lonely room over there — alone."

Alas, his cold was even worse the next day. The Marriotts had especially invited Harold to take the guests back to Chinkiang and have a visit there. Unfortunately, he was still too sick, so the three young women headed back to Chinkiang without him, but with a promise that if he was able to on the following day, he would come on over to a party at the Marriotts for all the foreigners in the city. The next day, Alice said not a word, but every time the doorbell rang, she looked to see if it might be young Rev. Hall. Right before the party began that evening, in he came, having been determined that the cold would not get the better of him. Harold stayed for the weekend, and then, they all made the short boat trip to ancient Jiao Shan Island and its famous old temple. Alice and Harold were both fascinated by the forest of steles and seeing the temple and artifacts dating back more than 2,000 years. Their evening was spent playing checkers and getting to know each other. Harold stayed until Monday and took the visitors to the train when it was time for them to leave. Alice's instincts told her very clearly that this was not the last she would see of Yangchow's newest missionary, and her instincts proved to be very accurate.

Language school was a few weeks away, and Alice was hoping that the impending danger from Japan would not prevent her getting there. The university had allowed a small stipend for a little language study this past year, but she was so limited in free time that her frustration over not being able to speak Chinese was constantly nagging at her mind. Ever since she arrived, Alice had wanted to spend more time in sharing her faith, and with so little language and so little time, her restlessness grew. She wrote a formal request to the Central China Mission requesting a transfer to evangelistic work, and they voted to approve and sent the request to the Board in Richmond. In turn, the Board made the request of the university, but they were loath to release their sterling teacher, and insisted she was especially appointed to work there. Furthermore, her workload increased as the school wanted her to teach advanced courses as well. Alice swallowed her deep disappointment, but her certainty that evangelism is where God was directing her did not go away.

The latter part of February 1932 was frightening; it looked like no one was going anywhere, for Shanghai erupted as a battlefield. Grace had come to Shanghai on business and could not get back to Chinkiang; no civilians were allowed on the trains. At least the two sisters could be together as they waited to see what would happen. Terrible bloodshed occurred in many parts of Shanghai, and there was a constant roaring of aircraft as planes continually took off and landed at the Japanese airbase next to the college. Occasional shells landed on the campus, but mostly the fighting was confined to Shanghai. The bloodshed was horrific, but by the first of March the fighting had ended and the Japanese were gone, although warfare in Manchuria was more deadly than ever. A temporary treaty was signed, and plans were made for classes to start again in September. Alice had heartfelt gratitude that she could really go on to Peking and study Mandarin.

Language school was both a challenge and good fun at the same time, and getting to visit the Forbidden City and the Temple of Heaven was like a dream come true. Nonetheless, the whole time in Peking, Alice found her thoughts wandering back to Yangchow. Letters between Alice and Harold began to go back and forth. Grace was an interested bystander to the beginnings of an unusual courtship. Alice did not mention Harold in letters home; it was all so new to her, and she didn't really know what she thought or felt. On the other hand, it was very evident that Harold Hall had a keen interest in pursuing a friendship with *her*. Sometimes just the thought of a romantic relationship sent her heart racing, and she began to think of all the implications. Frequently, Alice had to force herself to back off and let things just happen. This was hard to do for someone as disciplined, single-minded, and committed as she.

For more than fifty years, all missionaries who were able would take several weeks and retreat to either Tsingtao or Kuling, high above the Yangtze River, where the climate was better and the air fresher. This attention to mental health helped save many a missionary's career. Alice and Grace had coordinated their summer vacation in Tsingtao the previous year and were planning to do the same this summer. Each summer, a number of the vacationing missionaries used this time to brush up on their language skills, and Alice was delighted to think that she could continue her language study while vacationing with Grace. Then, a letter arrived in Peking from Harold, indicating that he was joining the Stamps in Tsingtao for three weeks in August. Alice left Peking for Tsingtao the first week of August, joining Grace for a family reunion, and a few days later, Harold arrived at the Stamps' summer cottage next door to the Wells sisters' cottage.

The next several weeks passed in a whirl, with language classes each morning, and Alice trying hard to concentrate as she daydreamed a bit about the rest of each day. The summer was indelibly printed in her memory, and she later recorded in her bride's book each day's activities:

August 13th — Alice was Harold's guest at the picnic

August 16th — Southern Presbyterian picnic on rocks

August 20th — Walk to "big mountain" (2 couples)

August 24th — Ride with Harold and the Thompson party

August 27th — With Harold to the Zimbalist Concert at the Grand Theater

August 28th — Sat on the rocks out on the Point

August 29th — Goodbye. Saw Grace off and rode home together.

A note at the bottom of the Tsingtao vacation included a common comment she got from four-year-old Winkie Stamps: "Alice, what for you all the time walk home with *Mr. Hall?!*" (I was amazed some eight decades later to read Mama's letters to South Carolina and discover that her first mention of "Mr. Hall" was in a letter written from Tsingtao in which she said, "Mr. Hall, the young fellow who's connected with our work in Yangchow, is staying with the Stamps.")

Now their letters became even more frequent, and Alice was back in Shanghai, teaching and grading papers, and doing a good bit of daydreaming on the side, although she still had not confided in any of her friends at the university. There was a special sparkle about her, however, on which several friends commented and drew their own conclusions. The last weekend in October found Harold visiting the university and staying on campus with a missionary couple. Alice recorded details in her book, savoring each moment of the weekend. Saturday evening included a movie together in Shanghai and going to the special service where the famed Dr. E. Stanley Jones was speaking. On Sunday, Alice enjoyed the worship service even more, for Harold was asked to preach. It was her first opportunity to hear him, and later on she enjoyed hearing all sorts of good comments about his fine message. That evening, prior to Harold's departure for Yangchow, they talked far into the night, and Alice recorded in her book, "Plenty of food for thought in the evening's conversation. Goodbye again!"

The goodbyes didn't last long, for on December 15 Harold was back in Shanghai for a long weekend, Alice enjoying his company every moment of the day that she wasn't teaching. They decorated the Christmas tree together and took in a Christmas pageant. Harold left with a promise from Alice that she would be visiting Grace in Chinkiang as soon as Chinese New Year arrived. There was a lot of speculation on campus by this time. It was clear to all the missionaries, and to Alice's close friends in particular, that there was a courtship going on here. Still, Alice was reticent and deflected most interested queries with a non-committal "could be."

The final weeks of classes before Chinese New Year 1933 were the longest of Alice's life. The massive pile of exam papers looked daunting, and concentrating was so hard that it sapped her energy. She was in a daze, realizing that the coming few weeks might literally change the trajectory of the rest of her life. And it did.

Harold and Alice the winter
prior to their marriage

Wedding Day, Shanghai, China
June 29, 1933

SEVEN

A GARDEN WEDDING

Alice woke early Thursday morning. Chinese New Year (the Year of the Tiger) — the biggest celebration of the year in China — had arrived. The constant noise of firecrackers during the night reminded anyone who might possibly forget the occasion. She woke up with a special sense of expectation, for Harold was coming over from Yangchow to spend New Year's Day with the Chinkiang missionaries. She had not seen him in over a month and admitted to herself just how exciting this visit would be. This morning, her early devotions, as was her custom, included reading the Bible and the missionary prayer calendar. (In the 1930s, Woman's Missionary Union would list the names of missionaries in a particular mission station all on one day, rather than on individual birthdays.) She found the list for January 26 included her name, and it gave her a happy thrill of anticipation to think of Baptist women all across America praying for her.

Pa and Cora Marriott rather fancied the idea of playing the role of Cupid — for although Alice never gave a hint, they were not blind. Nor was Grace. She knew her sister so well and could read the extra sparkle in her eye. Harold arrived in time for the big dinner of the day, and the handful of missionaries in Chinkiang enjoyed the holiday meal together in the Marriotts' hospitable home. When the guests finally departed in late evening, Pa Marriott adroitly arranged for everyone to be busy at some task, leaving Alice and Harold to the privacy of the living room.

The usual noise of revelry associated with the lunar new year continued throughout the evening, but the couple in the living room was oblivious. Alice's sense of imminent change had been correct: Harold proposed, and the two could scarcely find time to say all that was in their hearts. In typical, reserved Alice Wells style, she suggested to her brand-new fiancé, "Shall we wait one year from June to be married?" Harold's immediate response was also typical — an unequivocal, "No, let's marry *this* June, and God will provide."

He had good reason to call on God's provision, for just the week before, Dr. Maddry had responded to Harold's December letter. Maddry did not hold out any false hope, writing "the Board is not at this time in position to accept any new missionaries. We have been compelled to keep at home thirty missionaries this year without salary in an effort to balance our budget." Harold was not daunted. His call had not changed — as he wrote Maddry, "My call to China was so compelling that I could not but come." The same faith that brought him boldly to Yangchow assured him that God would provide for them as a couple.

By mutual consent, the newly engaged couple decided to wait a few days before telling the people closest to them. (In a letter Mama wrote to South Carolina the day *after* she became engaged, she did not mention the big news!) On Monday evening, Alice confided in Grace, who grinned from ear to ear, informing her younger sister that the look on her face had been giving her away all this time. The couple next told the Marriotts and the Stamps but were not making it official yet. In a quite unusual way, this was an engagement with an assortment of challenges. Foreign Mission Board policy dictated that if an appointed missionary married anyone who was not a missionary of the FMB, then that missionary had to resign. Alice's situation was further complicated by the fact that she was appointed at a time when missionaries were essentially not being sent out. Hers was an emergency appointment because of the request of the university. That institution was going to feel that her annual salary of $800 belonged to the school. What to do? The *two* would not be able to live on the money Harold's friends were sacrificially providing him each month. Harold wrote Dr. Maddry again in early February, telling of their engagement and desire to do evangelistic work together. Thus began a year of letters jockeying back and forth across the Pacific, with Maddry being in sympathy but finding no way to make it possible to appoint Mr. Hall. Not only that, but he confirmed the Board policy that should Miss Wells marry someone not an appointee of the FMB, she would be forced to resign.

None of the complications of reality daunted the faith and enthusiasm of the newly engaged couple. Love conquers all, and both were ecstatic about the future lying before them. Alice's head may have been in the clouds, but when her feet hit the ground back in Shanghai, she immediately sat down to write Dr. Maddry in Richmond. She knew Dr. Ray, the previous director, but Dr. Maddry was someone she knew only by name. Praying as she wrote, Alice explained the circumstances and asked Dr. Maddry to give real consideration to her situation, trusting it would not be necessary for her to resign, given that Harold was working in lockstep with the Yangchow mission. Having done all she could, Alice determined to follow Harold's philosophy of positivity. She smiled to herself, wondering if he, by nature, always tended to look at the bright side — or if, instead, it was simply a reflection of the great depth of his faith. Maybe it was a mixture, she decided.

March 10 arrived, and Harold came to Shanghai for the weekend, both feeling that the intervening weeks since February had been months, not mere weeks. Furthermore, the groom-to-be had a special purpose for this visit, for Shanghai was the best place in China to buy gems. The weekend was everything Alice could have wished, and more — for Harold surprised her with a beautiful engagement ring. She returned to the classroom on Monday morning, but it was like everything was on automatic; she felt like she was walking on air. In typical reticent Miss Wells' style, she did not wear the cherished ring but kept it locked in her trunk until they would announce their engagement. Each evening, she would unlock her trunk, get it out, put it on, admire it for an hour or so, then carefully return it to its little box in the trunk.

Alice wrote home in great detail about Harold and all that was happening, her biggest regret being the ocean that separated them and prevented the home folks from being with her on this all-important day. She shed many a tear over not having Papa to give her away, and her beloved Mamma having to miss all the wedding preparations, but over and again she would take a deep breath, renew her resolve, and remember that her commitment to sacrifice personal wishes and follow God's call also entailed sacrifice on the part of her dear ones. Their loving and supportive attitude was balm to her tender heart.

All the wonderful anticipation of engagement and plans to spend the rest of her life with her love did not keep Alice from diligently working with her students. She wrote home in early March of her special joy that semester. Her students, many of whom were also part of the fellowship group she sponsored, planned and prepared an entire week of chapel services, with Moonbeam Tong leading in the planning and being the featured speaker on the final day. Alice was thrilled to see their spiritual maturity and joy in their preparation and work, writing to her parents, "This has been a bright spot in the whole year for me."

In the same letter, she wrote of the battles raging in the north with the Japanese and the dreadful suffering among the civilians. She lamented, "And there seems nothing we can do but sit and wait and pray." She concluded, "Just one year ago tomorrow the fighting in Shanghai stopped. The devastation is not by any means repaired — and here this war goes on. We just wonder how much longer it will last."

Meanwhile, her closest friends — Hannah, Juanita and Libby — were all suspicious, and commented frequently that Alice surely seemed to be smelling of orange blossoms. They really turned up the teasing when Alice received beautiful flowers from Harold on her birthday. She was counting the days until the long first-term weekend, when she could take the train to Chinkiang. It was a "no fooling" April Fools' Day when she and Harold officially announced their engagement, and the combined mission stations of Yangchow and Chinkiang gathered at the hospital compound to note the occasion. The team of the Reverends Stamps and Marriott both labeled themselves as the marriage brokers, with Pa Marriott the more portly of the pair of Cupids. Both were as delighted as schoolboys to be asked to be part of the wedding party, with Stamps acting as best man and Marriott doing the prayer of dedication.

Back on the university campus, there was an official engagement party on April 16, with much good-natured teasing and the display of Alice's engagement ring, now out of the trunk and on her finger. One of her favorite professor colleagues, Dr. Hui Zu Ja, wrote a special poem for the occasion, with one of the stanzas echoing his good wishes:

Congratulations and best wishes, dear Alice;
We wish you every joy in life.
Our tragic loss will be Harold's gain;
For him you'll make a model wife.

Alice's closest friends, her fellow teachers, not only put on the engagement party but went in together and surprised her with a beautifully carved dark camphor wood hope chest. (It has a place of honor some nine decades later in our home.)

Wanting the dear ones at home to be as much a part of the experience as possible, Alice wrote about the party in great detail. Her angst in missing them came across in the letter home: "I long for a chance to talk with you. The joys that are mine would be still sweeter if only you dear ones could be nearer." She continued, "But here … I always remind myself that thoughts mind no distance. We are near after all." The following week, she wrote her mother, lovingly calling her "My own Miss Annie," and mainly writing about Harold and wishing the home folks could meet him. Normally not one to express herself openly, Alice did pour out her heart to her mother, saying, "Of course I know myself so well that I know it's Harold's imagination that makes him see some of the good things he *seems* to find in me. I've told him," she went on, "that he's fooling himself and all that. But I listen anyway, just like all he thinks is quite true. I'm sure his exalted opinion makes me anxious to live up to it."

Alice then described to her mother a bit of her feelings for her fiancé, writing in her typical understated style, "I can't afford to tell Harold all I think of him, so I have to take it out on you and others who are too far away to protest much. I guess you might have the idea by now that I think Harold is pretty near 'all right.'" She wrote discussing the wedding announcement her parents would send out and the names of those to receive one. She acknowledged her current absentminded condition, noting, "I just seem to get busier with school things and my attention is harder to hold. This is, I can't get my *work* done as fast as I sometimes do." She told those at home of the proposed wedding date of June 29 and explained that they hoped to go to Kuling for their honeymoon. Grace, as well as other friends, would be vacationing there as well — Kuling being a prime spot for a "cooling" holiday. In fact, the name had been given to the area by foreign visitors who discovered the cool highlands in the previous century, so the Chinese simply applied similar-sounding tones to the resort's Chinese name.

Alice's fellowship group of students gave a tea party in her honor, and their touching note of tribute brought her to tears. As one of the young men with beautiful English spoke for the class, she could not prevent the tears from slipping down her cheeks. He spoke of all of them feeling deep sorrow that she would be leaving the university and said, "You have been more than merely a teacher to us, and we do not know how to thank you for your kind help that we shall never forget." They next presented her with a beautiful engraved pewter tea service. Alice found herself flooded with emotion as she thanked them and tried to "help them face the future."

Grace and her teacher friends loved having a part in helping assemble her trousseau and plan the wedding dress. Shanghai's Madame Tang designed and produced her white lace wedding dress, and descendants in later years held up the lovely garment and wondered how anyone could be tiny enough to fit in the long, lace gown. Harold made reservations for them at Shanghai's most prestigious hotel, the Astor House, in the heart of Shanghai on the famous waterfront Bund. The Astor House had been right in the middle of the fighting the previous year but had survived fairly unscathed. Alice had passed the beautiful structure many times but had never been in it. The plan was to spend one night there and take a ship the next day up the Yangtze River to the Kuling area. Grace came from Chinkiang and spent the entire week in Shanghai, helping Alice pack and do all the last-minute things that needed doing.

Dr. R.T. Bryan, beloved by all Baptists in China, had been the first president of the seminary (now part of the university) and after retirement had come back to Shanghai to pastor Sallee Memorial Church along with three Chinese pastors. Dr. Bryan, who was nearing eighty, was honored to perform the wedding of Harold and Alice. Alice's university friends — Hannah, Juanita and Libby, joined by Annie Root of the university administration — were bridesmaids, and Alice's own Grace was maid of honor.

All the wedding party anxiously observed the sky at noon on the big day as it opened up and rain poured down, and the blustery winds looked ominously like a typhoon (what hurricanes are called in Asia). Alice somehow managed to calm her nerves, finish packing her trunk for the wedding trip, and lie down to rest. She surprised herself by actually falling asleep and woke up to see sun shining in the window. It was like yet another gift from heaven, the perfect setting for the late afternoon wedding in the garden at Dr. White's residence. The retired president of the university was now back as a professor of religion and was a special friend of Alice's. He was honored to stand in for her father, and as the wedding procession was played, escorted her to the rose-covered trellis where Harold stood beaming, with Dr. Stamps as his best man, and Pa Marriott on the other side of Dr. Bryan, the officiant. The timeless words of the traditional wedding vows were exchanged, Dr. Marriott prayed, and

Dr. Bryan smilingly pronounced them man and wife.

Not knowing if they even had financial support, with all sorts of unanswered questions lying out before them, realizing that the bride might have to resign her appointment — none of it dented the new couple's excitement and sense of joy at God's guiding in their lives. God had brought together a Southern girl from South Carolina and a young man born in Indian Territory, uniting them in China to henceforth serve as a missions team.

Harold Hall with believers he has just baptized

EIGHT

THE NEWLYWEDS

"Happy the bride the sun shines on!"

Some old adages must really be true. Alice Wells Hall was a radiant bride, and it showed to all those who gathered to wish the new couple Godspeed. She threw her bouquet, and the two left the wedding reception in a shower of rice and good wishes. Walking into the Astor Hotel, the two were oblivious to the splendor of its famous lobby, so excited they were to actually be man and wife. After a candlelight dinner in the Astor's restaurant, they sent a cable to Sumter to the home folks — only two words: *Just Married.* In her bride's book, she carefully saved the receipt from the Astor and the schedule/itinerary of the small ship that took them up the Yangtze.) That vessel was aptly named, in Chinese: *Wu Hu* (in English: Woohoo!). Their ship did not sail until about 10 p.m. the following day, so the newlyweds did a bit of shopping in Shanghai and even took an hour to visit an elderly missionary friend confined in Country Hospital. The elderly woman bragged for months about having a visit from her young friends who were actually on their honeymoon!

The trip up the Yangtze was all that a young couple in love could wish for — smooth waters, breathless scenery, and a large moon glistening on the water at night. They had leisurely hours to talk over the events of the week just past, and by tacit agreement, did not bring up the issue hanging heavily over their heads: How were they going to get the funds needed to continue Alice's support? They were in love — on their way to a fabulous month in Kuling — and something as practical as support could just wait. Alice smiled to reflect on the two earnest wishes Harold had expressed the day before the wedding. She wrote home to tell the dear ones: "Harold said he had been praying for two things: One was good weather, and the other, not to be scared." Both petitions were answered — and both at the last minute.

The following week, Alice wrote a long letter home postmarked Kuling, July 5, 1933. Her first words were: "Tomorrow is one week!" Then she described the experience of getting up to Kuling for the first time. The process could certainly be scary to anyone who had never been to such heights. Kuling was far above the Yangtze Valley, and it took three hours as each passenger was carried in sedan chairs on the shoulders of four to six bearers: She wrote: "I had dreaded the trip, for I knew there were sharp curves and narrow steep paths. But we had a lovely trip up — my first in a sedan chair." She went on, "We are 3,500 feet high now, and I'm just absolutely relaxed and ready to rest." She continued the letter on the following day: "My first thought this morning was — 'This is Thursday!' This is our first anniversary — we have been married one week, and it is a happy day!" Alice continued in her usual unconsciously self-effacing way, "Now the trip's over and we're in the beauties of the mountain — also Kuling. Once more I'm overcome with all the joy and peace and deep happiness that I do not deserve."

Grace also wrote numerous small details of the wedding and reception to the folks at home, sharing the little things she knew their mamma would love to hear. Grace noted, "You can hardly realize how many friends Al really *does* have, both missionaries and Chinese, and she has had to leave out a number she would have liked to have (at the reception) because it would be too big a crowd. And you can share the joy of knowing that our little Al is truly happy and is just growing sweeter every day if such is possible. I do see a change, though she is the same old Al in most ways — so thoughtful and appreciative."

The following week, Alice wrote a "happy birthday" letter for her father on his sixtieth, telling him that the day was also her second week anniversary. She added a personal note about her new husband, "Harold is kind, thoughtful, and loving to me. He's a consecrated Christian, and I look forward to going down, refreshed of body and spirit, to our little Yangchow home … to serve God with this loved one." It was obvious to her family in Sumter just how happy their daughter was. Alice's friends in Shanghai sent a clipping of her wedding announcement and the large picture that appeared with it in the July 9, 1933 *Shanghai Post.* A number of missionary friends were in Kuling, and all were thrilled that the "newlyweds" were beginning their lives together in such a beautiful place. Grace and several other friends arrived in Kuling in August, and Alice and her sister had opportunity for special times to talk in that most beautiful of settings.

Shortly before leaving their honeymoon haven in August, Alice wrote to her family about an idyllic day, "Harold and I went on a long hike together. There's a famous place — The Three Falls — but it's a day's trip. There is a steep climb, and many people take chairs and ride part of the way, but we decided to walk. We left about seven on a cool morning and got back about seven that night." Those at home could almost *hear* her happiness as she said, "We saw perfectly beautiful scenery the whole walk over. There were times we could see on either three or four sides the valley for miles and miles away. We took our dinner and bathing suits, and after feasting our eyes on the three crystal-looking waterfalls, we walked down a narrow path to the clear pool to swim."

As wonderful as the honeymoon had been, the new couple was equally excited about setting up house together. It was all a bit like living out a dream. Leaving Kuling on September 7, they took a boat down the Yangtze and traveled all the way to Chinkiang by the end of the following day. Grace wrote details to the family, explaining that Alice and Harold would stay temporarily with the Stamps while waiting for repairs to be made to their house, which was right next door. Grace wrote, "Now this week they are in Shanghai getting their furniture together, and in a week or so they can really get settled in their own little nest. Don't you know they are having lots of fun in it all?" She concluded, "Al has never seemed as happy as she is now and does not seem to worry over anything." And Alice wrote her parents: "At last — home — just us. Our own little house!"

Yangchow was a fascinating old city, rich in history. There was a fabulous old city wall, two miles on each of the four sides, about forty feet high. It was wide enough that two cars could stand abreast. One section of it even contained bricks with the imprint of the Han Dynasty, which predated the time of Christ. Alice marveled to hear that this was the city where Marco Polo had briefly served as governor in the 1260s.

But now the time had come, not only to begin their ministry together, but to address the thorny issue confronting the new couple: appointment and support. The two agreed that love was wonderful, and life was beautiful, and — you can't live on love. They sat down to put practical eyes on the situation facing them — the first big challenge for the two to work through as a team. By mutual agreement, they outlined the process from the beginning of the year until now — in their new home, but with only one salary coming in. There was some clerical error going on, because nothing had been done officially to rescind Alice's appointment, yet she was not receiving her monthly salary. Dr. Maddry had written in July that Alice's salary would continue until at least when school opened in September, but that hadn't happened.

Harold had first written Dr. Maddry in December of the previous year about making him a regularly appointed missionary, with his current support from friends being channeled to the Board. That was not possible at that time, Maddry replied. Harold then wrote in February about their engagement — and the correspondence across the Pacific started in earnest. Alice had heard from Maddry just before the wedding, stating that the Board could not see their way clear to transfer her to Yangchow as the university considered her salary part of *their* budget. The newlyweds managed to put this issue on a back burner during their honeymoon, although Alice wrote home saying, "I have never doubted God's leading us in this step. We've not taken it lightly, but as I know my own heart, we've waited on God. I am grateful for His love that is showered upon us."

Both knew the gravity of the financial situation at the Foreign Mission Board. Maddry wrote of the summer meeting of the board, reporting that the ledger told the news that by November 1, the Board would have a deficit of at least $10,000 with no relief in sight, so long and tenuous was the current depression. Maddry did add, "I wish from the bottom of my heart that I could write you a different letter, but I can see no way out of the difficulty at this end of the line. We shall simply have to make it a matter of prayer for divine guidance, and you young people go ahead and do what you believe to be God's will in the whole matter." In a follow-up letter, he stated that the Board had not taken any final action in the matter but were waiting and praying. Then in the next breath, he returned to the complications of the issue: The university was determined that it must retain Miss Wells' salary for another teacher. As the two read the discouraging news, they looked at each other with their hearts sinking a bit more. Then they brightened up again as they read on: "Many missionaries have written such gracious letters about your work. It is simply the difficulties confronting *us.*"

Harold was never noted for candy-coating anything, and in reading through the correspondence between himself and Dr. Maddry, it was clear he adhered to his usual direct and factual manner. He did find hope in Maddry often referring to, "if a way can be found," for Harold was personally dead certain that there *was* a way. As he replied to Dr. Maddry about finding a solution, he wrote, "The Lord has a way, doesn't He?" Harold then asked if there could not be found churches in the homeland to send support for Alice and suggested the Board try that approach.

Maddry had written Alice in July, "I wish for you great happiness. I only wish indeed that I could write you a different letter and say that we will be able not only to continue your salary but also take over Brother Hall's. But I am faced with the cruel necessity of keeping within the limits set by the Convention, and it is utterly impossible for us to find money unless the churches give it to us."

When Harold and Alice first began seeing each other some two years earlier, they developed the habit of ending each date by praying together. This became a habit, and when they married, they started each morning praying together. (Some twenty years later, I recall waking up many mornings to the soft sounds of my mother and father as they prayed. It was like a benediction at the beginning of the day.) In their new home in Yangchow, the young couple began every day in earnest petition together for God's solution to the salary and appointment dilemma. By nature, Alice was something of a worrywart, but Harold's certain faith that God had the answer and would provide it in *His* time buoyed her spirits each day. Alice wrote Maddry in response to a suggestion aired by him: "We are very much interested in the idea you set forth that if $800 comes from churches as a special fund for my support this next year that my relationship with the Board will be maintained. For, after all, it is this relationship that has grieved me to think of losing." Then she added, "I am praying that God will use me to fill a real place in the churches where Harold ministers, in the work with women and especially the young people."

In October, the Foreign Mission Board met, and Harold and Alice, far away in Yangchow, prayed earnestly the entire day. The matter of the Halls and their salaries and appointment was presented to the Board, and a motion was made to remove Alice Wells Hall's name from the list of missionaries. At this point, Dr. Hale Davis, president of Oklahoma Baptist University (Harold's Alma Mater) and Board member from Oklahoma, requested that the matter be *deferred* until he could consult in his state. Maddry wrote in a letter to Alice, "I am going to do my very best to raise the money for the support of yourself and Brother Hall in Oklahoma, and then we will take up with Brother Hall the matter of his appointment as a regular missionary." Their hearts were further encouraged because Maddry included with the letter an application for Harold to complete. It felt like evidence of his good faith.

At once, Harold wrote various friends in Oklahoma and, after a long night of prayer, he wrote to Dr. C.C. Morris, pastor of First Baptist Church, Ada, Oklahoma. That church's WMU had been a faithful monthly giver to his support fund these past two years. Consequently, stepping out in faith, Harold presented their urgent need to Ada's pastor. In a letter just one month later, he joyfully reported to his faithful supporters in Oklahoma and Texas, "In the Executive Session, the Far East Committee made a motion that Alice Wells be dropped as a missionary. But Oklahoma's Dr. Davis immediately made a substitute motion to the effect that FBC Ada, Oklahoma, pay Alice Wells' salary and she be retained as a missionary. The Lord used this as an opening to get me appointed as a regular missionary." He concluded the letter, "The Lord has done great things for us. HIS NAME BE PRAISED!"

Thanksgiving that year of 1933 was a time of special thanksgiving, for the appointment news from the Board became official in November. On November 30, Harold jubilantly wrote Dr. Maddry: "Your good letter just received. Our hearts are full of praise and thanksgiving because of the good news it brings us, namely the adoption of Mrs. Hall by certain churches in Oklahoma and the prospects of my adoption by the Board." The next letter from Dr. Maddry stated that at the monthly meeting of the Board on December 14, Harold Hall was duly appointed a regular missionary of the Foreign Mission Board. It was the season's best of all Christmas presents for the Halls.

Alice loved nothing better than trying out her Chinese and having opportunities to share the good news. She had loved her university students, but *this* was her calling. She told her parents about some of her early venturing into the villages and homes, often with one of the older women missionaries. She explained, "I just forgot my 'inferiority complex' about my use of the language. And by His strength, I found great joy and liberty in speaking quietly to women as I had a chance." She finished, "I came back home a happy woman because of that."

Christmas was a wonderful, relaxed time for Alice and Harold that first year of marriage, and they spent it with Grace and the Marriotts, as Pa and Cora were soon to leave on furlough. In those first months as a couple in Yangchow, even the angst of appointment and support was *not* able to put a dent in either their joy as a couple or in the work they felt called to do. Every day was exciting to Alice, and just seeing her husband at work and so fluent in the language gave her a thrill of pride. They were looking toward their first full year together with great anticipation for what God had ahead. Alice, the English professor, loved literature and especially the poets of the previous century. She favored Longfellow, and Harold was getting used to her throwing out favorite quotes. Counting their blessings that first Christmas morning as a couple, she used Longfellow's words to express what the year had been for her: "The heart, like the mind, has a memory, and in it are kept the most precious keepsakes." Her tender heart was full of such keepsakes.

Alice Hall with Sunday School girls

Arthur Bryan Hall,
age 5 months, Yangzhou

NINE

THE HALLS AT HOME

Alice often woke up feeling like she was living her dream. Here she was in the land to which God had called her, with a wonderful and devoted husband who felt the same calling, and together in their first home. For his part, Harold could scarcely take in so many blessings in one year's time, and now the aching loneliness was gone.

He wrote to Dr. Maddry about the great prospects in the work before them, of his joy in being associated with the venerated elderly Pastor Jang (Chang) at the main West Porch Church, and the privilege of preaching there in Mandarin each week, along with his preaching at the new church start where he had preached that first sermon. Harold explained that the greater part of their messages were to the lost who had never heard, but that he was very conscious of the need to feed and train the believers.

Two nights a week he preached at the main church, with mostly men from the street coming in to hear. Harold's real pleasure was in the young Christian laymen who were helping with the services. These new believers were gaining valuable training while experiencing a growing feeling of personally taking part in the work of spreading the gospel.

The young couple wrote to the Board about the great needs at the Baptist middle school, with its 1,000 students, none of whom yet knew the Lord personally. The field was wide open, but the workers were few. Along with all the preaching, visiting, and classes, both young missionaries studied the language as much as possible each day. Alice keenly felt her need for more study and a larger vocabulary; she was frustrated not to be able to express all that her heart felt. She met on Friday mornings with the women of the main church. Her language teacher helped her with the Bible study for each week's class so that, as she wrote home, "I can be able at least to keep up with where they are. I understand much of what they say, but it *tires* my brain to listen long, for I have to listen SO CLOSELY to be able to understand."

In early December, Alice wrote to her mamma that she was sitting by the fire because it was already so cold. They had invited Chinese guests for the evening meal, including Mr. Jyah (Gee-yah), their Chinese teacher. It was a great treat for everyone, since the guests had never eaten foreign food before. Alice explained that the Chinese normally do not have heated houses, so, as the temperature drops, they simply wear more layers of clothes. Then, if they go to a foreigner's home with a fireplace going, they burn up in all those layers of clothing. Alice and Harold courteously left the room unheated while Mr. Jyah and the other guests were there, but as soon as they departed, Harold scrambled to build up a fire. (Small wonder that my mother was thankful they didn't entertain guests every day during the winter!)

Alice sent a sketch of their little house to her parents, showing the study, living and dining room, and kitchen on the first floor, and upstairs, three small bedrooms. As was the custom, missionaries needed to employ household help in order to have time to study the language and do their ministries. Housekeeping was full-time work, with no other cleaning tools than a broom and cloths. The houses had a coal or wood-burning stove that took constant tending, and with no refrigeration, someone had to go to the market each day for food. Harold and Alice were able to employ a young cook named Jen Gwang (True Light), who was a believer. His wife helped with the house chores, but since she had no experience, it fell Alice's lot to train her. Alice smiled to herself to think that this was one way to be thrown in at the deep end in language learning, for the young couple knew not one word of English.

Most of Alice's letters home mentioned language study because it was so important to her and such a huge challenge at the same time. She wrote to her mamma, "It's slow work, but the Lord gives joy in trying it, for it is His work. I have told Grace I will undertake the Bible class she asked me to teach on 'women of the Bible' at the month-long Bible school coming up. The Lord will have to help me. Grace will be here, and it will be mighty good to have her that near."

Harold and Alice went together to the countryside several afternoons when spring arrived to take tracts and attempt to talk to the people about Jesus. "Some of them were too busy," she wrote, "and others greet us by saying that the country people can't understand, because most of them can't read." She concluded, "This is discouraging, but yet there's a fascination about it that makes me want to go again. We intend to do this regularly. There's usually *one* person who will listen!"

To one of Alice's letters home that spring, her husband attached a little note to say, "We are having a great revival meeting here." He told of the testimonies and confessions taking place and added in amazement, "Nothing but the power of God would lead folk to make the confessions some here have made." Then, in a special Mother's Day note, he wrote to Annie Wells, whom he had yet to meet in person, "Permit me to say thank you again for the sweet girl who is my wife. I say this not to be polite but because I feel it. Your son, Harold."

A new challenge came to the newlyweds their first spring, for their cook and his wife moved away. Alice had to temporarily handle the cooking and marketing, and it was like a baptism by fire. She developed an armed truce with the coal stove — its flue determined to stop up, and she wrote to her mother, "Yesterday the flue got clogged up again, and I was ready for tears. Even with Harold's help, the pesky stove was terrible." She continued by explaining they would have to find some help soon, for there was just not enough time to go to market, cook the food, do the Bible class at the Bible school for women, plus do her language studies. She added in an effort to sound upbeat, "Harold's very good to try to eat most anything I try." It wasn't just the marketing issue that confronted missionary wives. A myriad of things were taken for granted in America that just didn't happen in China. The nearest dental help was in Shanghai, a day's journey away. Drinking water always had to be boiled; there was no such thing as safe drinking water from the faucet. No refrigeration was available, so that made a problem with fresh milk. Even today, the list is long of conveniences that Westerners take for granted.

On a few occasions, Alice was able to go with Harold on country trips of several days or a week. She loved being in the villages, but she learned it was better to go before it got too cold, because when the floors were made of dirt, it was nearly impossible to keep her feet warm. It was worth the bone-chilling cold, however, to be able to share her faith with women and children, many of whom had never even heard the word "Jesus."

Already, Alice was as busy as her new husband, with his continuing language study, village evangelism, and preaching four or five sermons a week. For her part, Alice was deep in her studies and attending women's meetings. She wrote to her father, "I have another class at She Jah Chow Church, and my Bible classes are showing a real reason to take courage, I feel. Not that I'm doing a lot, but God is blessing in the work here." Their first year of marriage was all they could have wished for, and more. The two were not only deeply committed to the task before them but also totally committed to their marriage. All their missionary colleagues could see their happiness. It was contagious and an encouragement to the whole mission station.

Chinkiang and Yangchow stations worked in tandem on many ministries. Grace loved the work in the villages, and now that Harold was part of their mission, he could help. Sometimes Harold and a Chinese evangelist, and Grace and a "Bible woman" served as a team, going into an unreached village and staying a week or more at a time. Alice dreaded the nights when Harold was away but was deeply gratified to see what a complement he was becoming to Grace's village work. She and the Bible woman would witness to the village women, and Harold and his helper worked with the men. They made a great team.

Harold nearly had more on his plate than the day had hours. There was even more than usual to do now, for Harold was the only male missionary in either Chinkiang or Yangchow, since both the Marriotts and Stamps were on furlough. He loved the challenges, and daily gave thanks for his wonderful helpmeet. In no time, he began to wonder how he had ever made it without her. One of the most difficult parts of his time away in a village was that they both missed their morning time of prayer and Bible devotions together. It was a daily habit that bonded them for life. Harold crossed the Yangtze River many times between the two cities, baptizing, preaching, and doing station business in matters where the Chinese expected a man to direct. Alice would sometimes smile and think, how, just a year earlier, Harold had been a language student, not even appointed by the Board, and now he was essential to the two stations' ministries.

Early in 1935, good news came for Yangchow and the hospital. Dr. and Mrs. Robert Mewshaw, who had served for years in Kweilin in southwest China, were being sent to Yangchow. Much of the Baptist hospital had been closed off because there was no way Dr. Pierce could handle all her medical work and run the hospital at the same time. It was especially good news to Alice, because by early February, she was pretty sure that a baby was on the way. When she told Harold one morning in their prayer time, it brought him to tears. It was just nearly too good to be true. Alice was very aware that she was in her thirties, with a ticking biological clock. Thankfully, her nausea wasn't too bad, and they decided to wait a little while before sharing their exciting news or writing home to South Carolina and Oklahoma.

In April, Alice sat down to tell her parents and sisters the good news, feeling a little thrill of excitement as she thought of how excited her mother would be. Of the four sisters, only Alice was married, and Annie and Henry

Wells had no grandchildren. She wrote, "Now, I've been 'laying off' telling you something that means a great deal to us. It's this — in the fall, we look forward to a *little* Hall here in the Hall family." Her excitement bubbled over onto the paper as she wrote details, "I do not need to tell you of the deep joy that is ours in this hope. I told Dr. Pierce, and she and I both figure the date is late October. So you have about six months to enjoy with us this happy thought of (a son or daughter)." She ended, "I seem to be in a strange new world these days!"

As Alice wrote home each week, Annie Wells was astounded at all that her daughter was able to accomplish in any seven-day period. In one note Alice commented that she was usually up at six each morning, unless she was "awfully lazy." And what a lot a week did hold. Thankfully they had located a Christian woman to cook and clean, Mao (Mau) Ma, as they called her. It seemed to take a long time to just get a simple meal on the table, and it certainly did Mau Ma. Alice commented, "I'm rather slow, you know, and Chinese are MUCH slower than I." Harold's calendar was always full, and Alice's was the same. She told the home folks about a typical week, saying, "I've had my regular work — Monday prayer meeting, Tuesday and Thursday Bible class at South Gate, Wednesday class with inquirers at the main church, and Sunday morning and Sunday night more Bible classes." Harold would have as many as twenty inquirers in his men's group at one time, and it was highly encouraging.

Dr. and Mrs. Maddry made a long-anticipated trip to China in May, and it was a shot in the arm to the entire China mission. The Board's executive secretary was able to put new eyes on some problems and issues that needed a voice of authority to make decisions, and it helped the ministries of each station. After the Maddrys had visited Yangchow in mid-May, Harold wrote to his in-laws: "It was our privilege to have the Maddrys as guests in our home the two days they were here. Dr. Maddry brought new hope and encouragement to our work." Harold concluded by reflecting, "It is evidently time to give our Chinese brethren a greater hand in the work." (The wisdom of that philosophy proved so true in later years when China was closed to outside missionary influence as Communism took over the government.

Wells House, Tindal, South Carolina, 1929

Arthur Hall, rural mail carrier, Oklahoma, 1929

Harold Hall, pastor, County Line Church, Oklahoma, 1931 baptism

Dad and his car Oklahoma, 1931

Wells-Hall Wedding, University of Shanghai, June 29, 1933

Alice Wells on her wedding day, 1933

Alice and Harold on their wedding day, 1933

Harold in Chinese
chang paur

Wu family,
in Yangzhou
and Shanghai

揚州南門外三元巷浸會全體歡送牧師和家美全四臨別紀念影攝

一九四〇年青苗

Nan Men Wai Baptist Church, Yangzhou

WMU group in Yangzhou

Kiangsu Provincial Baptist Convention

*Aunt Grace with Rosalie and Arthur
and a friend, Yangzhou, 1940*

Grace Wells, Hawaii, 1943

*Grace Wells begins
publication work in
Indonesia, 1950s*

*Wahiawa Baptist
Church, Hawaii,
congregation with
the Halls, 1938*

George W. Truett with the Halls and Chinese leaders,
Sye Lyang Jye Church, Yangzhou, 1936

Arthur Bryan Hall, 1936
1 year old

The Hall family in 1938

*The Halls with Li Nai Nai
and friend, 1939*

*Arthur is reluctant to push
the cart, Yangzhou, 1939*

*Rosalie and Arthur
with Carolyn and Ralph
Cauthen, Yangzhou, 1940*

*Rosalie sleeping with a
bowl of Cream of Wheat,
Yangzhou, 1939*

Although missionaries were forced out, a strong church remained in China. It survived great persecution and emerged stronger and deeper than ever.)

Handling a full-time schedule and expecting a first child all at one time was a daily challenge to the Halls, and they were both looking forward to a few weeks in Kuling and wonderful fresh air and a chance to catch their breath, literally and figuratively. Alice said in a letter in August, "I'm feeling free here where the air is so pure and fresh, so different from the streets in Yangchow." Grace was in Kuling as well, and Alice smiled repeatedly as she watched Grace knit a beautiful little white sweater for their coming son or daughter. While in Kuling, she and Grace received exciting news from South Carolina that Henry Herbert, their preacher brother and his wife, had just had a son. Their soon-to-be-born baby would have a cousin about the same age.

The expectant couple returned to Yangchow refreshed, ready to jump back into their busy schedules and anticipate the imminent arrival of the little one. Most exciting to Alice was making definite plans for the baby's birth, and she smiled to think of the bounty of medical help the good Lord had provided for them. Dr. Mewshaw, Dr. Pierce, and Ruth Bracken, their friend and excellent nurse from the large Presbyterian hospital in Chinkiang, would be with her. Preparations were put in place for sterilization of all equipment, supplies, and clothing. By late September, Alice's body felt nothing but cumbersome. It felt like she was wading through rushing water just to pick up her feet and get from one place to another, so unwieldy was her body. In early October, Ruth Bracken came from Chinkiang to stay with the young couple, for who knew when baby might decide to come.

Meanwhile, Grace was sewing all sorts of little baby items and knitting in all her spare time. She would be listening for a message and come as soon as word arrived. Grace made plans to stay for a week or so in Yangchow. That way, she could keep the house running smoothly and allow Alice and Harold plenty of time with their new family member. Alice was ever amazed at Grace's knitting output, and wrote to their mother, "I must learn to do better myself, for I mustn't depend on Grace to keep the youngster supplied with sweaters!" Dr. Pierce and Nellie, her mother, made a little winter cover for the baby's basket bed. It was pink on one side and blue on the other.

The family in South Carolina got the first news in a letter from Grace, who wrote on October 15 of the arrival of Alice and Harold's son the previous day. Grace had received a message at nine that Monday morning: Come immediately. Writing about the day, Grace said, "As soon as I arrived, Mao Ma in the kitchen told me with beaming face that the baby had come, and I rushed on upstairs to see Al eating her dinner and the newcomer calmly eating his thumb." Then Grace related to her mother all the little details that she would want to know, explaining that Alice started having pains at midnight but thought they might be a false alarm. Soon realizing it was the real thing, Nurse Bracken went to work preparing supplies, and Dr. Mewshaw and Dr. Pierce came quickly. Harold was there to help the whole time, even showing some nervousness not typical to him. It seemed an eternity at the time, but really, it was just 10:30 on Monday morning when baby gave his first lusty cry, all six-and-a-half pounds of him fussing at the bright new world in which he found himself.

Alice's joy was evident in the letter she wrote two days later: "Bless the Lord oh my soul, And all that is within me, Bless His Holy Name!" She shared the excitement of this time in their lives and added, "If you could just see us in our new role as father and mother!" Alice introduced their grandson to the Wells family: Arthur Bryan, named for Harold's father, Arthur, and for Dr. R.T. Bryan, that grand old patriarch of the Central China Mission, who had performed their wedding ceremony. Arthur was fortuitously born on Dr. Bryan's eightieth birthday.

In November, Alice wrote home that a furlough time had been approved by the Foreign Mission Board for June the following year, so they would be able to meet their grandson when he was still just a little fellow. Her letters the next several months were full of both work and all the details of Arthur Bryan developing, growing, smiling, turning over, sitting up, and wrapping himself around everyone's heart. Now more than ever, there were simply not enough hours in each day, and Harold and Alice looked with deep satisfaction at their work, their precious son, and the exciting prospect of seeing family and dear ones after seven long years.

Alice and Grace Wells, Shanghai

TEN

THE REAL *ĀH YÍ*

Grace never shirked from hard work and a full schedule. She normally thrived on it, but suddenly it was a special pleasure to have meetings and tasks in Yangchow. Of course, all along she had enjoyed special times with Al and Harold, but now there was Arthur Bryan — and she was the epitome of a doting aunt. (*Āh Yí* is the general term for "aunts" in Mandarin, although there is a specific title for "aunt" on each side of the family. Grace was officially *Yí Mā* — her sister's side of family.)

She wrote Sumter the details of Arthur's first days of life, and of the many discussions of who he resembled ("Some say his Grandpa Wells!"). She speculated on his coloring, deciding he might end up a blonde. Grace lavished love on the new family member, and Alice would sometimes come to happy tears, thinking of the extra blessing that was hers in having real family here with her at such a special time in their lives. Grace tried not to dwell on the fact that her treasured young nephew would soon be going to America for the first time, so she cherished every moment she was around to spoil him.

On June 6, 1936, Grace wrote the family about seeing her little curly-haired nephew and his parents off for the United States, happy for them but rather sad for herself. She described how seven-month-old Arthur Bryan was captivating hearts everywhere, Chinese and foreign alike, with his endearing little toothless grin and his ability to wake up in a good mood and remain charming nearly all the time. She reported to her family waiting with such excitement to see their long-gone daughter and meet their grandchild, that, "He has just captured everybody's heart." Grace comforted herself by focusing on how excited her parents were going to be to meet Arthur and reminding herself that her own furlough would be coming up in a matter of months, and for a short time, *all* of them could be together.

Now, over eight decades later, I reflect on this "Aunt Grace" who played such a big part in my life. In fact, for the last few years of my childhood in China, she was the *real* Āh Yí who lived next door. It was such a nice feeling to know that, although I called nearly every woman in the China mission "aunt," this one special aunt really *did* belong to me. Next to Mama and Dad, Aunt Grace had the greatest impact on my life. She and Mama were so alike and so different. Aunt Grace was a wonderful example of the oldest child in a family, for she was a great boss — *bàn shr de*, as the Chinese would say. Her bossiness was the loving kind. She was a woman who could take charge and work with everyone, while at the same time helping them know how to be at their best. Mama, with her gentle and kind spirit, never liked to have to take charge, although she could do so with great skill when necessary. Mama was more likely to observe, assimilate, and pull the best out of others, so she and Grace were a great team.

The sisters experienced similar childhoods, both having the wonderful influence of godly parents and a grandmother and great aunt who nourished their spirits as well. Grace was born near the end of the nineteenth century, in 1897, and took to her role of big sister to four siblings like the proverbial duck takes to water. Her teacher at the little country primary school in Bethel district loved the way Grace would help with the younger children — and, for her part, Grace learned great teaching techniques from watching her own teacher and gained valuable teaching experience that she used for the rest of her life. Like her younger sister who followed her to China, Grace's first missions training came from Aunt Edith, who poured information about missionaries working in foreign lands into all the little Sunbeam Band members at Bethel Church. Edith must have found special joy in seeing two of them go around the world to share the good news with hundreds of children who had never heard. Grace graduated from Sumter County High School in 1914 and was the first female in the Wells clan to ever attend and graduate from college — graduating from Winthrop in Rock Hill, South Carolina, in 1918. Grace trusted Christ as a ten-year-old child and felt even then that God wanted her to go to China to share the good news.

In order to save money to attend the Woman's Training School (WTS) at Southern Seminary, Aunt Grace taught in a rural South Carolina school for a year. Then came the immediate need for a teacher at Connie Maxwell Children's Home in Greenwood. Aunt Edith was a beloved housemother there and contacted Aunt Grace about the need. For two years, Grace gained invaluable teaching experience while simultaneously being able to save enough money to attend the training school. She then headed for Louisville and two years of study, preparing for service overseas as evangelist and teacher. In constant contact with the Foreign Mission Board, Aunt Grace was focused on appointment to China in 1923.

The fulfillment of her dream of mission service became reality on June 14, 1923, when she was appointed by the Board to do evangelistic work in Chinkiang, China. Late in August, Aunt Grace headed across the country by train. It was her first transcontinental experience. The five-day journey from Sumter to Seattle was both exhausting and exhilarating as she drank in the scenes of America's West. Grace reported to the home folks, "Lucy (Yau) and Mary (Phillips) are here, too, and we are to room together on the steamer." After language school, Lucy and Mary were to be co-workers with Aunt Grace in Chinkiang, and it was hard to know who was most eager to sail. Both Lucy and Mary had been her classmates at the seminary. (Lucy, sponsored by Missouri WMU, had been the only international student at

WTS, and as if by divine planning, Lucy's home city was Chinkiang. She would be returning home, where her pastor father worked, and where she, too, would now work with her recently appointed classmates and friends.)

Grace told her mamma, "I can't realize that this is really Grace Wells here in the Hotel Gowman in Seattle." Four of her training school friends would be on the same ship with her, and that made it doubly exciting. In fact, there was a bumper crop of missionaries on that one steamer, both new and returning, single and married, some thirty-six of them. To make it even more special, the renowned executive secretary of Woman's Missionary Union, Kathleen Mallory, was to be on the *SS President McKinley* as well. Miss Mallory was embarking on an extended visit to two of Southern Baptists' largest fields: Japan and China. Grace felt privileged that among those missionaries was Miss Cynthia Miller, the nurse who had accompanied Lottie Moon on her final trip home in 1912. Grace was able to speak with her about that experience, and it was a bit like touching missions history firsthand.

The cluster of missionaries gathered around Miss Mallory on the ship's deck as they all waved farewell to the well-wishers on shore; many people had come to wish them Godspeed. Aunt Grace felt a thrill of excitement that afternoon of August 30, 1923, heading out to fulfill the mission to which God had called her. The *President McKinley* was a sleek steamer and held the record for the fastest trip to Asia of any ocean liner to date. In just a few short weeks, Aunt Grace wrote home her first impressions of her new adopted land, describing the amazing and crowded metropolis of Shanghai — the largest city in that land of large cities — and explaining that it would be her second home for all her years in China.

First on the agenda was language school in Nanjing, at that time the capital of China and only some fifty miles by train from Chinkiang, the city which would soon be home. Everything new assailed Aunt Grace's eyes in Nanking (Nánjīng). It was a fabled ancient city of China, several thousand years old, with a Ming Dynasty (1368-1644) wall and relics of a number of tombs belonging to famous Ming emperors from earlier centuries. Nanking had been China's capital for six different dynasties, and all about the city was an echo of its storied past that fascinated Grace and simply added to her appreciation of the country's significance in history.

Studying the difficult, tonal language presented a constant challenge, but determination had never been a weak point for Aunt Grace. She absorbed her lessons and studied for hours each day. Even during out-of-class experiences, she used every possible occasion she could find to practice speaking Mandarin with people in shops and on the street. She waited with great eagerness for the first holiday, because then she would have an opportunity to visit the city that would be her home — Chinkiang, part of the Central China Mission. Grace was thrilled to think of soon getting a first look at what was to be her field of service. The holiday break from studies finally arrived, and Aunt Grace was like a child at Christmas, looking out the window of the train as it neared Chinkiang — and home. Nearly 100 years later, I discovered the letter she wrote about her first impressions, and her excitement stepped out of the yellowed pages of her account. Recalling her first look, Grace wrote: "I got here Thursday p.m., and Friday morning went down the street with Mrs. Stamps, and we realized that *all* the descriptions of the narrow streets, the many people, the rickshaws, and the sights and smells had not prepared me for what I saw. You just have to *see* to believe."

Chinkiang would be home for her seminary classmate Mary Phillips as well, so the two traveled together for their first visit. That evening, the city church gave a reception for the new missionaries. Aunt Grace described the reception: "The new-comers sat on the rostrum in this crowded little room and listened to any number of Chinese speeches of welcome — all of which we didn't understand, of course." Aunt Grace added, "To our dismay, we had to respond!" Fortuitously, their friend and classmate from Chinkiang, Lucy Yau, was there. Lucy served as interpreter as Aunt Grace and Mary thanked everyone. Grace described in detail the refreshments — some of which were familiar, and others things she had never seen. Following refreshments, the church leaders gave Aunt Grace and Mary their all-important Chinese names. Aunt Grace's was a fairly simple task, for the Chinese like to find an auspicious surname that "sounds" a lot like the English surname. "Wells" became "Wei" (sounds like Way). Her given name was an easy one to choose, for "Grace" in the Bible is Ēn Dyān (Ūhn Dyānn).

Elizabeth Stamps, a seasoned missionary colleague, was their hostess and an old China hand. Knowing the importance of hospitality and eating in the culture, Elizabeth gave Aunt Grace a tutorial in how to use chopsticks. Margaret, the Stamps' winsome little three-year-old, loved demonstrating to her new Āh Yí the proper use of the eating instrument that looked to Aunt Grace like nothing more than two straight little sticks. She had never tried them before, and at first it felt clumsy and awkward. She was amazed, however, at how quickly practice made perfect. Grace's first real use of them came that night with her first true Chinese meal, and it was in dear Lucy's home in Chinkiang and great fun for all. On Sunday, she heard her first ever sermon in Chinese. Aunt Grace told her mother in a newsy letter home, "Mr. Marriott preached in Chinese, the first sermon I ever heard of which I could not understand a word!"

She also wrote to her mamma about the afternoon tea Mrs. Marriott gave so she could meet all the foreigners in the city and added, "I know it sounds strange to you to hear me call myself a foreigner, but I am!" The entire experience in Chinkiang made Aunt Grace acutely aware of the massive needs of the people in her adopted city, and she explained, "I shall be so impatient until I can really learn enough of the language to do even a little ministry. Don't forget me, dear people, for I need your prayers as I never before did for the task before me." Seeing Chinkiang and its vast needs, realizing her utter frustration at not being able to communicate in the language, and reflecting on what challenges lay just in front of her, were all daunting bits of reality to a young single woman in a strange land. But Aunt Grace was never one to back down from a challenge, and this challenge was God-given — and, God being her helper, she would meet it one day at a time.

Grace Wells in Zhenjiang

ELEVEN

THE WORK BEGINS

Language school was quite a task master. Sometimes Aunt Grace would chuckle and tell a fellow student, "It's days like today I wonder why I didn't go to South America and only have to learn Spanish!" Even as she said it, her classmates knew it was merely language frustration speaking, for Grace was totally committed to her calling to China. And, typical of language students, she was anxious to be "out there" and doing her job. At the end of May 1924, she wrote home about her first-ever experience of an annual mission meeting. She stayed on the campus of Shanghai College and had a great time rooming with her long-time friend Hannah Plowden from Sumter, who had finished training school a couple of years ahead of her. (The Wells sisters had known Hannah from childhood, and in a few years, Hannah would be a bridesmaid in Alice's wedding.)

Aunt Grace described a bit of her shopping experience in the great metropolis, including getting a little folding cot "that I can use in working in the countryside." The whole day of shopping sounded like a wonderful break from the monotony and discipline of school. Her letter explained that when she was about broke, she decided to quit shopping and end the expedition by "getting a chocolate milk shake at the Chocolate Shoppe." Downtown Shanghai was a good seven miles from the college campus, so she tried to get a lot done on a single trip into the city. On campus, Aunt Grace loved looking out the window of her bedroom on the fourth floor of the women's dorm and watching the ocean steamers moving up the Whangpoo River into Shanghai.

Then came the mission meeting itself, where she met for the first time most of the missionaries who comprised the Central China Mission, nearly ninety of them. She noted in her letter home, "There were lots of tiresome details of business, and yet, there were also *many* very important things in regards to plans for the work." As she heard the reports from each station, Aunt Grace was able to get an introduction to the scope of the work in that populous area of China — and it was massive. She commented, "I feel so woefully ignorant of it all. I did not realize before how many problems there are in mission work." Aunt Grace sounded rather puzzled as she observed, "Things that you feared before you came never materialize, for the physical and material hardships are not felt at all. But the *mental* problems arising every day are the real tests of a person's Christianity." She ended by commenting, "This is a new day in China, and some of the old methods of work cannot be used now. There are new responsibilities and perplexities."

Aunt Grace continued her studies that summer in Kuling and fell in love with the cool breezes, clear water, and cleanliness so unlike the typical crowded cities of China. Studying in that atmosphere was a pleasure, even if the trip up the mountain in a sedan chair was so scary that she kept her eyes closed a good part of the way. In August she wrote to Alice of plans for the months ahead. She was moving to Chinkiang in September and would be continuing her language school while also starting part-time in her work. That was what excited her. She reported, "I expect to have general oversight of the girls' day school and, to begin with, will teach maybe only one class in English." Grace sounded impatient when she commented, "Don't know *when* I'll know enough to teach subjects in Chinese in the Woman's Bible School where my *real* work will be. But others are learning — and so can I." She sounded a bit self-reflective when she commented to her sister, "I want to see if my inspiration here in the mountains will carry on when I get down in the valley and face some of the problems. There are plenty of them, and the more advanced and efficient our work becomes the more complicated the problems."

The mission station was planning for Aunt Grace to live with the Stamps, and she wrote of hoping she would not be a bother to them. She had already fallen in love with the Stamps' little ones. Margaret was three, and little George had just been born that summer in Kuling. Aunt Grace wrote to Alice, "George has just begun to coo and play, a well-developed ten-week-old boy. I just enjoy him so much."

Aunt Grace's introduction to Chinkiang and work on the field was not an easy, comfortable time. She was soon to discover that wars, threats of war, civil conflict were all the norm in China. In October 1924, a warlord from the north was approaching with a large army, and government troops from the south were also fast approaching. It wasn't long before fighting began. The British consulate was right behind the Baptist compound, and toward evening the British Consul sent word that the missionaries could shelter in the consulate. Aunt Grace had never experienced such a crisis and found that it gave new meaning to the truth of utter dependence on God. Her several days in the consulate seemed like weeks, and the sounds of fighting could be heard throughout each day. Then one morning they woke to utter quiet. The opposing forces had moved on toward Nanking, and the final fight for supremacy was fought there rather than in Chinkiang. Nanking missionaries were now in peril. Many had evacuated, but one missionary was killed. Aunt Grace was cautious about what she wrote home, not wanting to unnecessarily alarm the family. Thankful that the current crisis had calmed down, she was soon back to work.

In December, Grace wrote to Mamie ("Dumps"), her youngest sister, about Thanksgiving in Chinkiang with the main course being goose. She told Mamie about the constant presence of language study and commented a bit wryly, "I am still studying and suppose I will be to the end of my days and *still* never learn anything." She raved about the precious children she taught and said, "I have received a box of toys from some Sunbeams in North Carolina and will give them to the children at Christmas time. I want to have some pictures made of some of the dearest little children here for you folks to see. I'm just wild about some of them. One little girl, whose father is in the Bible school studying to be a preacher, is a little picture, but I could never catch the mischief in her little eyes with a Kodak shot."

Aunt Grace had more than enough work going on already: language study (which she recognized as being a lifelong learning) and heading up the girls' school — plus beginning teaching at the Woman's Bible School, which was a particular joy. Teaching there made her feel like she was directly investing in the lives of women who could, in turn, reach their fellow women with the message of salvation in a way a foreigner never could. Village ministry was another important part of her work. Lucy Yau usually accompanied her on country evangelistic trips. Lucy was not only a great companion and coworker in their village "itinerations," as Grace called them, but also a personal friend who could help her culturally in her understanding of the people to whom she ministered. Aunt Grace often reflected on the wise and loving investment of Missouri women in this young lady who so effectively worked with Chinese and missionaries alike. Cread and Cora Marriott had sung her praises to the WMU women of their home state of Missouri, and those women had raised the funds for Lucy's two years at the Woman's Training School, where she made top grades in her New Testament studies.

Aunt Grace's work was primarily in Chinkiang, but as often as possible, she and Lucy also worked with the Yangchow station in country evangelistic trips. By 1926, Aunt Grace was officially heading up the Women's Bible School (seminary extension) and teaching and directing teachers at the girls' school. Mission schools were key to teaching children Bible truths and becoming feeder schools for the University of Shanghai and the seminary.

Grace felt the enormity of the tasks before her and sensed a deep need for wisdom in using her time wisely. It did her heart good to see how the 75 Million Campaign of Southern Baptists (aided immeasurably by WMU and Kathleen Mallory) had invested in the wonderful new church structures in Yangchow and First Baptist Church in Chinkiang. She wished women in America could just see what their loving investment meant when it went to work overseas.

By 1926, wars and rumors of wars, plus danger from bandits, were growing, and Grace could sense the unease among the people. Both the Marriotts and Stamps had gone on furlough, making Mr. Napier the only man left in the Chinkiang station now. Whenever missionaries went on furlough, everyone else picked up more work. Not only was the extra work a challenge, but also Aunt Grace sorely missed the Stamps — especially little George. He had wound himself around her heart, and it was just like part of her family was gone. More than ever she longed for Alice to get there, but she knew her sister must first finish her seminary training.

In addition to a heavy workload and political unrest that was growing every day, Aunt Grace had some personal unrest. She had been having digestive problems for a number of months, and the diet she was forced to eat on extended country trips only added to the problem. The pain finally came to the point where she knew something was wrong and help was needed. Subsequently, she crossed the Yangtse to Yangchow and placed herself in the hands of Dr. Adrian Taylor, a brilliant surgeon, fresh back from additional studies in the US. A nasty appendix was the culprit, and a week after surgery, Aunt Grace was up and ready to get back to work.

She dearly loved the ministry, especially evangelism in the villages, where so often she had inquirers who had never before heard the name "Jesus." Her Chinese language skills were growing with each day of use, and in the girls' school, she was teaching English each day — a real drawing card for students, because everyone wanted to learn English from an American. Her special delight was teaching Bible in grades one and two — and she frequently grinned to herself, thinking that was just about her level of Mandarin, so it was a perfect fit. At the women's Bible school, as she taught New Testament, she felt like she was making a personal investment in the lives of those women who would, in turn, reach their villages and communities with the good news.

At the same time, in the midst of all that seemed "normal," conditions in the countryside and city both worsened quickly, with refugees fleeing the fighting and crowding into Chinkiang, hoping to be more protected there. Yangchow was somewhat out of the main danger zone, but Chinkiang, being only fifty miles from Nanking and a major port city, was at high danger. Chinkiang was at the confluence of the Grand Canal and the mighty Yangtse River, where American and English gunboats were in the harbor.

Aunt Grace tried to write the home folks of the current situation in a way that would not alarm them too much. She briefly outlined for them the causes for the conflict. It was basically a civil war, with the Nationalist forces of the north now opposed to the leadership of the Nationalists in the south under the direction of General Chiang Kai-shek. Mixed in with all of that was the Communist threat, although ostensibly the Communists were working *with* the Nationalists — both of them opposing the ever-growing threat of a militant Japan that had eyes on controlling all of China. To further confuse the situation, the Soviet Union was secretly backing the small Communist element with an eventual end goal of seeing all of China controlled by Communism.

The greatest suffering was among the poor people: thousands were slaughtered, young girls and women raped, property randomly burned and destroyed, and soldiers taking whatever they wished, both food and property. The women in the Bible school, and even the young girls in the girls' school, were living in daily fear and were careful never to be alone on the streets. Aunt Grace's heart ached, and she felt so terribly helpless.

Generalissimo Chiang began what he called the Northern Expedition that year, with a goal of capturing the large cities and subduing the warlords, persuading them to join him. For their part, the Communists didn't trust Chiang, because he made deals with conservatives and with Western nations who were friendly. On the other hand, the Communists were anxious to promote a popular revolt among the poor people. Before the year ended, Nationalists had taken Hankow. By early 1926, the Southern Nationalists were headed toward Nanking, leaving vulnerable a large community of foreigners, missionaries and businessmen alike. Nanking was only fifty miles from Aunt Grace in Chinkiang, and the consulate warned all foreigners of the danger. Chinkiang's main mission houses were located right in the heart of the foreign concession — with the French consulate to their right, and the British right behind the Baptist compound. All were vulnerable to attacks from either army in the civil conflict.

Aunt Grace met with her missionary friends, and they talked and prayed through what they must do. There was no way to protect their property; all they could take with them was possibly one suitcase and a small trunk. Aunt Grace was careful in her letter home not to sound too terrified, which she personally admitted to herself was more like what she really felt. Strangely, however, she later recalled that along with the terror was a rather indescribable sense of the presence and protection of the Lord, something she had never experienced in such a way in her nearly thirty years of life. She put what she could in her meager baggage and felt a fatalistic sense that the rest was surely expendable — it was just "stuff."

What would happen to them? What should be their next move? All these questions roiled around in her heart and thoughts as Aunt Grace hastily packed what she could and prepared to get to the wharf and safety. Often in theory, she had declared that she was willing to suffer and to put her life on the line if necessary. Well, now it might be — and she felt a strange sense of inevitability in what was going on. Truly, only God knew what lay ahead. She had no way to know — she could only trust. As Aunt Grace packed, she began humming one of the grand old hymns of the faith, and it brought a strange peace in the midst of her tumult: "When we walk with the Lord in the light of His word, What a glory He sheds on our way, When we do His good will, He abides with us still, And with all who will trust and obey." She firmed her chin, straightened her back, picked up her suitcase, and did not look back.

On advice of the US Embassy, Aunt Grace and most of the missionaries prepared to temporarily evacuate to Japan — Grace thinking all the time of her women students and those vulnerable young girls at her school with no place to go for safety. She sometimes felt like she herself was sitting on a bomb of emotions that was just waiting to explode.

It was almost two months before Aunt Grace was able to freely write a few details to the home folks and relate how she had gotten out of Chinkiang. She explained that she and her fellow missionaries were still in Chinkiang when the Northern soldiers moved out of the city (ahead of the Southern soldiers on their way in). The little band of Baptists had waited to evacuate because the Napiers, the only missionary couple then in Chinkiang, had two sons in school fifty miles away in Nanking. Mail and telegraph connections were all cut off, so they had no way of knowing where the boys were. They just knew Nanking was in immediate danger. Aunt Grace wrote, "We got word to get on the gunboat as things were going to happen soon. We left our homes on March 24 and stayed for two days on the wharf by the gunboat until we could get a boat to take us down the river. We finally found a steamer with room for us and were escorted down river by a British gunboat. But," her story continued, "when we arrived in Shanghai we found things *tense* and nobody sure of anything." The Napiers learned that their sons had been evacuated from Nanking and sent for safety to Japan. Shanghai itself was in imminent danger of fighting, and no one felt safe.

Sure enough, Aunt Grace and other missionaries were temporarily sent to Japan for safety. She explained, "The future looks very dark for our work, and I wish they'd send us all home for the present, for I feel so useless sitting here spending money when if I were at home I could work and not be an expense to the Board." She ended the letter by explaining that it looked like things had settled down enough in Shanghai for her to return and maybe teach there, while she waited to see if she could go home to Chinkiang. Aunt Grace was certain of one thing — and that was uncertainty.

Grace Wells, 1926

TWELVE

WARS AND RUMORS OF WARS

After tense months of anxious waiting in Japan, the US Embassy gave the all-clear for Americans to return Shanghai but to expect a tense situation. Aunt Grace wrote to the family, "We have heard since we left that our houses have been looted and occupied by soldiers and that there is great anti-foreign and anti-Christian feeling. Luckily we got out all our personal belongings early, and only the furniture and big things were left to be looted." But on a more ominous note she added, "Many in Nanking lost everything and almost their lives. One missionary was killed by a man who was robbing him, but his wife and two children got on a boat headed home the other day, and they seemed so brave."

At least from Shanghai Aunt Grace could monitor the situation in Chinkiang, hoping to get back to her work there. Consequently, she returned to China in September and described her jumbled feelings in a letter home, "I'm not anxious to be back in Shanghai but it looks as if the Lord is leading that way and it may be best to stay nearer the work in case there is anything I can do." She concluded, "Anyway, I've stopped worrying for I know that if I do my best to follow, I'll be led." She sailed into Shanghai harbor to find a city much on edge. The terrible Shanghai Massacre of April 12 had left a thousand new problems in its wake. General Chiang Kai-shek had managed to purge the Communists who had incited the labor unions to attack the government. However, Chiang's forces had killed thousands before taking over control. Chiang was supported by western governments, and American and British ships with many troops remained in the harbor. Only the international settlement had escaped the bitter fighting — but everyone was on edge, and nationalist soldiers were everywhere. Grace wrote to Sumter about the soldiers pressing men into service to carry things for them, and that "they take anything they want, like shoes and eats from the shops. It's mighty hard on the poor people, and it is affecting our schools some, for a lot of the little girls are afraid to get on the streets with so many soldiers."

Confusion reigned in the city, but Aunt Grace agreed to teach at the North Gate School. Chinkiang was in far worse shape than Shanghai at the moment, and she didn't know when she might be able to return. North Gate school was completely supported by the strong North Gate Church, Shanghai's oldest, and a living tribute to Dr. Matthew Yates, the missions pioneer who had founded it in the 1800s. Miss Willie Kelly, with her amazing skills in the language, was becoming something of a legendary missionary herself. Miss Willie was director of the school and the single most influential person in the venerable congregation. She was delighted to have the skills of Grace Wells to teach and serve as an inspiration to the young girls attending.

Grace wrote to her parents, "Foreign troops are still being landed in Shanghai, and that scares the Chinese and at the same time makes them mad. Both factions are trying to get the other side to do something to start things with the British troops, but so far Britain has been very patient." She was getting reports from Chinkiang all along, and news was discouraging. Mr. Marriott was there to try to keep an eye on the work among the Chinese Christians and protect the property. It took all he could do to keep soldiers from occupying the mission houses, and things were so dangerous, she wrote to her parents, that "he sleeps in his clothes in case he has to leave suddenly." She added, "I don't see what the future holds — the near future anyway. I do believe that the Lord will bring good out in His own good time, and His kingdom will be strengthened."

The newspapers were full of news of the "Red Terror" that was sweeping parts of the country as Communist bands were burning, robbing and killing in villages and small towns throughout entire provinces. Aunt Grace taught in North Gate School the remainder of 1927 and in 1928 as well, since Chinkiang was still too dangerous for foreigners. She was more than busy with her schoolwork, helping lead the missionary society in the North Gate Church, plus assisting with smaller churches. In a different type of work, many evenings the missionaries in Shanghai led Bible studies for the countless American sailors and marine corpsmen, some from the American ships in harbor and others posted in the city. These men were hungry for fellowship with other Americans. Any number of young American men were lonely, and many were eager to study and learn Bible truths.

Several of them became regulars at the fellowship groups, and one in particular was impressed with the vibrant young woman from South Carolina with the shiny dark curls and intriguing Southern accent. Walter, a handsome young sailor, seldom missed a fellowship time, and he brought numerous others with him. (Nearly sixty years later, Aunt Grace, then close to ninety years old, long retired and living in South Carolina, showed me a picture from her "China trunk." She gave her little self-deprecating laugh — the laugh she always had when she was a bit embarrassed — and handed me a small snapshot. I took it, looking into the smiling face of a striking young naval officer, then looked askance at her. Aunt Grace ducked her head a bit to one side and said, "That's Walter." I frowned a bit in puzzlement. She gave her little laugh again and murmured, "He was my fiancé." My eyes got big, and I said, "What?!" No details were forthcoming; that was Aunt Grace, always reticent about herself and her feelings. She simply said, "It just wasn't to be. I needed to be where I was." She said no more, and I knew better than to probe. Aunt Grace had never spoken a word about Walter in the fifty years I had known her. (Now, more than thirty years after that revelation, when going through the hundreds of letters Aunt Grace and my parents had written sixty or more years earlier, I found her letter talking about Walter and recalled that moment in South Carolina when Aunt Grace had given me just a tiny glimpse into her heart.)

In late 1928, during her final months of teaching in Shanghai, Aunt Grace wrote, "We had just gotten the fire to going and settled down when three of the sailors came in and stayed through supper. Then we all went to the Beacon for a service and social." Two days later in the same letter, she said, "Walter is gone — left very unexpectedly on a transport that sailed yesterday. He had only about two hours' notice to get ready and get on the ship. It surely seems strange to feel that he won't be in every evening." (There was so much more left unsaid than spoken, and I wish I knew more about Walter and all that went into Aunt Grace's decision to remain at her post when there had been such a pull in the direction of her heart. Seeing this reference to that long-ago moment in her life helped me understand that she never divulged her heart even to the dear ones at home.)

It was providential that Aunt Grace was so busy, for it likely kept her from dwelling on "what might have been" and getting on with the work at hand and that to which God had called her. She was grateful to be able to get back to Chinkiang, even if only briefly, prior to time for furlough. There were masses of refugees in the city, and uneasiness among the population was very understandable, considering the state of politics and the economy in China. Grace hoped that her presence would serve as a comfort to the Christians and provide something of a sense of normality. The Stamps were still on furlough, and nearly everything they possessed had either been looted or destroyed during the fighting in 1927. The Marriotts were on furlough now as well, so Grace and Mary Philips were the only ones in the station. They did receive some assistance from the handful of missionaries who had returned to Yangchow. Faithful Lucy Yau had made it through the fighting and was still active at both the girls' school and the women's Bible school. It crossed Aunt Grace's mind many times during that final year that "normal" might never return in China, for who knew what "normal" was by this point?

Back in Chinkiang, Grace reflected on the months of teaching in Shanghai with a certain sense of accomplishment. In the midst of all of China's turmoil, she still had the satisfaction of knowing she had been able to meet a real need and plant the gospel seed in scores of young hearts. Nonetheless, she was more than glad to be "home" in Chinkiang and directing and teaching at the Baptist primary school for girls again. The women's Bible school was still in temporary hiatus; she greatly missed that opportunity, but it gave her more time for village work — and, in spite of the great physical difficulties in that type of travel and teaching, the village time was rich in personal fulfillment, as she was able to share the good news with hundreds of people who had never heard it . Some of her country work was "out stations" on the railroad line linking Chinkiang with Shanghai. Women's work had never been touched in these out-stations before, and when she and Lucy Yau first began, the pastors in the city discouraged them, saying it wouldn't do any good. However, they kept right on, and in the first year had already organized two Sunbeam Bands and were ready to organize a Woman's Missionary Society.

Aunt Grace wrote a long letter telling the family about the trials and troubles encountered on the country pilgrimages, but mostly describing the rewarding moments that made the troubles worth the effort. In March 1929, she reported: "The trip was not an easy one as we went all day by boat and reached our city by ten at night but had to get up at five to take *another* boat. And that meant unrolling and rolling up bedding to use during those few hours as I did not *dare* use the cover at the Chinese inn. When we came to the town, we were welcomed by the pastor and his wife and given the best they had. Lucy and I put up our cots in his study, which was a small room with one window and a dirt floor. But we had some very good meetings in spite of *cold* damp weather, and we hope that some souls were saved. Many listened to the gospel, and we hope the Spirit will use His word to convict their hearts."

Aunt Grace continued with her account, "We stayed there six days and then went by boat to the next town. Here, the pastor and his wife gave up their own room for Lucy and me. But, my, this room was dark. It had a window opening on a sort of open hall, but all the light came from a tiny skylight overhead. And at night, the tiny lamp did not give enough light to even read by." She finished on a positive note, "But the women came in great numbers and listened oh so well. It is a place which has the name of being especially given to idol worship and superstition. But the Spirit had prepared hearts to listen. A number [of the women] professed faith in Christ." (As I read Aunt Grace's letter some ninety years later, I marveled at her attitude, to say nothing of her fortitude. From the standpoint of a different millennium, those conditions sound both primitive and harrowing, but it was the joy of her heart, and her favorite type of ministry.)

Sometimes the two young women went as a team into what Aunt Grace called the "real country" where the gospel had never been preached. The great joy there was encountering eager listeners, and some would invite them into their homes to tell them more. She wrote home, "One lady heard us and said she wanted the people in her mother's village to know about Jesus and pleaded with us to go there. It was a longer walk for her than for us, for she carried a baby and had bound feet — but we were glad we went, for the people were so happy to see us."

And it was furlough time! Had she really been on the field six years? Some days it seemed like twice that long, and others, when she saw the crying needs surrounding her, made her feel that she had done so little, and the time had just flown. She continued to hope that in spite of the Board's financial situation, Al (the family's pet name for Alice) would soon be able to be appointed. It seemed like a lovely dream, to think of having a piece of her real family in China with her, and she prayed daily for that to come about. Furlough came — and she could never have imagined the emotions that flooded her heart upon first seeing the coastline of America over the horizon as her ship neared Seattle. She stood on the deck of the vessel, her eyes welling with tears. Surely that was nothing compared to the overwhelming sensations that brought her to tears of joy when her father met her at the train station. They could scarcely get enough of hugging each other, patting one another's backs as if to say, "Is that really you?" Jumping out of the car when they reached the Tindal farm, Grace flew into her mamma's arms, and she thought she would never let her go. But, here was precious Grandmà, looking a bit more fragile but smiling and weeping with joy, and dear Rhett, with suspiciously damp eyes. Aunt Grace was so buoyed by the sheer joy of being home that she scarcely slept that night. She lay there for a long time, giving thanks to God and determining to absorb and enjoy every moment of the family time ahead of her.

And, as if her cup of joy needed to simply overflow a bit more, in June, Al sent a telegram from Tallahassee, where she was campus minister at the college, announcing the news that had just reached her from the Foreign Mission Board: She was to be appointed for China! Grace thought to herself, *Now I can enjoy every moment at home, and know at the same time that when I return to my work, my sister will be there, too!* She recalled how often Mamma would say to her brood of children, "I know you like to think you can have your cake and eat it, too!" In this case, Grace felt a new burst of joy; she felt she could indeed have it both ways.

Harold Hall with Sunday School children, Yangzhou

THIRTEEN

WAITING

Thinking about Aunt Grace's first furlough in 1930 and the great joy she felt at being with family after nearly seven years in China, causes me to think about how much Mama and Dad looked forward to their first sight of America and family, after spending six years in China.

In January 1936, Alice wrote that word had come from the Board indicating they were to go on furlough in June. She described it: "To think of seeing you all makes me feel all jumpy inside, like Christmas holiday coming when I was away at college. No, it's a deeper feeling even than that!" In the next breath, she wrote, "Harold has so much scheduled for the spring, I don't see how he can get it all in." Her own schedule was packed full as well. The Bible classes with girls from the church were meeting at the house with her now so she could be with the baby, and, of course, the girls loved that. Alice's heart overflowed with a sense of fulfillment whenever she thought about the girls who had come to faith and were growing steadily in their depth of understanding.

In addition to the couple's full days, guests were on the way. Dr. George W. Truett, president of the Baptist World Alliance (and pastor of First Baptist Church, Dallas) and Dr. J.H. Rushbrooke, BWA officer (and later following Truett as BWA president) were to spend a weekend in March in Yangchow. She told her mother, "I'm delighted for our people here to hear a message by Dr. Truett. He is to preach at Syi Liang Jye (the large church) and then meet with the Yangchow missionaries."

Some two months later, on June 19, Alice wrote from on board the *SS President Taft*, "I'm coming as fast as I can towards you. I just can't push this boat along any faster." She ended the letter on her usual tone of excitement, "I don't yet realize how near I am to America, home, and you! It seems too good to be true!" Since they were coming across the continent, it was logical to stop first in Oklahoma, where Alice met her in-laws for the first time, along with Harold's sister, Mellie, and her husband and family. It was obvious that Georgia Hall adored "my only boy," as she called Harold, and the whole Hall family fell in instant love with the baby and with Alice. A short time later, the three of them headed for South Carolina in a car a good deacon friend had helped them purchase at cost. Alice had never driven, so Harold did the driving, and she had her first experience of traveling cross country for over a thousand miles with an eight-month-old infant. (This was before the days of disposable diapers, so it was an interesting experience — and one she would have several times during furlough.)

When their faithful little car reached the state line from Georgia into South Carolina, Alice felt her heart rate accelerate. She was actually in the same state with her beloved family, after seven years with not a look at those dear faces. By the time they turned off the main highway onto the small road close to Tindal — she could hear her heartbeat in her ears. The baby had fallen asleep, but as the car slowed down, he roused and look around. When they turned onto the little unpaved road leading up to the house, Alice was close to having her anticipation boil over into happy tears.

They drove up in front of the white-framed house, the front door burst open, and out poured the entire family. Alice had imagined this scene for years, but reality was much more joyous than her anticipation had envisioned. She grabbed Mamma close, and the two wept together. Then the same joy was repeated with Daddy, and even he could not control his emotions. Grandmà, a bit frail but with a huge smile, tenderly held her grandchild close, and then there were Rhett and Dumps and Aunt Edith, as quiet as ever, but overflowing with emotion. It took a good ten minutes for anyone to become coherent, and for Alice to introduce Harold for the first time to his in-laws. Everybody wanted a piece of little Arthur, and he basked in the attention.

Furlough was exhausting and wonderful all at the same time. Trying to juggle some family time, coordinating with the two families living so far apart, and speaking to groups and churches made Alice and Harold realize that they would have to return to the hectic schedule of Yangchow in order to get just a bit of rest. Sadly, in the midst of an already busy time, Alice suffered a miscarriage. She was not far along, but she and Harold had been ecstatic at the thought of one more child. At age thirty-six, Alice was very aware that her biological clock was ticking inexorably, and they both grieved over this loss. At the same time, seeing old friends, meeting new ones, and sharing experiences from China was a thrill. It was also good that they were extremely busy, for there was little time for brooding and worry.

Alice was especially happy to have experiences like they did in Shawnee, Oklahoma, where Harold had attended Oklahoma Baptist University. There was a School of Missions where a team of missionaries spoke in all churches in the area during a two-week period. At the end of two weeks, both Alice and Harold were completely drained, but they had stored up wonderful memories. Alice was so happy to meet for the first time many of Harold's college and seminary friends, especially those from Southwestern Seminary that helped support their friend who had gone to China on faith.

Another highlight was attending the state convention, where the featured speakers were Dr. Maddry, president of the Foreign Mission Board, and Kathleen Mallory, executive director of Woman's Missionary Union. Alice wrote to Sumter, saying, "Dr. Maddry spoke last night, a great speaker and truly our friend. When we came to the platform at the beginning of the service, he walked clear across and greeted us." She continued reporting: "Miss Mallory brought a message tonight, and it was so good to see her again." And she ended by telling about George W. Truett's concluding service. He spoke to a crowd of more than 2,500 — and many more people stood outside the auditorium, for there was no more room.

Grandmama Hall kept the baby for those weeks, and Alice could scarcely believe how much she missed that child. She had brought along a big picture of him and "talked" to it frequently during each day. The hardest part of furlough for her turned out to be such times as this when she had to leave her baby for several days or a week at a time.

The furlough seemed a whirlwind, with family time plus deputation work speaking in many places. All the time, both were missing Yangchow and wondering what was going on there. Grace tried to keep them posted, and a recent letter had said, "I feel like we must do all we can while we are at peace here. Nobody knows what to expect, and there is a very pessimistic attitude." Harold and Alice felt torn, anxious to get back to their work, yet at the same time deeply thankful to be with family while they could. A highlight for both of them was a week spent in Ada, Oklahoma, with First Baptist Church, the church that paid Alice's salary through the board. Both of them treasured all the opportunities they had to see old college and seminary friends and bond again with America. There was no way around it though: China had changed them. A big part of their hearts was there, but then, they realized that this was how it should be, for their love for the Chinese people was a God-given gift.

While they were still in America, Grace arrived on her second furlough, and on their final trip to South Carolina, Harold and Alice had a chance to see her on the American side of the Pacific. The whole Wells family listened in delight to hear the three old China hands get caught up on news of the dear ones in Yangchow and Chinkiang. Grace informed them that she was a regular joke to all the missionaries in her area because of her excitement over going home. She declared, "I am even more thrilled than I was the first time — guess I'm getting old!"

It was a blessing that Harold and Alice had learned a few things about changes of plans. It had just about become a way of life, and here it came again. They headed to Seattle in August 1937, with reservations to sail on the *SS President Grant*. They had left for the long trip across the continent, aware of the uncertainty of sailing. Conditions in China were steadily worsening, yet Alice and Harold were like the rest of the China missionaries due to return to their work — anxious to get back and work while they could. They left Oklahoma on Tuesday August 10, for Seattle, knowing that Dr. Maddry and the Board might wire them that they couldn't leave on schedule. Arriving on August 13, they went first to the shipping office to see if a wire had arrived with instructions. Nothing had come, so they checked into the hotel with plans to sail the next day.

Early Saturday morning, a cable came from Dr. Maddry in Richmond. Dr. Rankin, head of the mission in China, had cabled that all missionaries in Central China had come from the surrounding areas into the foreign concession of Shanghai for safety. Maddry suggested that the group delay sailing, but let each missionary make a personal decision. The Halls decided to wait at least two weeks until the next ship was to sail. The situation was complicated by the news that Americans were not being allowed to leave Shanghai by train or boat to go further into China, because troops were carrying soldiers only. They might get to Shanghai, and then not be able to go on to Yangchow.

Conditions in China only grew more tense, so here Harold and Alice were, in limbo, sitting on the West Coast, waiting. When word came again in two weeks that missionaries headed to Shanghai needed to "wait and see," the little family of three sighed, packed, and headed back to Oklahoma to wait. All the angst of goodbyes had been gone through. Now it would happen again. Word spread that the Halls were temporarily still in the United States, so they filled their time with speaking and helping in churches. Waiting was hard, and hearing confusing reports out of China made it even harder. Their hopes would rise with good news, and then the next day, reports of further Japanese occupation sent their spirits plummeting. Grandma Hall was doubly unhappy that they might well be going into harm's way, and her face held a perpetual look of anxiety. Dr. Maddry contacted them frequently with the latest news available, and that helped.

On Thanksgiving Day, it dawned on Alice that she was going to have another child. She was a mixture of joy and angst, and Harold echoed her feelings. This is what they had hoped for, longed for, but the memory of her recent miscarriage was haunting. It was the worst and best of times — but it was what it was, and they were in God's protecting hands. Then shortly after Christmas, Maddry wrote saying that Dr. Rankin felt missionaries could return to the field with the understanding that they recognized from the outset that times were greatly uncertain, as was the future.

So eager were Harold and Alice to return to Yangchow that, as they prayed and thought through the issues involved, both determined that they should go. Their two-year-old was oblivious to the drama going on around him. Just give him his little hammer, and Arthur was a happy boy. Alice declared to the family that he was "enamored of his hammer." He even insisted on taking it to bed with him.

Alice was so queasy by this time that the very thought of getting on board a rolling ocean liner made her stomach make an extra roil. Even at the best of times, the ocean had to be glassy smooth for her to find her sea legs and keep her stomach calm. However, she consoled herself with the thought that a voyage wouldn't last forever, and the ship they were able to board was stopping first in Honolulu. That gave her some assurance for relief along the way. With hopes high, the little family of three said their tearful goodbyes once again, leaving with the sight of Grandmama's stricken face haunting their minds.

The last of January 1938, they arrived in Honolulu. Never had Alice been so happy to see land appearing on the horizon. Her optimistic thought two weeks earlier was that the ocean voyage would not last forever. As she wrote to her parents after recovering enough to write, she assured them it only *felt* like forever. "We had a *rough* voyage," she wrote. "The SS *Matsonia* looks pretty but has a reputation for rocking. ... They need to change its name to *rocky*," she suggested. "As to our feelings those days — the less said, perhaps the better. Arthur Bryan lost his dinner to the fishies one day and was satisfied to stay in bed the next day as well. Even Harold was quite miserable," she explained, "but I was the one violently sick." Being an expectant mother didn't help the situation with her stomach. The sight of Honolulu in the distance literally brought thankful tears to her eyes. In two weeks' time, they had come from snow on the ground to sunny skies and balmy breezes.

They stepped on shore, only to learn that a telegram from Richmond awaited them. It was not welcome news. Japan had occupied Yangchow; at the moment, it was uncertain as to whether missionaries would be allowed in. "Wait and see" was the message. The news rocked their minds and shocked them all at the same time. It was devastating — to be thinking they were on their way home to Yangchow, but suddenly, the door slammed shut. However, the handful of Baptists in Honolulu welcomed the Halls with open arms and wanted them to be interim leaders at the little Wahiawa Chapel, part of the beginning of Baptist work in the islands. Gordon McDonald, a Baptist layman, had started a Sunday School at Wahiawa, just out of Honolulu, and was thrilled that a minister had come who could help in the interim to get a little chapel going. Many of those attending were young Japanese who understood English, and several had already come to faith. It was a vibrant young group, hoping for some pastoral leadership. Disappointed as Harold and Alice were that their work in Yangchow was temporarily inaccessible, they were relieved to know they could be useful while they waited. Harold was also eager to preach, even if it was in English. Alice was grateful for firm ground under her feet for a change, and a stomach that had quit tossing. Their two-and-a-half-year-old was thrilled to be able to run around again on firm ground and play with his hammer.

There was a neat little apartment over the chapel building, and on the bottom floor, the small chapel and four Sunday School rooms. They began teaching and preaching at once, all the while listening to daily news about the situation in China. A number of adults attended the services, for quite a number of young Americans were stationed at the nearby Pearl Harbor base. In fact, Wahiawa was just a mile from Scofield Barracks, home to 12,000 US military personnel. Alice found her greatest joy in teaching the young people. These were bright and eager students, wanting to learn biblical truths; the Halls could not have known how God would use one of those youth in years to come to skillfully lead Hawaii's Woman's Missionary Union. Another youth was a promising young elementary student named Dan Kong, who grew up to pastor Hawaii's leading Baptist church, Olivet, and serve for years as a convention leader. The Halls' seven-month investment of time in Hawaii was time well spent.

Not knowing what to expect — when, how long they would be here, or if the coming baby would be born at sea (although Alice had nightmares over that thought) — they found a doctor in Honolulu. Dr. Roberts, a Naval doctor and teacher of the men's class at the Honolulu church, agreed to be her doctor. Honolulu was about twenty miles from Wahiawa, so they drove in for her visits and decided when the baby was due, they would stay in Honolulu so as to be close to Queen's Hospital, where Dr. Roberts worked. The family at home asked if they had chosen a name, and Alice hedged a bit by replying, "We've thought something about a name, but it's hard to think very definitely till we know if it's a he or a she."

Even when they waited, they became deeply invested in the young people of the chapel. Alice wrote home about their love for this temporary stay: "The work with this mixed crowd around here is certainly interesting — we love our young people. Pray with us that many of them will be won." In May she wrote: "We've learned that Dr. Vance and Dr. Pierce have been able to return to Yangchow, and that gives us hope for our early return. After all, it is the work to which God has called us, and we've been 'champing at the bits.'" And still they waited — for permission to return to China, *and* for baby to arrive. May came and went, and still they waited. Surely it would be soon. Once again, faith needed to step into the moment and sustain their courage. Wait they would, and hope.

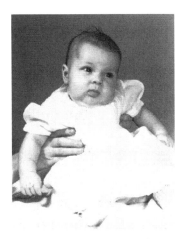

Rosalie Ann at 2 months

FOURTEEN

AND BABY MAKES FOUR

Mama was always the most patient member of the family. However, some things could try even her patient soul. By the time May was nearly gone, Dr. Roberts suggested she stay in Honolulu to be closer to the hospital. Mrs. Takahashi, a dear church member who lived in the city, wanted the family to stay in her home, and she thoroughly enjoyed spoiling the mother-to-be.

It was a revelation to me over eight decades later to discover Mama's letter written the first week of June and read about my arrival in the world. After reading about her experience, it is small wonder she had no more children! She wrote home that from Friday until Tuesday, they mostly relaxed, walked, ate, talked and slept "with one eye open." Tuesday afternoon, Dr. Roberts asked her to check in at Queen's Hospital and he would start things going. After the procedure, he told her that pains would likely begin in an hour. Her pains only waited twenty minutes and lasted from then until shortly after midnight. It was early morning, June 1, when

I arrived, eight pounds, two ounces strong.

Many decades later, when going through old letters and the baby album Mama meticulously prepared, I cringe at all the early references to size and appetite. However, part of it is likely due to comparisons with my brother, for he had been a finicky eater. Mama seemed highly gratified that her second child was not. She wrote to South Carolina family, "And what about the tiny one? She has a double chin, (underlined) bright sharp eyes (when they're open) and dark brown hair. The nurses say she has a fine disposition, and we hope she keeps it up." She ended by telling them the baby's name: "'Ann' is for her two grandmothers, and 'Rosalie' because we like the name." Early the morning of my birth, Dad sent a cablegram to both sets of grandparents, who, in turn, notified the mission board. Mama stayed in the hospital ten full days. All these decades later, that sounds extremely long.

Mama's next letter described Arthur's first look at his sister. Dad brought him to the hospital to pick us up, and his little head popped out of the car window. With big eyes he asked, "Is that *Syau Mèi Mèi*?" (little sister). As soon as we were settled in the car, he demanded, "I want to see her feet!" After a moment or so, he pronounced, "Nice baby!" Mama described me to the South Carolina relatives, "She's a fat darling little thing; her skin seems quite fair, and she still has a big appetite!" They tried putting mittens on me (according to the letters) to keep me from sucking my thumb. It didn't work.

I can remember many years ago Dad telling me one of Art's cute sayings. Dad was teasing him one day and asked, "Did you know you had ancestors?" Art piped right up, "Yes. Rosalie Ann sister." Glancing through that letter recently, it warmed my heart to read, "Arthur Bryan calls her 'our' baby and 'my baby,' and shows her his toys."

The day Mama and Dad returned to Wahiawa, a cable came from the Board saying they were cleared to return to China, even with so many unknowns. Reservations were made for them on the SS *Empress of Japan*. Both were thrilled to finally have some concrete plans, although they knew it would be hard to leave the chapel and all the friends they had made in Hawaii. Not only was their passage booked, but Grace was going to be booked on the same ship. Mama was elated. The ship arrived August 24, and departed the next day, allowing Aunt Grace just a few hours to go to Wahiawa and meet the church folk. Her big excitement was meeting her only niece for the first time. Mama later told me that the moment I first smiled at Aunt Grace, she instantly became my willing slave.

Shanghai seemed much as it had been, other than the unbelievable amount of red tape all foreigners had to go through with the Japanese military. Up country in Chinkiang and Yangchow, the Japanese presence was going to be even more restrictive, and changes were occurring everywhere. Many of the church services had to be conducted in the homes of the missionaries for the time being, and it was a different way of life. Yet in spite of restrictions, rules, and intimidation from the occupying forces, among the hearts of the people there was a great stirring. Many came to faith and were discipled and then baptized. The difficulties of working under Japanese occupation were well worth the pain because of the attitude in the hearts of the Chinese, who realized their desperate need of a Savior. Dad and Mama had a wonderful sense of being "home" again and back where they belonged.

Mama occasionally found a way to send letters on an American or British ship, which meant she could write more frankly about what was really going on under Japanese occupation. After they had been back in Yangchow for about two months, she sent word: "We write carefully from here, for incoming and outgoing mail is all subject to THEIR censors. And please be careful that anything in letters unfavorable to the Japanese be kept quiet. In other words, if facts are made public and by any chance came back to the authorities over here, they might make things hard for the person who wrote them." She explained further, "Things are so uncertain as to the future of the work; we are grateful every day for the privilege of witnessing here *now*."

She wrote of the heavy schedule Daddy was maintaining, wanting to preach and teach at every opportunity since all the missionaries sensed that they were working on borrowed time. Dad had several young men who were very promising Bible students, like twenty-year-old Wu Ji Shau, who seemed a truly anointed young man. He came from a strong Christian family, with an older brother already in ministry. Dad wanted to pour into young Mr. Wu and other promising young students who would, in turn, be able to do so much among their own people. All the missionaries had an increasing sense of the ticking clock, realizing that it was just a matter of time until they and the other missionaries were forced out. Mama was having her Bible class girls come to the house twice a week, and as she wrote, "I do feel that they need to be studying regularly, and it's a joy to have them." She explained one of their problems under Occupation: "The Japanese military police told Harold decidedly he could not go to our South Gate chapel to preach. Things are not peaceful in that section of the city. There is still much suffering," she continued, "People who lost all they had will not have an easy time this winter. We try to help them in any way we can." Yet in spite of the angst and tension surrounding both the suffering Chinese and the missionaries who wanted to help all they could *while* they could, there were bright pockets of hope — as God's hand at work was evident in the eleven churches and chapels now active in Yangchow.

Dad and Aunt Grace were able to make several evangelistic trips to the villages, and Mama never liked to be by herself while Dad was away. Occasionally a missionary friend would come stay with her, and it seemed to ease her mind. Dad and two Chinese helpers went on one particular trip, and Aunt Grace and Lucy Yao went to work with women in the villages. In this little town, there was an empty upstairs in the pastor's home, so Dad and the helpers slept in one room and Aunt Grace and Lucy set up their cots in the other. Aunt Grace wrote that this trip was an easy one for food, because the pastor's wife was a good cook and took care of the meals for the week. Normally on village missions, Aunt Grace and her helper would have to fend for themselves about food. It gave a real boost to the pastor to have the missionaries come to work with the ones who were already believers, and foreigners were always a draw to bring in new ears to hear.

Mama tried to write home about once a week, but sometimes that wasn't possible. We two children were a handful, in addition to language study and all the Bible classes she taught. Her letters home revealed that I began talking long before I crawled. The Chinese tended to carry children around most of their first year of life, rather than letting them get down where it was dirty. But after all, the vast majority of homes had dirt floors so that is very understandable. Li Nai Nai was a nanny *(amah)* for me when Mama was studying or teaching, and evidently loved to spoil little ones. I was a prime candidate. My first words were in Chinese of course, "Da Da" *(Bah Bah)* for Daddy and *"Um Mā"* for Mama. These many years later, I love being able to read Mama's letters about those long-ago years back in China. I can sense the sheer delight her two little ones gave her. She described to her own mamma the fun she had in watching us play together. Art would fall on the floor to make a big noise, and I would slap the floor with my hands and squeal with pleasure. I called him *Guh Guh* (big brother) and he called me *Syaú Mèi Mèi* (little sister). He informed Mama one morning, *"Syau Mèi Mèi* is a sweet baby." I wished many times in future years that he had remembered that early sentiment!

Mama recorded my early language tries in the baby book she kept. Evidently, I loved having visitors, for they invariably indulged me. Clarabel Isdell was Yangchow's newest missionary and principal of the large girls' school. She enjoyed practicing Chinese with a two-year-old but ran into a snag one day as she watched Mama dressing me. Clarabel picked up a sock and asked, *"Shr nide wādz ma?"* I shook my head no and answered, *"Bu shr* (no)! *Shr nide wàdz,"* letting her know she had used the wrong tone and said the wrong thing. (Amazingly, nearly two decades later, Clarabel was the only person present at our wedding who was a long-time personal friend of both the bride and the groom — one of life's strange coincidences.)

Evidently, one of my favorite pastimes was eating. When we went to the Stamps for a meal, Elizabeth always fixed a lovely little children's tea table for Art and me. Mama told me in later years that I would eat my food at the kiddy table, then come clamber up on Mrs. Stamps' lap and say, *"Wo yàu dyan syīn"* (I want dessert). Mrs. Stamps doted on little ones, for her George was a teenager now, away in school and almost ready for college. Their only daughter, Margaret, had tragically died when only four. That was followed by the blow of losing their youngest son Winston (Winkie) in 1936. He was just nine years old. Winkie contracted flu and was gone in a day's time. The shock was nearly overwhelming. Ever after, Aunt Elizabeth shamelessly spoiled us.

One morning when Mama couldn't locate me, she went next door — and, sure enough, I was at my little Chinese friend's house, having a second breakfast with her. Mama got there just in time to see me reach out with my chopsticks and pick up a crispy little piece of something and crunch down on it. She was horrified to learn it was fried grasshoppers. That was the end of my spontaneous breakfast visits.

Even during trying times with constant surveillance from the occupying forces, Dad and Mama had a steady stream of joy in their work. They had added a new chapel to their other work. It was thriving and had already found a new and larger place to meet, one that was well-located to attract new people. Interspersed with the satisfaction of ministry, however, was the constant tension in the atmosphere. They had to be extremely cautious in what they said and did. As Mama wrote, "We can only live one day at a time and be thankful for continued opportunities. I know we are more fortunate than most of the world just now."

Aunt Grace loved to have meetings scheduled in Yangchow, for that meant she would have family time and could be with the little ones. She wrote home that "Mei Ann's (Rosalie's) first phrase was 'Gay Wo' (give it to me)." The Bible school for men and women in Yangchow was thriving just now, with students eager to learn, and Dad and Aunt Grace both taught there and were constantly aware that their own days might be severely limited. However, these young people would still be there to share the message. This gave the work a real sense of urgency. Mama was also teaching English to some promising students, and, like all the missionaries, praying that these hours investing in young lives would pay heavenly dividends. Dad was teaching a class titled "The New Testament Church," and the text was in Chinese, written by Miss Janie Lide of the Shantung (Shan Dong) mission. Miss Lide had lived with Lottie Moon when she first arrived in China and was like a piece of mission history herself.

Mama always filled her letters with little everyday tidbits that she knew the family would love to hear. A Chinese friend from the newest chapel gave the family a young canary, and Art and I were thrilled to watch it flit around. The folks had a little portable organ they used at the various chapels and kept at home in-between services. Mama was noted for playing *only* in four flats, and, accordingly, would transpose any song to that key. Little Miss Canary began singing along with Mama and the hymns, much to the delight of Art and me.

Restrictions did not grow fewer; instead, some new rules were added all along. Everyone treaded softly and worked hard at being discreet and cautious. Dad and Mama were always conscious of the fact that their days were likely limited in China. Foreigners had to get passes from the Japanese military to travel anywhere, and travel by train was closely monitored. Right before Christmas, Dad and the other teachers went with the Bible training school students to do evangelistic visits in the out-stations and surrounding villages. It was a first for several of the students and a wonderful training experience. Mama wrote Sumter to say that in one village, they walked part of the way and took rickshaws the rest. At one point, Dad got out and pulled the rickshaw and let the rickshaw man ride in his place. It was likely the first time that man had ever had such an experience. Mama wrote, "This is a wonderful time to work, and we rejoice in every chance to work for him. NOW is the time, and it's a privilege to be here!"

Mama felt especially blessed at Christmas to have "real family" in China with her, and that Christmas was spent in Chinkiang with Aunt Grace. Even as they savored every moment, all the adults were aware of the fragility of conditions and understood that their opportunity to be there and preach the gospel was not likely to last much longer. For some reason, Dad and Mama were allowed to return to their work with South Gate Chapel, and they made good use of each chance to work there, knowing that it could change at any time. Because of censorship, Mama left a lot of things out of letters. Talking about the children seemed safe enough and she loved to include details, as in one letter she mentioned that Mei Ann (me) had gone on strike and would not put on her shoes, but she loved playing with her dolls. Arthur Bryan still favored his hammers and had finally learned not to hit people, just nails. I heard him called Arthur Bryan so often that my baby version was a shortened *"myan."*

Mail was becoming more sporadic, and a lot of their mail was not reaching them. Mama frequently wrote of "the missing mail." The summer of 1940, rather than try to go to a cooler clime, the four of us spent several weeks with Aunt Grace. She was in the large mission house at Yin Shan Men (Silver Mountain Gate), and it was far cooler than our little Yangchow place. With everything on summer schedule and meetings only sporadic, it was a welcome break. Mama especially enjoyed it because Aunt Grace indulged her niece and nephew all she wished, and Mama looked on and smiled and rested.

My parents felt like a broken record when writing to family in America, because nearly every letter was full of "we don't know how long we can stay," or "the situation grows increasingly tense." Rumors of imminent war breaking out between the U.S. and Japan kept everyone on edge. Dad and Mama were still able to carry on their heavy workload in the various chapels, but more and more frequently they heard the question: "When are the foreigners going home?" Dad was engrossed in his classes at the Bible school at the main city church. He had thirty young men, and several of them did "on the job training" by assisting Dad in village work and numerous chapel services. A young Mr. Hu "with a big, deep good speaking voice" was preaching, too, as was Wu Ji Shau, whose winning personality and gentle spirit were combined with a fine mind and many skills. Dad happily invested in their lives, always thinking of what the road ahead would look like for them, with war bubbling on the horizon.

By this time, Japanese soldiers stood guard at the hospital compound gate, and all the coming and going of the mission family was duly noted. One day, for no apparent reason and right in the middle of a busy nearby street, Dad was apprehended by Japanese military police and taken to their nearest precinct. Dad had to go through a Chinese interpreter who understood Japanese to try to discover what was going on. He later told Mama that he had to admit to some heart palpitations, for the occupying force was just looking for a way to cause trouble. After hours of questioning, Dad was very reluctantly allowed to return home; he was a bit shaken as he related to Mama and the concerned mission family what had happened.

It was shortly after this that Mama and Dad had a scare on my behalf. Art and I were endlessly fascinated at the way the Japanese soldiers would snap to attention and salute one another. One afternoon, Mama heard some commotion at the gates and hurried to see what was going on. She knew Li Nai Nai had taken me out on the compound for a walk. Sure enough, I had approached the gate, stopped right between the two Japanese guards, snapped my feet together as I had seen them do, briskly saluted and announced (in local dialect and little girl pronunciation), *"O sz dah Buh Bun bing!"* (I'm a big Japanese soldier). Mama, her face red, forthwith got me home in a hurry.

To add to the uneasiness of the times, Dad had some physical problems going on, and numerous exams and blood tests were trying to find the problem. That, plus the political tension brewing ever stronger, forced my parents to decide what they should do about the immediate future. They wished the problems would all just go away, but that wasn't going to happen.

Rosalie and Arthur, 1939

FIFTEEN

WAR

Daddy and Mama tried to keep life as "normal" as possible in such a tense atmosphere, but uncertainty hung over each day like a dark, gray cloud getting ready to dump on the hapless souls on the ground. We children were oblivious, and for that my parents were thankful. Mama tried to keep a positive tone in letters home, and the work was highly encouraging — with real responsiveness, especially among young people. Not wanting to alarm the family in America, she wrote as usual about the doings and sayings of us two children. She reported, "Mei Ann is Chinese in language and food, for she insists on rice, wanting it three times a day." Mama continued, "She usually understands English but invariably answers in Chinese. Some things she simply understands much better in Chinese." She wrote that my favorite remarks were *"Dà ni,"* (hit you) and *"Shr wŏde"* (it's mine). For his part, Art was happily bilingual.

Dad's health was an increasing problem and a cause for concern, for neither the doctors at the Yangchow hospital nor those at Presbyterian

Hospital in Chinkiang could find his underlying problem, even with multiple blood tests and various injections. At the same time, the work was a daily blessing because of the great responsiveness of the masses of people now living under foreign occupation. In November 1940, advice came from the US Consulate for all women and children to leave the country, as well as any men who had physical problems. A large ship was scheduled to arrive in Shanghai to be used as a special "evacuee" ship, and hundreds of people were preparing to leave on it. Mama wrote to South Carolina, "I still do not feel like leaving the work yet. After much thought and constant prayer, I've written to the mission office in Shanghai that I don't feel that God is leading me to go on the ship next week."

There were several special meetings and revival services going on, and with doctor appointments and a hectic schedule, Dad was busier than ever. There was another ship scheduled to evacuate foreigners the end of December or the first of January. Mama wrote home, "If there should be a shaping up that looks like a number ought to go, our whole family may go. But we just don't know now." The letter rang with both uncertainty and hope as she explained, "Nobody wants to be caught here if America and Japan go to war, but we all want to stay as long as possible and *still* have a way to leave." She finished with what was clearly their dilemma, "If His will is for us to go, we want to go, and *when* He says 'go.'"

When time came, saying goodbye to their Chinese friends and all those they loved at the churches was a wrenching experience, to say nothing of all the planning and packing that had to take place. Daddy went through the house looking at the various rooms and devising a plan. There was a tiny room upstairs that might be able to be sealed off without its being obvious. For several nights he worked on the project, and when the room was sealed off and the walls repainted, Dad thought it could possibly work. They put everything in the room that would fit, including little mementos and family keepsakes they could not possibly take with them. Knowing the chances of the room remaining undiscovered were slim to none, they still felt like it was worth a try. Goodbyes were laden with tears, although thankfully Art and I didn't have a clue. We were just excited about going "on a big boat."

On January 1, 1941, we were aboard an American ship, and Dad reflected on what he had written to Dr. Rankin (the area director in Shanghai): "The one big question is how long before world conditions permit our coming *back*. The extra year we HAD to be away from China is still fresh on our minds." By the end of the month, our family was back in Oklahoma. Reunions were bittersweet: joy at seeing family, but grief over leaving the work they loved.

The first order of business was Dad's health. Appointments were set up at the Baptist hospital in New Orleans, so they soon traveled there, hoping to determine the problem and possibly start treatments, although surgery sounded like a possibility. It took considerable time to discover that Dad had a severe case of oriental amoebic dysentery (a condition that plagued him much of the rest of his life but didn't stop him).

Mama was beyond excited to think about going home to Sumter and introducing her mamma and daddy to their only granddaughter. It was worth the tiring trip, although they could only cover about two hundred miles a day. It was an extra challenge to travel more than a thousand miles with two little ones. All the discomfort of those days on the road vanished from Alice's memory with the first sight of Mamma and Daddy and the dear ones there. They were frailer than four years earlier, but so dear that she wept with joy. Her parents' elation over seeing Arthur again and meeting their granddaughter warmed Mama's heart and made her cry even more. The weeks spent in Sumter were like a dream, and those special times were some of the earliest memories of my childhood. South Carolina held a special fascination for me, and I loved the farm — all of "Aunt Rhett's chickens," as everyone called them; the fat, jolly (and dirty) pigs snuffling around; a herd of milk cows and several horses. It was a whole new world.

Most fascinating, however, was my grandparents, aunts, and ninety-three-year-old Grandmà. She had her special soft chair in the parlor, and I loved to sit at her feet and listen to her talk, of course just understanding about half of what she said. It was becoming a bit unhandy now, in America, to be speaking Chinese all the time, and no one outside Mama, Dad, and Art understanding a word I said. Mama told me that one evening shortly after we got there, I got down on my hands and knees and went growling up to Grandmà and said, "*Wo shr yige dah law who. Wo yau chr shau ni.*" Grandmá looked taken aback and asked, "What did the child say?" Arthur, with all his five-year-old wisdom, was my faithful interpreter. He explained, "She just said she's a big Chinese tiger, and she's going to eat you up!" I could tell Grandmà loved me anyway. Nevertheless, as a matter of self-preservation, I soon picked up English. It was a lot easier than having to depend on Art all the time.

I was especially enthralled by Granddaddy's candy jar on the parlor mantel. It was shaped like a triangular cone sitting on a pedestal, and he kept it stocked with peppermint candy. Granddaddy seemed to be the only one in charge of that jar, and every evening he would get it down and give us children a piece of peppermint candy. That jar now sits on my mantel, and I smile and think of my grandparents every time I see it. Grandmama Ann was the quiet one with a loving hug when I got near her side. Her sweet smile reminded me of my own mother's smile, so it was instant love. One of her specialties was peach ice cream, and no one has ever made it quite like Grandmama.

Those early days often flash back in my mind, and I recall the first time I ever met an African-American. A family friend from the neighborhood came to see the returning missionaries and meet their children. She reached down to pick me up and hug me, admiring one of my thick golden curls. I stared at her in wonder and reached up a tentative finger to brush down her cheek, then inspected my finger to see if the color came off. She got a huge laugh over this "foreign" American child who couldn't even talk with her.

Granddaddy Hall had retired from his mail route, and he and Grandmama moved to Pryor in northeastern Oklahoma. Pryor served as something of a headquarters for Dad and Mama as they did deputation work, speaking in churches and conferences while waiting to see what would happen in China. Mama mostly cared for the two of us and did some speaking in the general vicinity while Dad traveled. They were hoping to hear at any time that they could go back to China. (There was no way anyone could predict the world conflict that was about to erupt and rage for the next five years.)

Art and I adjusted quickly to life in America, and I speedily learned to communicate in English. Just across the street from Grandmama and Granddaddy's was Gail Jones — exactly my age — and she soon became my buddy. I found a lot of things different in America. There were no walls around our houses, but neither was there a Li Nai Nai to satisfy my every whim. There were sidewalks in this country and ten-cent stores! For the first time in my life, I attended a Sunday School class in English and loved going to Pryor's First Baptist Church. Of course, when we were in South Carolina, Bethel was our church, and everybody there seemed to know everyone in our family. Mama and Daddy were able to work in a visit to the nation's capital along with a speaking trip, but, regrettably, I wasn't old enough to remember that first visit to Washington. Mama told me in later years that they went quietly and reverently into the rotunda at the capitol, walking around looking at all the statuary. After a number of minutes, Mama said I just plopped down on the floor and announced, "Ma's tired!" Wish I could personally remember that piece of history.

Then came December 7, 1941, and the world changed forever — literally. Pearl Harbor was bombed. Hundreds of Americans killed. Dad and Mama heard the news on the radio shortly after returning from worship that Sunday morning. They looked at each other, and their first reaction was: "China. How can we hope to go to China now?" All America echoed with President Roosevelt's words: "A day that will live in infamy." Pearl Harbor changed the whole equation of what my parents were going to do. No longer were they anticipating quickly returning to their calling. America was at war. The next months were full of turmoil for a whole nation newly at war. Dad and Mama prayed most earnestly about what they should do. Within weeks, Dad set into motion plans to pursue enlistment in the US Army as a chaplain.

Meantime, my parents were deeply concerned for Aunt Grace. She was now living in a country occupied by a declared enemy of the United States. Not only were they unable to talk to her, all mail service was cut off, and for the next eight months, they knew nothing directly. The Foreign Mission Board was able to get occasional word on the situation in Yangchow and Chinkiang, and cabled worried family members in the United States that missionaries were interned where they lived but could not leave their compounds. That was relief in one way, but shock in another. Aunt Grace and a Methodist missionary friend interned together in the large mission house, and we later learned she was allowed no visitors and no mail. Thank God for loving Chinese helpers who remained with her and did the marketing. Mama sat down and cried when in late August she received a letter from Aunt Grace, written from aboard the evacuation ship the *SS Gripsholm,* somewhere in the Atlantic Ocean. The remaining Yangchow missionaries were also on that ship, and a total of thirty-eight Baptist missionaries were traveling with her. Aunt Grace began by assuring the family that she had not been in physical danger, although they'd had no idea what was going on in the world. Her last letter had been from Mama, written the previous October! Aunt Grace was safe — and the entire family was overjoyed.

In late April 1942, Dad was scheduled to leave for officer training and then chaplaincy school at Harvard. Fortuitously, the house next to Grandmama and Granddaddy became available for rent, and we moved in. April 27, however, was a day that has remained in my memory ever since. Dad was trying to get everything shipshape in our rented house prior to heading to officer's candidate's school, and he and Mama went downtown in Pryor to run errands. I was four years old and loved "going." The folks refused to take me on this business outing, and I proceeded to cry; Grandmama kindly just let me cry and get over it. She was busy watching the sky. Georgia Hall was an old hand at reading weather signs in the atmosphere, and it felt and looked like trouble. She could "feel it in her bones." Ominous storm clouds gathered, and the winds grew stronger.

She called to Granddaddy, "Arthur, hurry up; we've got to get the children to the storm cellar." But Granddaddy *never* hurried, nor did he this particular afternoon. Grandmama grabbed Art and me, one by each hand, and headed across the street to the neighbor's underground cellar, with Granddaddy coming dragging behind, clearly reluctant to come. The rains became fierce and the winds were gusting before we got to the cellar door, and it was difficult to get inside. We and the neighbors sat on dusty, old benches lining the sides of the cellar. To this day I remember the musty closed-in smell, the sounds of fierce storms outside, and Grandmama's anxious face.

Meantime, in downtown Pryor, Dad ran his errand to the plumber's store, finished up, and came out to go to the hardware store two doors down. As he reached the door, he looked up, saw the funnel — and ran into the store, yelling, "Get under tables in the middle!" Everyone scrambled for cover, huddling together in terror as the tornado ripped right down Main Street. The store's front and back windows were totally shattered, and much of the furniture blown away. Miraculously, Dad and the employees in their shelters survived with only a few scratches.

Pryor was devastated. Sixty people in downtown Pryor lost their lives. The plumber, whose store Daddy had just left, perished in the wreckage. Mama, sitting in the front seat of the car praying, was untouched. Every one of the car's windows was shattered, except for the small section where Mama was. She sat in abject terror, and then thankfulness, knowing that God had spared her life. Within minutes, here came Dad, equally unscathed but petrified that Mama had been killed. One of Mama's first coherent thoughts was, "What if we had brought Rosalie with us?" That was the first of many times I experienced the protection of the Almighty; it is something you do not forget.

Off Dad went to war, and that was the beginning of three years of travel, uncertainty, and nearly constant change. All those army posts and moves got jumbled up in my mind. Certain memories stick out, of course. Occasionally, Mama went with Dad — and sometimes all four of us could travel together, usually living in a large rented room where Dad's army post was located. I remember some of the names: Fort Polk, Fort Screven, Fort Pickett in Blackstone, Virginia. That post was at Christmastime, and I remember Mama putting up a little tabletop tree, and Art and I waking up Christmas morning to find little presents nestled in its branches. Years later, Mama told me of the angst she endured on that assignment. Right after Christmas, Dad abruptly received word one afternoon that he must ship out for overseas that same night, destination unknown. Mama said she got the landlady to stay with us while she went with Dad to the train station. He threw his duffel bag on and stood on the platform at the end of his car, talking with Mama as long as he could. Mama later related that as the train began to slowly pull out, she held his hand and walked, then ran, alongside the moving train. Her last words to him were, "The eternal God is our refuge, and underneath are the everlasting arms."

The three of us remained a few weeks in Blackstone. I recall the gas mask drills in the city park, where mothers and children were drilled in how to put on the gas masks in case of chemical warfare. Those were trying times; in retrospect, I know Mama was deeply worried, but she never let it show. We returned to Pryor, and Mama waited from day to day, and sometimes week to week, for news from Harold.

Everyone became familiar with ration books. Mama saved some, and I recently unearthed one of my first ration books, dated May 1942. Each family member had a book. When I was five years old, Dad was assigned to Fort Hood in Texas, and we boarded with a local family, all of us living in one large room and sharing the family's kitchen. My two big memories of Temple, Texas, are starting kindergarten and quitting kindergarten. It started off as fun and games. I do recall the day a fellow kindergartner bragged to me that she was perfect. Not to be outdone, I informed her, "I'm perfect, too!" My conscience smote me fiercely, and I cried when confessing to Mama that night. I well knew I was far from perfect. Mama consoled me, but it was the beginning of my realization that I needed help in my life. There were things I couldn't do on my own. Then one day, I abruptly decided to "quit school." Mama was puzzled; I loved school. What was going on? I informed her the teacher said we had to learn to read, and I refused. Mama was highly amused, for she knew how much I loved books — but she didn't push me, and I did quit. That's the last time in my life I recall not wanting to read!

We attended a large church in Temple, and one of my brightest memories is Sunbeam Band each week. There were maybe fifty or so children in

Sunbeams, and I loved the stories. All too soon, however, we had to leave when Daddy was sent to another army base. It was back to Oklahoma for the time being, and real school. First grade left a few memories with me, some better than others. I had a drill sergeant of a teacher, but Miss Quinn knew what she was doing, and learn we did. I loved reading. Go figure. I recall three reading groups: the blue birds, red birds, and yellow birds. I mean, we kids knew what was going on. The blue birds were the good readers, and the other birds were in descending order. Strange — the child who quit kindergarten over having to read was by now a voracious reader. The clearest memory of first grade, however, is one I could do without. It was Christmastime, and all our class took part in a Christmas program. Along with about four other first-grade girls, I was holding my swaddled baby doll as we sang "Away in a Manger" for our audience. To my horror, excitement meant I needed a bathroom break right in the middle of "the little Lord Jesus lay down His sweet head." It couldn't be helped. I crept back to my seat after the song, leaving behind a little tell-tale puddle. All these years later, the memory remains clear.

Going to South Carolina was a favorite event for Art and me. We loved time on the farm and all the routines there. In 1943, the whole family grieved over the death of Grandmà, but what a privilege that I had been able to meet this amazing ancestor and learn at her feet. South Carolina meant helping Aunt Rhett feed her chickens; never would she eat chicken, for they were like friends to her. There were many tenant farmers in the Tindal area, and they would frequently come to Aunt Rhett's little store on the back porch and buy maybe two stamps or a pound of sugar or sometimes a few envelopes and a candy bar. Ten o'clock on weekday mornings were always to be anticipated in summertime, for Granddaddy would bring in a big ripe watermelon and everyone took a break.

Mama often read portions of Daddy's letters to us. By 1944, his favorite lament was obvious. In one letter he spelled it out, "Seems to take a long time to win a war," and in another, "If wars just wouldn't last so long." Surely there soon had to be a breakthrough. The world was weary of war and death.

Rosalie and Arthur in the park, Zhenjiang, 1940

The Hall family in 1943

SIXTEEN

VICTORY

War felt like a permanent fixture of life. Mama was a rock of stability for Art and me. She worked hard to keep life on an even keel so we children could live as "normal" a life as possible in the midst of world chaos. Daddy came and went, occasionally coming for a short furlough, but frequently he was at a destination unknown to us. At home in Pryor, Oklahoma, my favorite part of church was Sunbeam Band. Sunbeams went up to nine years old at that time, and I loved learning about children in other countries. There was also growing in me a dawning awareness of my own sinfulness and shortcomings. Mama was never "preachy" with Art and me, but we had learned enough about Scripture and the message of salvation to understand this was a personal thing. Art had accepted Christ as a young student in Temple, Texas, and I began to think about my own need for a savior.

I clearly remember the evening in our living room when everything seemed to come together in my thinking. Dad was somewhere overseas, Art was at a friend's house, and I told Mama that I knew I was a sinner and I needed to do something about it. Mama let me take the lead and talk it through. I recognized how good my parents were and how they loved the Lord, but it had dawned on me that their faith would not take the place of personal faith on my part. I remember Mama praying, and then I voiced my own petition, telling Christ I knew I was a sinner and I needed Him. *Please come into my heart*, I prayed. The miracle of grace occurred in that simple act of a child's faith. I have thought so many times since of how no matter our age, or location, or circumstances, the way each of us comes to saving faith is as a child does — simply trusting Christ and His free gift.

As the months and years dragged on, it seemed like Dad had it right — this war was going to last forever. Rationing didn't go away either. I vividly recall how excited Art and I were when a playmate told us that the corner grocery store three blocks away had just gotten in some bubble gum! Out came our ration books and we hurried to the store, each of us rationed to one precious package of Fleer's Double Bubble. I chewed each piece for days, saving it each night for the next day, making every piece last until it was so hard I could no longer chew without pain. Of course, when we were able to go to South Carolina to visit Mama's family, we took the ration books along. During one of Dad's overseas tours, Mama, Art and I spent several months on the farm in South Carolina and stored up bright memories of that special summer. Aunt Edith had retired by then and was back on the farm. She made the most heavenly batter cakes (pancakes). Try as I may, I've never been able to duplicate them.

Aunt Rhett not only cared for all the chickens and ran the back-porch store, she also collected just about everything: tobacco tags, postcards, Confederate money, and, most of all, stamps. Art and I loved to sit with her at night around her little card table and use her big round magnifying glass to look at the unusual markings and postal marks that made a stamp special. Granddaddy would pass around a peppermint candy from the mantel candy jar, and occasionally Aunt Rhett would play a song on the melodeon. I was mesmerized. Then Aunt Mamie, home for the summer from teaching kindergarten in Columbia, would tell us the story of the melodeon and all sorts of interesting tidbits of family history and lore. She and Aunt Rhett were fountains of family information. They especially delighted in taking Art and me to the Wells family cemetery and regaling us with tales of ever-so-great-grandparents as we walked from marker to marker. It's small wonder I've always been fascinated with history and genealogy, American and Chinese alike. Aunt Grace was working in Hawaii now, a missionary at Wahiawa, the very church where Dad and Mama had served in 1938 and where I was born.

Mama penned a steady stream of letters to Dad, and he faithfully wrote several times a week. In one letter he spoke of getting away from base, and said, "As always I feel good when leaving camp and bad when coming *back* to camp." Art and I enjoyed hearing bits and pieces of trivia about life at some faraway fort. Often Daddy lived in a tent. He mentioned in one letter that their company had a barber chair made from an airplane seat with a hydraulic jack underneath to raise and lower it. Arthur thought that would be a fun place for a haircut. The troops had set up a tent where Dad could give counseling and comfort to the men in the company. Often, he would go to the nearby field hospital to visit injured troops. Sunday chapel met in a tent set up just for that purpose. Mama had a big smile on her face when she read in a letter he wrote in February 1944, "I've had a good day today. Being on the prayer calendar of WMU for February 20th helps. I do believe in prayer!" From somewhere overseas in August, he wrote, "This mud is terrible and awfully sticky. Now we have a little hut built, and it will be much better than living on the mud." He added, "The front of my hut is about twenty yards from the chapel. If I get to live in it a few months, the labor will be well spent. On the other hand, if the time is short, I'll be sorry I built it. Would love to live on a floor for a while; living on the ground and in the mud is trying."

I still remember Christmas 1944. It was lonely without Daddy there. I could tell Mama was sad, but, as usual, she worked hard to make every-thing good for her two children. As we sat around the tree that Christmas Eve and read the Christmas story from the Gospel of Luke, Mama injected cheer into her voice and announced, "I just feel like *next* Christmas, all of us will be together again." It turns out we were, but a lot of things had to happen in the world before Christmas 1945.

We sometimes knew where Daddy might be and sometimes just had to guess. In February 1945, he sent Art and me a letter from Fort Knox. The skies were full of dirty smoke most of the time, he told us, because they burned soft coal. He explained, "Everything gets dirty, and it most makes one sick to breathe it. We don't have it tough though," he added, "like the men do on the fighting fronts. I'm sure glad the Russians are making headway on their march to Berlin. Maybe the war in Europe will be over in a few months. After that it will still take a year or more to whip the Japanese." Then he wrote in March from Denver, Colorado, on his way to the West Coast. A few days later, he sent a note especially to me and talked about the beautiful mountains he was seeing. He ended by saying, "We will all be very, very happy when the war is over and the daddies can all come home. May the Lord bless and keep you all of the time."

Soon Dad wrote from Camp Beal in California, but he did not know how long he would be there. Dad's letters always had tidbits in them that we found funny. He wrote: "We have about 40 beds on this floor in our barracks. One officer near me snores very loud." Near the end of March, he wrote from "Somewhere on the West Coast," because he was not allowed to give his location. It appeared that the company might soon be shipped out overseas. Daddy's next destination proved to be various small islands in the Ryukyus and then Okinawa. One of the bloodiest battles of World War II was conducted there in the spring and early summer with more than 150,000 total casualties. More than 12,500 American soldiers were killed and many thousands more injured, some with permanent disabilities.

The US victory in Okinawa was won at great cost but proved to be one of the straws that broke the camel's back for Japan. Dad's unit was one that moved in following the battles, and the destruction and mayhem were horrible. Everything was in chaos. Often Daddy was not even allowed to date his letters, and occasionally they read, "Somewhere in the Ryukyus Islands." One of the good features of military effectiveness was fine mail service, and that was a blessing to the soldiers living in such terrible conditions. He wrote that he had a lot to do there, adding, "To have something to do is most encouraging." The chapel services were well-attended, and Dad loved being able to boost the spirits of men who had been through so much.

He wrote one night, "I am now permitted to say that we are somewhere in the Ryukyus Islands and that we have occasional air raids, though these are not nearly so bad as I expected." (Dad told us when he got home that chaplains were not allowed to carry weapons, but when those air raid sirens sounded, he got his trusty rifle and put it by his side in the jeep.) We got a good laugh when Dad wrote about his food: "We had a delicious supper. It is refreshing to find G.I. cooks who know *how* to cook. I have found the percentage very small."

Then Daddy's letters in July and August 1945 gave a hint that things might be coming to a tipping point in the war. On August 1, Dad wrote that several men were helping him "build a shack," because he had been living on the ground for four weeks. He added, "Also hope we are here long enough to make building it worthwhile." The next day his letter reported, "We are having a typhoon — my, how these tents do flap." The next line was cut out of his letter by the censors, so all of us were curious as to what bit of news was cut out. Dad feared the typhoon would blow his tent down, which would make the beating rain hit them mercilessly. At the time, we were spending the summer in South Carolina, and all the family was curious as to just where Dad might be. He could only say: "Things are a bit uncertain for us, but that is normal in army life. The only certainty is uncertainty. It will be *grand* when this is all over."

August 5, Daddy quoted from a friend in Oklahoma who had written saying, "The war will be over soon, and all the boys will be home." Dad loved the sentiment but thought it too optimistic, explaining that "an invasion of Japan will take time and cost precious lives, and not a few of them." Nonetheless, being the optimist he was, Dad tried to inject a bit of humor into most of his letters, and those often dealt with mud or with army food. He finished this particular letter by writing: "This is the best G.I. mess I ever ate in. These men cooked *before* they came into the army. They are not blacksmiths turned into cooks. This mess is too good to last." He finished on a wry note, "It probably won't!"

Then a noteworthy letter arrived, dated August 9 and headed "Somewhere in the Ryukyus." Dad began: "We are very happy here over the discovery of the new bomb and of Russia's entry into the war against Japan. Surely they can't last long now. Maybe they will have sense enough to surrender before they are wiped out." He continued: "Everyone expects to get home earlier than he had thought. However, it will take months after the war is over, and it is not over yet, but things look mighty good." It was clear that Dad and the soldiers on the ground had heard the news about the first bomb, and the *second* was dropped the actual day he wrote the letter.

August 14, 1945 became widely celebrated as the day when the world learned that Japan was surrendering. September 2 (now called V-J Day) marked the official surrender that set off great rejoicing throughout the free world. Both Mama and Dad, though far apart in miles, had the same initial thoughts: first, that God willing, they would soon be together again, and second, now they could begin planning to return to their calling in China. There was no way yet to determine when Daddy might be discharged, so again they played the waiting game. However, Dad experienced a real serendipity those last months in the Far East. He was permitted to hop on a military flight going into China and was able to be the first missionary on the ground to send some preliminary information to the Foreign Mission Board about the Chinese Christians, churches, and mission property.

Mama, Arthur, and I returned to Oklahoma and school, and we waited each day for the postman to come to see what news we might hear from Daddy. Mama wrote to Sumter the third week of September with an update. The censors had finally quit reading all their mail, so Dad was able to write a few details. He explained that he had landed on Okinawa on July 5. His division had stopped over twelve days on one little island on the way and eleven days on another. She told her parents: "Harold says if they'd landed on Okinawa three days earlier, they'd have had a major battle star. I'm not worrying about missing that star!" Dad explained that there were still many Japanese soldiers hiding out in caves on Okinawa, some of whom didn't realize the war was over.

And still, we waited. I started second grade and thought I had the prettiest and best teacher in the world, Miss Hudspeth. She was young and vibrant and endured rambunctious children remarkably well. Now, along with Sunbeam Band, I was old enough to join Brownie Scouts. I loved the Brownie uniform and wearing the cute little beanie cap. I even got a Brownie ring at Christmas. Best of all was the feeling of "belonging." I have only one clear memory of any of our Brownie troop activities. A TB sanitarium for sick and elderly veterans was located not far from Pryor, and we Brownies took on a project to make paper spittoons for them. (Yes, spittoons!) They had no barf bags, so we girls learned how to fold newspapers in such a way as to form a pocket, and these could hang on their bed rails and provide a convenient place to spit. I secretly figured that many of them enjoyed chewing tobacco and used their newspaper spittoons to take care of the tobacco drippings. (Making that little paper pouch is a skill I have passed along to Sunday School children and GAs for decades now. They find them really handy for holding cookies and candies.)

Occasionally on a weekend, we were able to go to Coweta where Aunt Mellie, Dad's only sister, lived. She loved to spoil us. Uncle Victor was short, stocky and jolly, and our cousins Willa Dean and Leroy, a few years older than we, would let us play in the large attic in their fascinating old house. It looked like something out of the Victorian era, with its turrets and decorations, and we were captivated by all the nooks and crannies in the attic — the boxes there were full of old cast-me-downs and a funny-looking Victrola. I could get in one of the little turrets and look out the window, pretending to be a princess in the tower, looking out over the kingdom.

I enjoyed America and its comforts and conveniences, loving time with family and having a good time playing with friends in a place that was open and free and without confining walls. Yet, I missed China and home there, and all that was familiar from those early days. Mama had packed and brought my favorite little blue enamel cup. I loved that little cup and used it every day. It was a piece of China and "home" to me. (Seventy-five years later, that little cup still sits in our China cabinet, reminding me of my roots.) Mama indulged us with Chinese food quite frequently, although it was time-consuming with all the chopping that was necessary. Our favorite (and still is to this day) was *jyaŭdzs* (called "pot stickers" in Chinese restaurants in America). We ate them steamed or boiled, and Mama's *jyaŭdzs* were always our favorites. Art and I often had contests to see who could eat the most. I blush to admit that I won the record, having consumed forty of them in one sitting. (I have already admitted that I was a *sturdy* child!)

Finally — Christmas of 1945, and Daddy was able to come home. We all celebrated and rejoiced. It seemed like Mama could not keep from smiling all the time. Art and I did, however, have to adjust to a bit of "army" discipline from time to time. When Mama corrected us, the look of sadness in her eyes was sufficient to make us repent at once. However, when Daddy spanked us, it was an event. I clearly remember one signal day when punishment was clearly due. Art and I were making beanie flips with wood and strips of old rubber, and we got in a royal argument over who was doing what. I assured Art he was wrong. I must admit that on this occasion, I was the guilty party, and, sure enough, Daddy heard us going at it. Here he came. When Daddy had his jaw set and clenched, I knew to watch out. I steeled myself to receive the just rewards of my folly. Art angrily explained my crime, and Dad turned and came toward me while I gulped and awaited my spanking. Amazingly, he looked at me with stern eyes, took a deep breath, cocked his head to one side, and pronounced, "Well, I guess we'll just love you and keep you." I remember that glorious moment of undeserved mercy more than *any* of the spankings I received during those growing up years.

During the months after Daddy returned from overseas, he and Mama spent most of their time planning their return to China — China and home. But there was so much to be done to prepare for another five or six years away from America. Mama ordered our Calvert Course (correspondence school) material: third grade for me and sixth grade for Art. By mid-summer, plans were firming up, shopping began, and so did the hard part — the goodbyes. I learned something those many years ago: Goodbyes are never fun, and practice does not make perfect. Goodbyes hurt. But I was a child, and there was adventure just ahead. The next two to three years of my life would prove to be the most impressionable ever — both the most exciting and possibly the most dangerous.

Boarding the SS General
Gordon, *December 6, 1946*

SEVENTEEN

HOME TO CHINA

When I start thinking about the pre-Communist years back in China, my memories are a bunch of jumbles — all tumbling around in no particular order. Those times are so imprinted on my brain that they remain vivid, much more so than subsequent years. The final visit to Sumter and Mama's family was a mix of joy and sorrow; I didn't realize then how this was simply a foretaste of how frequently those two emotions would swim around together in my heart for all the years ahead — times of wonderful reunion mixed with the sadness of goodbyes. For Art and me, the implications of the years to come were not obvious, but I look back and think how Mama and Daddy must have felt, as they left another piece of themselves behind and moved forward to fulfill their calling. It is the look in the eyes of dear family members that lingers in my heart to this day. Not only the called,

149

but those they leave behind, are part of the sacrifice of service.

There were several farewell parties in Oklahoma with our church, our childhood friends, and with family. Mixed with the farewells, we packed. Art and I each had a new footlocker, and we could pretty well pack them as we wished. I was mostly practical but did manage to surreptitiously slip in a few items that Mama would have thought unnecessary, but I considered essential. One of the last things packed came from the final farewell party. The place had been decorated with countless yellow balloons, both large and small. I took home about ten little yellow balloons filled with "American air." I was leaving America, and by now I loved this country and wanted a piece of it to go with me. Carefully arranging the items crammed into the footlocker, I managed to make room for six perky little yellow balloons, putting them under the top tray where they would not be noticeable. *There, I thought, I am taking some American air home to China!* I guess Mama was too busy to check the contents of my footlocker. I could just imagine what she would have said: "Balloons?! In that valuable space? They'll pop anyway!" But she didn't look, and I didn't talk — and American air went with me to China. In the ensuing several years, about once a month I would quietly open that footlocker — squeeze a little balloon to see that all was well — and sigh with relief. I still had some U.S. air!

Art and I thoroughly enjoyed the long train trip across the continent, seeing lots of America on the way — from soaring mountain ranges with snow on the peaks to roaring rivers that flowed forever. We loved the berths where we could stretch out at night and be lulled to sleep by the constant click-clacking of the wheels of the train as we sped west. Strangely enough, I clearly recall a little boy of maybe four or five traveling to California with his mother. I was noticeably happy that *my* mama was not like his! She fussed on the poor little tyke from morning 'til night. He was charmed by his favorite toy, a little airplane, and he would go up and down the aisles "flying" it in the air. His mother fussed about everything he did, and if he got near a window, she would shrilly warn him to get away. Alas, in a moment when her head was turned, the little fellow put his hand out a window to let the breeze help him fly the plane — and, yes, it whipped out of his hand and quickly out of sight. His mother could say nothing but: "I told you so! You naughty boy! Now you have no plane — serves you right!" I looked up at Mama and whispered, "I'm so glad you never talk to me like that!"

The skyline of San Francisco finally appeared in the distance. Soon we would sail! But, wouldn't you know, just the week we arrived, a maritime strike began. No ships could sail. We were to have been in San Francisco three days. It turned into three months — September, October, November. Our family of four lived in a single room in the Mark Twain Hotel, in downtown San Francisco. Dad had a cousin who lived about an hour away in Novato, and we would go visit on occasional weekends for a break from the city. During the months in San Francisco, Art and I loved going to the posh new Emporium and taking our first-ever rides on an escalator. The Golden Gate Bridge has an indelible place in my memory. That giant structure gleaming in the sun rather symbolized the possibilities that America offered. Our favorite place to eat was the Clinton Cafeteria. There were all sorts of marvelous dishes from which to choose, especially choosing from twenty or more desserts! Decades later, I still recall the afternoon Dad commented on "Rosie having the largest bill, since she got so many items." Art loved teasing me about it, chanting, "Tubby, tubby, tubby!" so I piously determined to have the *smallest* bill our next trip there. The next time we went, I deliberately got one small cup of vegetable soup for eleven cents, and, yes, I was hungry for a good number of hours afterward.

There was a "midget convention" in San Francisco while we were there. A large number of little people from across the country converged on the city. This was a new experience for Art and me, and we learned not to stare but to smile and greet them as we passed. Art was an ardent baseball fan, and, since he was a Brooklyn Dodgers fan, I was determined not to be outdone, so I quickly adopted the St. Louis Cardinals as my team. (To this day, I love the Cardinals and can tell you the names of some of the former greats — like Stan "The Man" Musial and Enos Slaughter.)

Art and I had to make our fun wherever we found it. Both of us were taking a new pair of roller skates to China (in spite of the fact that there wasn't much of any place in China to use them — no sidewalks to be had).

Meantime, we found a good use for them in San Francisco. We couldn't go skate on San Francisco sidewalks, but when there was no hotel staff around, we would skate up and down the halls. Although the neighboring hotel guests were not too impressed, we became quite proficient skaters.

My most vivid memory is of the hotel maids, one in particular. We had a corner room on the eighth floor, and just yards from our window was the maids' supply room where they would come for a break each morning and each afternoon. Nearly every day, Art and I would see this regular maid as she had a soft drink, or, more frequently, took a cigarette break. I don't remember who had the idea, but we had a supply of straws and toothpicks from the Clinton Cafeteria and were pretty skilled at shooting the tooth-picks through the straws. On one particular day, we carefully observed our maid coming for her break, and, taking care not to be seen, waited for her to come over to the window for a smoke. Just as she put the cigarette in her mouth, we both shot our missiles — and, right on target, the cigarette went flying out the window. The look on her face was priceless. She gave a yelp and clutched her heart. We two culprits quickly ducked out of sight and wondered what story she related when she got home that evening.

All of us were anxious for the maritime strike to end. Dad went to the shipping office nearly every day, and Dad and Mama did a bit more shopping and crating of supplies. On November 23, Mama finally wrote to Sumter to report that the strike was soon to be over, and, God willing, we would be sailing on the SS *General Gordon* on December 6. Sure enough, two excited children and two equally relieved adults went aboard the *Gordon* and sailed the following day. The China adventure was about to begin!

Quite a number of missionaries were on their way to China, either returning or going out for the first time. James and Martha Belote and their children were headed to Canton. Jimmy was eight, my age, Teddy was a four-year-old rounder, and little Ginger was a cute toddler. Brand-new appointees were Ruby Wheat and Marie Conner, who were headed to Yangchow, and Fay Taylor, who would work with youth in Shanghai. Aunt Fay was a favorite of mine, and on the voyage she had Sunday School for the MKs and played games with us. Poor Mama got seasick from the first day and was miserable most of the trip, especially when we ran into a typhoon not far from Japan. I remember sitting at a dining table and clinging to the table to keep from sailing across the room. Oranges and apples were rolling everywhere. Mama stayed in her bunk and didn't want to hear a word about food. One positive thing occurred on our trip overseas: I stopped a lifelong habit. Ever since birth I had sucked my thumb, the last five or six years only at night when no one could see. Daddy put the fear of the Lord in me, describing some of the nasty oriental diseases that a thumb could transfer to my stomach. It did the trick, and in self-preservation, I broke myself of the habit. Another event on the journey sticks in my memory, for as we drew near the Aleutian Islands off the coast of Japan, we saw a smoking volcano. This prompted Art and me to send a message while at sea. Each of us wrote a note and put it in a soft drink bottle, sealing it tightly and sending it out to sea. I still wonder where our notes went.

Of all times to get to a new country (or at least one no longer familiar), we arrived in Shanghai on Christmas Eve, 1946. Mama wrote the family two days later, calling this the roughest voyage she had ever experienced, but rejoicing over finally being back after a six-year absence. We spent Christmas with the Cauthen family in Shanghai. Dr. Baker J. Cauthen was secretary to the Orient, and his wife, Eloise, a China MK. Their two children, Carolyn (the oldest) and Ralph (my age), were familiar to us, for they had visited us in Yangchow six years earlier. Poor Eloise — here it was Christmas Eve, and a whole family was thrust upon her. We were there an entire month, trying to get our baggage through incredible red tape in customs. I have an idea Eloise never realized that much entertaining would be part of her job description. In subsequent years, when we went to Shanghai for mission meetings or for other occasions, we usually stayed with the Cauthens, and enjoyed being with other kids because there were so few foreign children in Chinkiang where we lived.

Aunt Grace arrived from Hawaii on New Year's Eve and thankfully was able to get her goods through customs more quickly than we. The last day of January we finally arrived in Chinkiang. Art and I were beyond excited to see our new place. All of the big old mission houses were built in the

1880s to accommodate a lot of people. Now, how to furnish ours? Aunt Grace would live next door, but most of the furnishings she left behind in 1942 were long gone. Dad went over to our old house in Yangchow to see if possibly the little hidden room had escaped the sharp eyes of the Japanese soldiers. It had! Art and I felt like it was Christmas all over again as Dad brought home the furnishings and personal items that had survived untouched. Some of the "secret room" items became furnishings for my bedroom, a large room on the side of the house facing out to the front yard and the old French Consulate on the right. Our front yard was about the size of a football field, and beyond that was our Yin Shan Men Church, the largest of Chinkiang's churches. It had been built by gifts of WMU women and Baptists in America. Pastor Jang (Dzang) Chang Qun and his family lived there, and his daughter, Aiteh, became my closest Chinese friend. (Seven decades later, we remain friends. Aiteh has lived in South Carolina for the past thirty years.)

It felt wonderful to be back in China. My memories were mostly subliminal; after all, how much can a three-year-old remember distinctly? It just felt *natural* and normal to me — seeing all the masses of people; watching coolies trotting through the streets bearing their burdens on a pole with a balancing basket on each end, full of whatever they were hauling, from geese to turnips; rickshaws calling out for fares — *"Lai lai"* (Come and let me take you); and hawkers all over the walkways and in the streets. It was cold wintertime, so there were street ovens with roasting chestnuts for people to buy by the bag. Other round, black ovens were filled with hot sweet potatoes, begging to be bought, and my favorite — *shau bing* (sesame bread) about four inches long, with a handy little hole in the middle — came piping hot from a round oven right there on the street.

Art and I had brought our bikes from America and were soon riding up and down the city streets. Each day we saw hawkers touting their wares, partially clad little toddlers running around, and cartloads of goods hauled by eight or ten men pulling the heavy loads. The men sang a chant as they pulled, and we grew used to hearing them chant in sing-song fashion, *"Syau yang gweidz lai"* (Here come the little foreign devils), over and over again. We would just grin and wave. We were the only foreign children in our city of about half a million people, so the two of us became accustomed to all the stares. We became friends with several traffic police along our route and would smartly salute them when we rode by. They came to know us and would give us a grin and a salute in return.

Our mission houses were on the side of Yin Shan (Silver Mountain), and from Aunt Grace's balcony, we had a grand view of the ancient street just below. Along the street was a bazaar where a wealth of little outdoor stalls were set up to sell just about anything you might want. Up and around the corner on the "ancient street," as it was called, was a twelfth-century *dagoba* (an upside-down pagoda). I thought it was fascinating — looking something like an ice-cream cone turned upside down. Out beyond the street and its intriguing bazaar, with all sorts of odds and ends for sale, was an open area, sort of like public fairgrounds. All kinds of activities took place there, from a tooth-pulling booth to a mobile Chinese opera, complete with stage and clanging cymbals. Then beyond the public square and in the distance was a stunning view of the great Yangtze River, one of the most famous, and sometimes deadliest (when it flooded), rivers in the world.

Behind our Baptist compound was the British Consulate, quite a large area with a number of houses surrounding the consulate building itself. The favorite part of the place to Art and me was the big gun emplacement by the road in front of their compound. It had a giant muzzle facing out to the Yangtze and had seen a lot of action during several wars over the past 100 years. Aunt Grace could remember its ominous boom from the civil war days in the 1920s.

I loved going in the little shops on the main thoroughfare leading up to our compound that was located at the end of the avenue. One of our first tasks was to have Chinese chops made. Chops are clever little oblongs with your Chinese name delicately carved on one end. It was your official signature, and mine made me feel like a name really matters. (I still have that little black chop and can still stamp my name with it.) When shopping, we learned right away never to pay the asking price for anything. If you did, you were immediately pegged as a *"da bidz"* (big nose, as all foreigners were dubbed). The shopkeeper started with an astronomical price, you countered with a paltry alternative, and would come to some sort of happy medium. When I bought any fabric, I knew to say, *"Fahng yidyan"* (add a little).

Art and I both loved Chinese food — not the far-out types like sea slugs or pickled jelly fish, but the everyday noodles, veggies, and, one of my favorites, pickled turnips. I know it doesn't *sound* good, but it is simply tiny, baby turnips soaked in soy sauce. It's the perfect condiment for a hot bowl of steaming rice or noodles. We knew to request Chinese food when Daddy had gone to the countryside for outstation evangelism, because when he came home, he wanted only American fare, and forget the eggs. For a week or two at a time, he would be in the villages, sleeping on the floors in his sleeping roll, and eating eggs soaked in soy sauce and nothing but local Chinese food. Every time Daddy came back from village work, he would wait until the first sunny day to air out his sleeping roll. It needed hot sunlight to get rid of the bedbugs and vermin that came home with him from every village trip. As children, Art and I thought village trips sounded like an adventure. However, Daddy endured difficult conditions because of the blessings inherent in sharing the good news with a multitude who had never heard.

Mama worked with a Bible woman and Mrs. Jang (Dzang), our pastor's wife — or Jang Shr Mu, as we lovingly called her. Pastors were known as "Shepherds," and their wives, "Mrs. Shepherd." Mama and our pastor's wife would visit in homes with women who did not know about Jesus, first getting to know them and then presenting the good news. Jang Shr Mu, Aiteh's mother, was even busier than Mama, because she had six children to care for; however, she made time for these important house visits. Three of her children were younger than Aiteh, so my friend often cared for her younger siblings. Her oldest brother she called *Guh Guh* (older brother) and her older sister was *Jye Jye* (older sister) and younger ones, *Mei Mei* (little sister) and *Dee Dee* (little brother.) Thus, I, too, was a *Mei Mei* and Arthur a *Guh Guh*.

Nothing was simple in China like it was in America. Even something as unpleasant as going to the dentist meant a trip to Shanghai. Arthur and I found the trains a lot of fun, with the little doilies over the back of our seats and glasses of tea for each passenger. A steward would come around and pour hot water over the tea leaves in the glasses. Of course, the water might not have been boiled so we weren't allowed to drink it, but we always took along our own boiled water. Also, we could buy a little lunch tin with rice, a pork chop, and a soy sauce egg. On this trip for dental work, we combined it with Easter and a visit with the Cauthen children. That meant two whole days off from school!

Actually, school was pretty enjoyable. The Calvert Course was a terrific homeschooling program, and with Mama a professor and Dad a whiz at math, Art and I were most fortunate. We would each study in our own room, and only in the mornings, because working individually, learning went much more quickly. Every month we took exams sent out from the home office in Baltimore, and teachers there graded our work. They were no slough-offs either. We had to work hard. Calvert Course was geared to move quickly, and in third-year Calvert, I covered both the fourth and fifth grade math texts, advanced reading, world history, and art history, along with science texts. I still have several of those textbooks. Nothing topped reading and history, of course. How could you *not* like history, living in the middle of one of the world's oldest cultures? And, that is exactly what the name China, *Jūng Gwo*, means — the Middle Kingdom.

I especially loved my reading textbooks. One of them I have kept for seven decades. In it is one of my favorite stories — the true story of Madame Chiang Kai-shek and how she rescued her husband, the president of China, from the Communists and war lords in what came to be known as the Xian Incident. In 1947, I had no inkling that many years later I would actually see Madame Chiang up close and personal.

Late that year, the foreign population of Chinkiang grew. Cleo Morrison came to live with Aunt Grace and work in evangelism, and a young family fresh from language school in Peking, Clyde and Alcie Jowers and their two adorable little boys, Tom and Harry, arrived. We had Methodist missionaries in the city, but they had no children. There was also a Presbyterian hospital. Wonder of wonders, just about the time the year ended, news came that a Presbyterian doctor and his family were soon moving to Chinkiang, and they had three children! More children was like a Christmas gift soon to arrive.

*12th century dagoba — two blocks
from mission houses, Zhenjiang*

EIGHTEEN

CHINKIANG

I had no clue what this Christmas would hold for me: It was not a present under the tree, but a man on the steps, that changed the trajectory of my life. Until reading one of Aunt Grace's 1947 letters earlier this year, I had forgotten how excited I was about that first Christmas in Chinkiang. In one of her letters written before Thanksgiving, Aunt Grace talked about the holiday season: "Rosalie has bought most of her gifts already out of her allowance. She goes out on the streets, sometimes alone, to buy them herself. She's been shopping off and on for two months!" It was such a treat to have my "real" aunt in the house next door. Not only did Aunt Grace knit all sorts of sweaters and caps for me, she also taught me to knit. Every time I ply my knitting needles, I smile and silently mouth, "Thank you, Aunt Grace!"

Thanksgiving also added to the excitement of the season, for there was a special conference going on for our association's churches, and a number of guests and speakers came. Dr. Charles Culpepper, president of the all-China seminary in Shanghai, was the featured speaker and our guest. Mrs. Cauthen also came with Carolyn and Ralph, and between the two households we hosted twenty-two visitors.

The following month brought the Christmas morning that changed the course of my life. Those moments with the leper on the front porch are seared into my spirit in such a way that it is no wonder I remember nothing else about that pivotal day. These decades later, I smiled upon reading Aunt Grace's letter written Christmas night when she said, "Rosalie gave me a dear little individual tea pot which can also be used for soy sauce." She also told the family about a Christmas play put on at the church that evening by some men and boys, saying the church was packed and so noisy it was hard to hear. About the play itself, she explained, "They love to put on these plays and act out the Bible stories. This story of Joseph was a revelation of interpretation!"

That following year in Chinkiang feels like a story I read somewhere — and yet, I know I experienced it in reality. I have to forget about the sequence and remember the moments. Strangely, my years in Chinkiang sometimes come to me in voices, maybe in English, sometimes in Chinese, and I can still hear their echoes. We did get that "Christmas present" in the form of other foreign children — the Moffett family. Penny was my age; her brother, Sandy, was the same age as Art; and the Moffetts had a younger sister, Mary Leighton, as well. Now Art and I regularly rode our bikes over to the Presbyterian compound where they lived. My friend, Aiteh, and I played in a more oriental fashion, and Penny and I played like we would have in America. Aiteh and I sometimes played with a small bouncy ball, just a little larger than a tennis ball, and would throw it between our legs back and forth and try to maintain our balance. Aiteh was much more adept than I. Penny and I decided we needed a club, although I already had one "club." I was a GA, which stood for "Girls Auxiliary" in those days. Since I was the only American girl around Chinkiang that first year, I was the sole GA, and Mama was my leader. I loved working on Forward Steps, memorizing Scripture passages and learning about the organization of WMU. There was also plenty of scope for doing missions projects right there in Chinkiang. I thought it was wonderful to be an MK and part of my parents' ministry.

Penny, however, was a Presbyterian, and GAs was outside her orbit, so we decided to form our own club. It would be a secret one; boys were not allowed, and they could try to guess our secrets all they wanted to. We named the club "JUG" (Just Us Girls), and the guys never did figure out what JUG stood for. The boys, of course, countered with their *own* organization. They dubbed themselves the "Chinkiang Mounted Police." I always assumed their "mounts" were their bikes.

Penny's doctor father was related to the Honorable Leighton Stuart, the US Ambassador to China. Nanjing (*Jing* means capital) was just fifty miles up the railroad line, so the Moffetts saw their uncle quite frequently. Dr. Stuart was for many years president of Peking University, and later was imprisoned by the Japanese for more than three years. He subsequently was named US Ambassador and was highly respected by the Chinese nationalist government. I was excited to learn that Ambassador Stuart was coming to Chinkiang to be honored at an afternoon reception/tea. Wonder of wonders, even the foreign children were invited. I was beyond excited. However, I all too vividly recall my teatime debacle. Trying to be mature and sophisticated that afternoon, I graciously accepted a cup of tea and decided to sweeten it with sugar and milk. Then, not even thinking, I squeezed in a liberal portion of fresh lemon — and, of course, the result was instant curdling. My face turned red, and, feeling about three years old and no longer gracious and mature, I moved quickly to dispose of the strange mixture. Why is it that such silly memories are the ones that stick to our minds like pieces of Velcro?

That summer, one of the wealthiest families in the city had their number-one son home from university in Peking. Only the very intelligent and wealthy went to this most prestigious of universities, and Mr. Chen, the student's father, was justly proud of him. While he was home for the summer, his father wanted to help him hone his English language skills and proceeded to ask my father if his daughter could come be the son's tutor one day each week. Dad felt this might be an opportunity to introduce Christianity to the family, and of course I was excited. I would be a ten-year-old teacher! Dad helped the gentleman understand that I was not to receive compensation, and Mr. Chen reluctantly agreed. Dad also suggested that we use the New Testament as our textbook, and the father agreed to that as well. I felt so grown up to have one of the fancy private family rickshaws sent to take me halfway across the city to teach the university student.

The house was fascinating. It was old Chinese style with many courtyards. I learned that Mr. Chen had four wives living in the different courtyards. My student was the number one son of the number one wife, with whom I had tea the first time I went. (You can be sure I had learned my lesson at the embassy tea. No more lemon.) The young student conducted me through the maze of a house. I'm sure my eyes were wide the whole time. For our lessons, we sat in the family tearoom/parlor, which was furnished with shiny black lacquer furniture richly inlaid with mother-of-pearl art. As our parents had agreed, I used the New Testament as a textbook. We read the Gospels and then conversed in English about what those verses meant. I had the satisfaction of seeing his vocabulary expand, and his pronunciation improve by the day. At the end of that summer, the father honored Dad's request not to pay me, but instead sent a gift: a huge basket of an expensive Chinese delicacy — 100-year-old eggs, the Rolls Royce of Chinese delicacies. I don't know the method of preparation, but these were large duck eggs treated with some seasonings and liquid, then buried for a period of time. They were considered the epitome of excellence. Some were buried for a number of years — those were the most expensive. When you slice one, it looks like layers of an oil slick, with lots of green, brown, yellow, and charcoal colors. Its taste is something best left to the imagination. Guess who didn't eat any? However, our Chinese friends were thrilled to get them, considering them a huge treat.

It sometimes seemed strange to have household help, but Mama could never have done her work without them. With no refrigeration, and having to go to market daily, her time would have been consumed. We loved Lu

Er (Second Lu, meaning he was his family's second son) and his wife, Lu Saudz. They were believers and a part of my parents' ministry. It's so ironic that a child wants to do those things she "can't" do; whereas, if they are required of her, she would likely fuss and balk. For example, for some strange reason, I loved to iron, and occasionally Lu Saudz would indulge me and let me have a turn. (I still like to iron. Go figure.)

Our Chinkiang Baptist mission station now grew with the arrival of the Jowers family. I was elated at no longer being the youngest MK in the mission; Tom and Harry were little fellows, and Alcie (who did not spell her name as did my mother Alice) was expecting a third child. That was the most exciting news, because she promised to let me help with the baby when it arrived.

The Jowers moved into a house quite close to us, one on the property of the former UNRRA headquarters. The United Nations Relief and Rehabilitation Administration offices were just beyond the public square near our compound, and earlier in the year they closed down operations. UNRRA had been distributing relief supplies and assistance to war-torn China since the end of World War II, but now they were moving out. That meant the foreigners in the city received their remaining food supplies, mostly items that the Chinese populace didn't care for. Our allotment included cases of powdered milk (which came in very handy), various canned goods, and a lot of paperback books, which Art and I thought was the best part of all their surplus. One item made an indelible impression on me — a case of gallon cans of asparagus. Somewhere between growing and canning, those asparagus spears had grown mushy and highly unappealing. Dad said, "It's healthy food. Eat it." My father was not a turning back kind of person, so of course I ate it. To finish off the incident, I got really sick that night, and ever since, no asparagus — ever.

The Jowers, on the other hand, were a great addition to our mission station. Not long after they arrived, Alcie Jowers went to Presbyterian Hospital, and Richard was born. I was so excited. Now the Jowers had a Tom, Dick, and Harry. Aunt Alcie (as we kids called her) let me hold him and even help with his baths. This was better than any doll, and I dearly loved dolls. I remember a strange occurrence at their place. One morning they came to the gate of their compound, opened the door, and there was a dead rooster lying on the entranceway. Strange. None of us could figure what that might mean. About a week later, upon opening the gate, there lay a dead piglet. Stranger and stranger. The following week was a shock. They opened the gate to discover a dead baby lying at the doorway. The authorities were called, of course, but no one ever found a reason for the various objects placed on their doorstep.

Little Dick was a special delight, but I also loved my dolls. Mama had been meticulous in bringing many books along for birthday and Christmas gifts for the years ahead, but dolls weren't on her list, and I kept hoping for a new doll or so. Hardly anything approximating a real doll was to be found in our city, but I didn't give up hoping. And then came the news of a contest. The leading English-language newspaper in China was the *Shanghai Evening Post*. It was our main source of Chinese and foreign news, and each one of us read it every week. Art and I liked the comic strips the *Post* ran each week, especially Dick Tracy. In those days, one of the characters in Dick Tracy was Sparkle Plenty, the daughter of B.O. Plenty and Gravel Gertie. I thought she was beautiful. Then a Sparkle Plenty doll was introduced, complete with beautiful blonde hair. The *Post* ran a contest: to win the Sparkle Plenty doll, all you had to do was fill out the enclosed application, mail it in, and a winner would be drawn. Perfect. I just *knew* that they would draw my name. I waited — and waited some more. One day I received a letter from the editor of the *Post*, explaining that I was not eligible to be in the contest because I didn't live in Shanghai. I was one more heartsick child. This was awful. Then I read further, and the editor said, "However, we are going to send you a consolation prize, and her name is Mei Mei." I was both pleased and puzzled. Mei Mei? The next week, a package arrived for me, something of an event for a ten-year-old foreign child. I opened it up and there was the most beautiful handmade Chinese doll, dressed in typical red clothes with silk cloth embroidered shoes. It was instant love, and seventy-plus years later, Mei Mei is still living in our house. I treasure her far more than I ever would a mass-production doll!

Mei Mei usually remained at home when Art and I made jaunts on our bikes. We liked to go to "Methodist Hill," as we called the compound where their Chinkiang missionaries lived. To get there, we rode through a kind of country area where the houses were tiny, made of mud with thatched roofs, and crowded close together. Near this village was a large graveyard. In the typical graveyard, there were mounds of dirt piled around, each marking where a body was laid to rest. The path through the village led through the graveyard, and we often speculated on the graves and their ages as we road through the mounds. Ancestor worship was a way of life here, and frequently we would see grave mounds with food offerings laid out for the dead ancestors to enjoy in their spirit world. On many occasions we would stop to look at a particularly old mound, where part of the piled dirt had washed away over the years. Frequently, we saw part of a coffin that had deteriorated over time, and we could see bones, and even hair, inside the rotting wood. We found it rather sad that time did this to a grave. We dubbed that area Death Valley.

Passing through the village one day, we saw a little lady sitting on a stool in front of her hut, and she unwound the strips of cotton binding her feet and rubbed them to ease the pain. We were shocked and saddened to see her poor little deformed feet, all the toes crushed down to one tiny point. Art and I knew that the custom of foot binding had caused suffering for the women of China for hundreds of years. Chinese men considered tiny feet in a woman to be beautiful, and "lily feet" were supposedly a sign that a girl was from a "wealthy" family and didn't need to work. Mothers were forced to begin binding the feet of the little girls when they were three or four, and the pain was excruciating. Once the bones of the feet were broken, with all the toes pushed together and forced into a tiny point, the child could never again walk without pain. It was a daily sight in the streets of Chinkiang to see old women, even some middle-aged ones, hobbling around with a cane. The government had outlawed the custom over thirty years earlier, but thousands in the countryside had kept binding girls' feet for many more years. I recall telling Mama that night that I surely was glad foot binding wasn't an American custom! Thankfully, Aiteh and my other

Chinese friends did not have bound feet.

The foreigners in Chinkiang (most of them missionaries) would have a joint service about once a month. However, First Baptist Church, where Aiteh's father was pastor, was our home church. The floors in the sanctuary were cobblestone, and I remember how cold my feet got in the wintertime. Homes and buildings in China were typically not heated, so parents put layers of clothing on their children to keep them warm; the colder the weather, the more the layers. Aiteh always looked dainty in her many layers, but she was a petite sprite to begin with. On the other hand, I looked like a winter bear with lots of layers. Art and I were grateful that at our house we had an old wood heater, and we didn't have to wear lots of layers there. I've often seen the little toddlers in their many layers walking around at church or on the streets. If they fell, the padding protected them from injury. They could just get up and start over. Chinese mothers didn't use diapers; the little one's trousers were cut open at the bottom seam for convenience, and they were allowed to use the floor or ground wherever they were. Sometimes we needed to watch where we stepped, but Art and I became used to this and didn't think anything about it.

Our Chinese churches had both deacons and deaconesses. In our services, the men sat on one side and the women on the other. Deaconesses passed the offering bags to the ladies, and deacons to the men. I wish I could forget the dreadful Sunday when Pastor Dzang (Jang) asked Art and me to sing a duet in English. Arthur was even more reluctant than I, but we decided to be agreeable and get it over with. We agreed to sing "What a Friend We Have in Jesus," and we got up there before an expectant audience. To my horror, when we began "What a" my mind somehow switched songs, and I came out with, "What a fellowship, what a joy divine." Knowing the words, I bumbled on, but poor Arthur, caught off guard, mostly fumbled and stumbled through. I don't think he ever forgave me, and I can't say I blame him.

Often, Dad baptized men and women at our church. There was a custom there, that following your profession of faith, you spent some weeks or months in an "inquirers" class. This aided people coming from

Buddhist backgrounds and no Bible knowledge to be discipled and grounded in biblical truths. One particular Sunday morning, there was a tiny, elderly woman who hobbled on her little bound feet to the baptistry. Dad instructed her on how to bend her knees. Well, it didn't work. She simply refused to unlock her knees. I can still picture Dad's frustration; he finally just took a deep breath, put his hand on top of her head and pushed her into the baptismal waters. She came up smiling.

In stark contrast to the warmth of fellowship at our church were the funeral processions that all-too-frequently passed down the big street in front of our compound. For some reason, Sunday seemed to be the most auspicious day for funerals. The wealthier the family of the deceased, the more elaborate the procession leading to the cemetery. White was the color of mourning, and families would hire professional mourners, all robed in white, some of them riding in rickshaws and others walking behind the casket. The richer the family, the louder the wails. I recall many a Sunday morning being awakened by those haunting moans. A type of band using cymbals and playing in minor keys would accompany the mourners with musical background. I was astonished as I recognized a pattern over the months and years; the favorite tunes played were "Massa's in the Cold, Cold Ground" and "Bringing in the Sheaves." How very sad, for these were people who had no idea what a *sheave* was and knew nothing of the God of love who gave comfort in the hour of death. I never heard or saw a funeral without being reminded, *This is why our family is here. We want to share hope.*

Mixed in with Dad and Mama's ministry was the ever-present sense of unease and apprehension about the political realities of China. How long would they be able to continue their work? Every trip Dad made into the villages made him wonder if this might be his last one. Ever in their minds was the refrain: "Work, for the night is coming." Each evening on our shortwave radio, we heard more disquieting news about Communist encroachment on nationalist territory. The Communists were already in control of North China and fast moving in our direction. As my parents prayed each day, they asked God for insight so as to "apply their hearts unto wisdom" and share the good news while they still could.

Rosalie and Arthur with the Moffett children
(Presbyterian MKs), Zhenjiang, 1948

NINETEEN

A LAND IN TURMOIL

Often on a free night, Aunt Grace and Cleo Morrison came over to our house and talked with Dad and Mama about the fighting that was coming closer every day in the form of Communist encroachment from the north. In her letters to America, however, Mama was always careful to assure the family that, whatever they might be hearing on the news, "don't be anxious." At least for the moment, central China seemed safe enough. To our north, in Honan province, however, the US Embassy had already warned Americans with children to leave. A clear indication of unrest was inflated prices. The cost of everything continued to skyrocket, and inflation was terrible. At one point, the exchange rate went to 12,000,000 Chinese yuan for one US dollar. Then overnight, banks printed *new* money and changed the rate to 4 to 1. Missionaries learned that as soon as their monthly salaries came, they needed to buy all the food and supplies needed for the coming month, because within two or three days, the month's salary would be next to worthless. Some missionaries bought staples, then invested the rest of their money in something of value for future security, like antiques and items that would not lose their value.

Nevertheless, life seemed pretty normal to my brother and me as we studied, went to church, and played with our friends. Those years back in China are like a kaleidoscope of mental and visceral impressions. I can still picture the sights on the streets as Art and I rode our bikes over to the Presbyterian compound, and particularly as we pedaled past the Grand Canal. The canal had been a major engineering feat over 1,000 years ago, and it connected China and its vast waterways. Hundreds of people lived on houseboats on the canal, and just about everything took place in its muddy waters. Women cooked on the deck of boats and did their washing with water from the canal, and children swam and frolicked in the swirling waters. I often thought what a fit Mama would have if Art or I were to go swimming in the canal, for its waters were never clear. The Grand Canal never smelled fresh. Some of the smells of China defy the imagination. Words can't do them justice. Nonetheless, there is some fragrance or scent that I have often encountered in years since, and that particular scent instantly brings back a veritable flood of memories. I always voice to myself: *China! That smells like China!*

We loved having company. On the few occasions that "Aunt" Fay Taylor could come to visit, we always had a fun time. I loved her surname. It sounded "missionary" to me, for Hudson Taylor, the famous founder of the China Inland Mission in the 1800s, had spent his last years in Chinkiang. He was buried in the European cemetery not half a mile from our house. Taking a picture of Aunt Fay at the large tombstone honoring Hudson Taylor felt like an historic event to me. All of us speculated that Aunt Fay just might be kin to Taylor. Art and I delighted in showing this favorite aunt the special pieces of history that made Chinkiang famous. She told us that living in Shanghai seemed to her like living in a sophisticated European city. But Chinkiang, she assured us, was the *real* China, so we made a point of showing Aunt Fay our sights. A ferry took us to Jiao Shan, often called the "Floating Jade Island," standing in the middle of the Yangtze River. Its famous temple was more than 1,000 years old. Art and I were OK with the main temple and all the smaller ones dotted around, but we were more fascinated by the caves where soldiers had hidden out in the various wars that had plagued China for hundreds of years. There was also a crumbling old fort, built in the 1800s, that was used during the Opium Wars. If we had known more Chinese history, we would have appreciated the little island's famous forest of steles, second only to the iconic stele forest in Xian. There was certainly enough to see on Jiao Shan to intrigue Aunt Fay, and she never forgot the outing.

We also trained Aunt Fay in a bit of real "cultural information," letting her know how to deal with stares. She never had that problem in Shanghai, with all its vast number of foreigners. We informed her that in the *real* China, you need to know how to deal with peoples' curiosity. "Aunt Fay," I earnestly explained, "don't let it bother you if they stare. They are just curious about your hair and light eyes and pale skin. If it *gets* to you," I suggested, "just stare at their feet, and pretty soon, they will quit staring at *you*." Aunt Fay tried out that theory, and, sure enough, it worked perfectly.

Even everyday life was never dull around Chinkiang. There was always something to do, or someone coming, and something interesting on the horizon. There were also serious moments, and ever since the encounter with the leper on the steps, I would spend time thinking about how to get ready to share the good news. Realizing I would need to know how to explain to Chinese people in their own language that God loved them, I tried a little character study. I don't know that any of it "stuck" very well, but it was soon evident that reading Chinese was a mountain of a challenge that would need to be climbed. The tones of Mandarin were no problem; I heard them all the time, so they came naturally. Characters were a different matter. Why couldn't those old scholars 5,000 years ago have developed an *alphabet* like we have in English, rather than inventing about 45,000 different characters? Chinese characters don't run across a page from left to right. They start on the top right and march down and up. Just like with the university student the previous summer, I used the Chinese New Testament to try to teach myself some characters. It was a slow go, but I was soon able to recognize the characters for basic words like: *Jesus, God, love, believe, come* and *trust*.

One would think that by age ten or eleven, a person would have learned enough about proper behavior to prevent frequent punishment. However, I had occasional lapses. Sometimes it was easier to be mischievous than upright. On one such occasion, and I can't even recall the infraction, I knew that retribution was coming. Interestingly, this time Daddy thought a bit before reacting. No spanking, no banishment to my room, but something quite different occurred. Dad looked at me rather thoughtfully, pondered a bit longer (sort of stretching out the agony), and then said, "Rosie (occasionally he used the shortened form of Rosalie), I want you to memorize Romans 12:1-3 and then come quote it to me." God knows, that is the most wonderful and useful "punishment" I ever had. How many times in the intervening decades has that passage from Romans come to my rescue and served as a reminder of how all Christ's followers are to "present themselves a living sacrifice." A number of years after the event, I reminded Dad of his "punishment" that worked and thanked him for it.

Winters could be bitter in China. Our province was in a somewhat moderate zone, but with so little heating in buildings, including churches, I sometimes thought my feet would never be warm again. Thankfully we had houses with indoor plumbing, but we had to use wood and coal to build fires under the water heater. This made it difficult to have a constant source of hot water. Vivid memories persist of the dead of winter and huddling around the wood and coal-burning heater in the family room in order to keep warm. When it got really cold, we would pull out the old tin tub, haul it into the family room, fill it with hot water and take turns getting a bath. I had "first turn" one time in four.

The lyrics of the poem "All Creatures Great and Small" must have penetrated my mind at some point in childhood. I loved lots of little creatures. However, cockroaches never made the cut. China was full of them — plus various and assorted scorpions and stinging creatures both

*Arthur and Rosalie
in Yangzhou, 1939*

*Arthur and Rosalie wield
their chopsticks, 1940*

The Halls in Yangzhou, 1940

Arthur and Rosalie, 1941

The Hall family in 1941, newly returned to America

Arthur and Rosalie with their dad

The Halls in 1944 in Texas

Family portrait, 1945

Rosalie and Arthur with their mother in Temple, Texas, 1944

Rosalie, 1945

Captain Harold Hall, 1945

Scouts Arthur and Rosalie Pryor, Oklahoma, 1946

Rosalie (on third row between two boys) with her first Sunbeam Band, Temple Texas, 1944

Arthur and Rosalie with Aunt Grace, Zhenjiang, 1947

Arthur and Rosalie with their dad, Zhenjiang, 1947

Rosalie and Arthur in their front yard, Zhenjiang, 1947

Rosalie in Chinese chi paur, Zhenjiang, 1948

Rosalie and Penny camping in the front yard with Miss Daisy Maiden, 1948

Rosalie with Chinese friends in Su Zhou, 1948

Harold and Alice Hall in Wichita, Kansas, 1957

*Carl and Ora Hunt in
Albertville, Alabama, 1957*

*Bob and Rosalie,
Albertville,
Alabama, 1957*

Alice and Jody, 1961

Alice, 1962

large, small, crunchy, or slimy. Nor did I appreciate what I dubbed the "Hazardous Household Guest." One particular night, quite like any other, Arthur was asleep in his room next door to mine, I in mine, and Dad and Mom in theirs right beyond my own. We always felt secure in knowing that Dad was so close, for we had absolute trust in his ability to protect us; after all, nothing seemed to frighten him, for he was a take-charge kind of dad.

The house was quiet with all of us settled down in peaceful slumber. However, in the dead of night, I became aware of noise next door in Mama and Dad's room — stumbling around and voices. I was instantly awake. Jumping out of bed, I made my way to their room and cautiously opened the door. At that moment, Mama switched on the light, and there was Daddy, hitting something on the floor. "Got it!" he exclaimed with satisfaction. What was IT? Sidling closer, I saw "it" was the most enormous red and black centipede I'd never hoped to see. Dad told the tale: Something had roused him, something tickling his ear. Half-asleep, he flicked it with his fingers, thinking it was a pesky mosquito. He settled back down and then came *another* tickle. He knocked it away more firmly this time, but it didn't leave. Now something was on his hand. Jumping up, he shook his hand back and forth, and then Mama turned on the light, only to behold the intruder.

My heart was pounding madly by this time. Dad tried to sound reassuring, "It's OK, but we'd better check. I hear that centipedes like to travel in couples." (Comforting thought.) He turned their bed upside down, and, sure enough, underneath the mattress lay centipede number two. It soon met the same fate as its mate, but none of us got much sleep that night.

Another creature was a pleasure to me, however. Of all things, it was a little white rat. Someone from the church gave me the little "pet," and I kept her in a special, roomy cage, fed her every day and watched her run endless miles on a little wheel in the cages, never getting anywhere but seeming to profit from the exercise. Still another bunch of "creatures" were the silkworms Art and I kept for a short time. We fed them mulberry leaves and watched them wiggle around but gave them away when they began spinning silk from their cocoons. After all, they needed a home where someone knew what to do with the fine silk they produced.

My favorite creatures, though, were Lad and Lady. I saved up allowance money, the folks pitched in to help, and I proudly went to the pet shop and picked out a pair of lovebirds. Lad was a brilliant green, and Lady a gleaming blue. I loved those birds and enjoyed hearing them chatter with each other. They lived together in a nice large cage stationed right by the big window of my bedroom, looking out over the yard and the French Consulate up to the right. By this year, 1948, the French had closed their consulate offices and moved out because of threatening war. Chinese soldiers moved into the building, lots of them, and it was usually noisy in that direction. I can still remember the morning I was at the window feeding Lady and Lad when I heard an unusual burst of noise from the direction of the consulate. To my horror, a group of soldiers had tied a dog to a tree and were stoning it to death. I ran crying to Mama, and she explained the sad truth that often in China, hungry people would kill dogs and eat them. I've wished ever since that the memory of that morning would quietly fade away, but it never did.

Art and I both enjoyed spinning Chinese tops. Art was always better at it than I — but, with practice, I learned to get the little wooden top with a wheel just on one end, balanced and spinning on my string attached to two sticks. The tops made a lovely humming sound when you got a good spin going. They are aptly named "wind cows" (feng nyou), for they made a bit of a roar. We sometimes saw Chinese teenagers throw them high in the air and adeptly catch them on a little groove on one tip. I could never quite get there, but it was fun trying. Art had gotten a BB gun for Christmas, but, to tell the truth, there wasn't much scope for using a BB gun in China. One morning, he and I were standing on Aunt Grace's balcony, which overlooked the ancient street with its interesting stalls below, offering about anything you could imagine for sale. One stall just below our balcony sold towels and washcloths, and we noticed that the lady running it was doing quite a brisk business. About that time, Arthur spied a sparrow sitting on the telephone wire running down the length of the street. Thinking that would make an interesting target, he cocked the gun, squinted his eye, and fired. Would you believe, he actually hit the sparrow; it didn't fall, but its little feet hung on to the wire as we watched with wide eyes, blood began to drip slowly down on the towels on the cart below. Oh dear! Both of us ducked out of sight, and, in short order, the fussing started. That little shop lady was *not* happy, and I can't blame her. Art did not report the incident to Mama and Dad, and I felt guilty about it for a long time.

There was another shooting not long after that which made a much deeper impression, and one I have relived in my mind a thousand times. China was in great political stress by this time, with refugees fleeing from the north, spilling over into our city — and often with no place to go. Everyone was living with uncertainty, never sure of what tomorrow might bring. Propaganda was everywhere, with the nationalist government vilifying the Communists who were taking over more and more provinces to the north. With Nanjing, the capital, being so near, everyone stayed on edge. Occasionally, some Communist soldiers would infiltrate our area, and no one knew what to expect from that danger. One morning, Art and I were on the balcony playing some sort of game when we heard a loud commotion in the public square just beyond the ancient street. There was the sound of marching and drums. Curious, we went to the edge of the balcony and looked out over the square. Nationalist soldiers were marching a bound and gagged Communist prisoner to the square, where they proceeded to stand him up, lined up a firing squad, and executed him on the spot. That moment of horror is permanently etched in my memory.

Increasingly, propaganda billboards went up, blazoning messages about the horrors of Communism. The billboard my mind's eye still sees is of Chinese people — men, women, and children, bound and gagged, and kneeling blindfolded — with Communist soldiers standing behind, executing them one by one. I began having frequent nightmares, often waking up with a racing heart and in a cold sweat, dreaming that Mama and Dad were bound and gagged and were going to be shot. So strange, what memories can do. Fifty years later, on occasion I still have that same nightmare.

All during our time in Chinkiang, the footlocker stayed at the foot of my bed. Every month or so, I would check to see if the balloons still held any "American air." Yes, three or four of the balloons still had a little, and I would sigh with satisfaction. Our schoolwork was a steady part of daily life, and I confess to liking to study. Being able to choose my own reading was always the best part. The folks had brought the Book of Knowledge for reference work for us, and there was always something new to be found there. That was way before the days of the internet highway, and we were thankful for some reference material. I wish I could remember all that knowledge now; alas, sometimes the brain leaks.

Art and I managed to go into business together. It was very "short-lived," but fun while it lasted. We thought a local English newspaper might be both fun and profitable. After all, there were Baptist, Methodist, Presbyterian, and a few independent missionaries in Chinkiang. We decided to name it the *Chinkiang Herald*. Getting several "subscribers" at ten cents an issue, we quickly set to work. Art would do certain feature stories, and I would write on various topics of interest. Alas, due to my lack of fact-checking expertise, our journal was so short-lived that it didn't make it through more than two weeks. I meant to report about the famous Joe Lewis, world champion heavyweight boxer, but I mistyped and called him John L. Lewis, whose fame lay in the area of labor unions. (Neither one of us did much proofreading.) Art was furious — and, once again, I couldn't blame him! I was pretty mad at myself.

The bane of our existence, at least as far as Art and I were concerned, was our massive front yard. Just picture a football field and think of trying to keep it free of weeds. Nearly impossible. But that didn't keep Dad from trying and from enlisting the whole family to do its part. Art and I detested pulling weeds. I've never like yard work since, and I guess I blame Dad for that! In reading one of Aunt Grace's letters from that time period, I could just see the smile on her face as she wrote home about our family out there in the yard pulling weeds. She told the home folks, "Arthur Bryan says, 'There's no future in this!'" One lovely memory of the big old yard remains. Aunt Grace's missionary friend of many years, Miss Daisy Maiden, sometimes came to do work in the Chinkiang area and would always stay with Aunt Grace. Miss Daisy was a great sport, and she would go camping with the two of us. Art and I thought it such fun to set up our pup tent, fix sleeping rolls, camp out with Miss Daisy, and have "breakfast" outside the next morning. This was a fifty-year-old woman indulging two young children and making a lifelong impression on our hearts.

One morning as I was out digging up weeds and muttering about it under my breath every few minutes, I made a discovery that gave me a little thrill of excitement. While using a little trowel to dig up a pesky weed, I unearthed a little oval-shaped stone that looked the color of jade. I sat back on my heels gazing at it and imagining that maybe, once upon a time, it had belonged to some young girl in an emperor's palace, and she had used it to adorn her hair or her fingers. In that moment, visions of archaeology danced in my head, and I thought how wonderful it would be to dig up ancient treasures. Most young girls in the 1940s thought about growing up to be a nurse or teacher, but my burning ambition was to be an archaeologist. In more recent years, I have thought about that little piece of green stone and compared that experience to digging up missions history and what sheer delight in discovery that has become.

And then, it was time for more change. Here in the midst of political and military turmoil, Art was preparing to go to Shanghai to boarding school at SAS (Shanghai American School). On the days Art and I had a royal quarrel or so, I sort of looked forward to him leaving, but mostly I was sad to think of my only brother away in Shanghai. So much change was occurring, and who knew what was going to happen next in China? And yet again, the only certainty was uncertainty. With no way of knowing what might lie ahead, we were all living on tenterhooks.

The Halls in Zhenjiang, 1948

TWENTY

MORE CHANGE

Mama and Art were busy packing and planning for boarding school, but Art and I decided to make a last visit together to our favorite pagoda at Jin Shan (Gold Mountain) before he left. This was our stalwart Chinkiang landmark, with its mixture of towering pagoda, huge ferocious looking idols standing guard at the first temple, and the aroma of incense permeating the entire temple complex. In all the decades since the 1940s, I can never inhale the scent of incense without automatically thinking about Jin Shan. The complex typically had a vast number of saffron-robed monks moving around and was always crowded with people giving money to earn heavenly favor by burning incense before the idols.

Those four huge guardian idols standing in the outer temple gave us shivers every time we visited. Jin Shan was beautiful from a distance, but up close a sense of barren hope surrounded us. For some reason, I always felt an unmistakable sense of foreboding in the temple's atmosphere. The Jin Shan pagoda was 1,700 years old, and for young legs, provided a nice challenging climb up its nine levels of towers. Climbing up the winding stairs to the summit provided a breathtaking view of the entire countryside. The mighty Yangtze looked like an undulating snake, winding across the green landscape below. (Of course, it was also made physically breathtaking by the long climb.) It was a satisfying final visit to Jin Shan, and with the precarious political climate in China, Art and I wondered if this might indeed be our last time to climb the pagoda.

Then it was time to leave for Shanghai and Shanghai American School. I was pretty excited to be able to go along and see Arthur settled in his dorm room. Aunt Grace promised to take good care of Lad and Lady while I was away. (In a letter home, Aunt Grace wrote, "The lovebirds are nice, but noisy, and I don't want any of my own!") I wondered if Art felt a little sense of aloneness as we left him at the school, but if he did, he didn't let it show. On the train trip home, however, I felt a bit hollow on the inside and wondered why change is so hard to deal with. A special trip with Mama and Aunt Grace was coming up, though, so I had that to look forward to. Meantime, as was a monthly custom, I checked the American air in those yellow balloons. Two of them still had a bit of air, and again I heaved a sigh of satisfaction. For some strange reason, I found this reassuring.

Of all the work Aunt Grace did, whether teaching in the Bible school, working in the local churches, serving as principal of the Baptist primary school, or leading WMU ministries, her favorite ministry was village work. She gained great satisfaction from pioneer work in small villages and towns where she could lay a spiritual foundation and share the gospel with people who were hungry for good news. Aunt Grace made it sound exciting, and rather romantic, as she described the women and children and their lives and homes. Even the living conditions sounded fun, although, of course, they were not. More likely they were a huge challenge. I recall after one trip, Aunt Grace described making pancakes on a little oil burner, and she grinned and said, "It was as much fun as camping out!"

On this particular exploration trip, Mama and I went with Aunt Grace to Dan Yang, a small city on the railroad line between Chinkiang and Shanghai. Aunt Grace called it "village work," although there were some 60,000 people who lived there. She and her Bible woman and Dad and a pastor colleague frequently went for a week at a time to Dan Yang; however, there was no missionary in the village full-time. Now the three of us went to look for a place to rent so she could live there and begin a permanent work. I secretly felt this must take just a bit of extra courage, considering conditions in China. She found a little place to rent, and she also rented an empty teashop near the heart of town for a place to teach and have services. Aunt Grace felt a new burst of enthusiasm at being able to engage in the type of ministry she loved so dearly.

There was another kind of ministry going on in Chinkiang just then, and visions of that work are still vivid in my mind. For all the time we had been back in Chinkiang, there had been refugees fleeing from Communist domination in the north. Most of them arrived in Chinkiang already destitute, and by the fall of 1948, tens of thousands more poured in, for the Communists were slowly and steadily pushing south. Waves of refugees fled in their wake. Quite close to the area Art and I dubbed "Methodist Hill" was a vast area of hilly, barren, open space. Mennonite relief workers came to Chinkiang and set up a food service in that open area. We would go and stand on a nearby hill, looking out over thousands of ragged people standing in line. Many of them waited twelve or more hours each day in order to get bread and a bit of rice or porridge. The very sight was heart-wrenching. Those refugees were barely staying alive, just subsisting on very little food. Pathetic little tents and cardboard huts dotted the nearby hills, and the Mennonite workers valiantly helped the masses as much as they could. My young mind tried to make sense of all that I saw. Here were thousands of families fleeing the enemy. When they got as far as the ocean — then what? Where could they go for safety? We foreigners held a passport that allowed us a bolthole, a way to safety. They had none. That was one of the many times in life I have confronted the question: *Why?* How can such things be? Why can't life be fair? There were no good answers to such queries. Nor are there now. I'm still learning about faith, hope, and justice. It must be a lifelong learning process.

My ensuing several months were full of wondering if I would ever get to go to my favorite places again or see my friends anymore. I went once more to the area where Pearl Buck lived as a child, looked at her house and wondered if it was my last time to see it. Inflation was running rampant, and the poorest people were the ones who suffered the most. I literally saw people go to a store pushing a wheelbarrow full of money. The whole wheelbarrow-full might not be worth more than ten or twenty dollars. Poverty had always been a problem in China, but it was now in epidemic proportions. On one day, $100,000 in Chinese yuan could be worth about five US dollars, but the next morning it might be worth a dollar.

I took consolation in the familiar and found stability in my studies. At least this was one thing that proved consistent. Then one morning I woke up, and Lad, my beautiful little green lovebird, lay lifeless in the bottom of the cage. I cried bitter tears over the loss of that lovely little bit of sunshine and worried about how lonely Lady must be. As usual, I found a small bit of consolation in checking those little yellow balloons, and, yes, two of them still had a bit of American air.

Dad and Mama were facing a tough decision. The US Consulate was strongly advising Americans in central China to leave promptly, especially those with children. News from the north was growing ever increasingly ominous, and who knew what was fact and what was rumor? Chinkiang's proximity to China's capital city of Nanjing further intensified the danger of remaining. My parents were so torn. They loved China. They loved their work. They felt called. Yet, at the same time, if the Communists took control, it could well be that the presence of "foreign friends" could make life even worse for the Christians in our city. Aunt Grace returned from Dan Yang and her new ministry. She, Cleo Morrison, the Jowers, and my parents all faced the same dilemma. Yangchow missionaries were in an identical quandary, and they met and prayed, agonizing over the next step. I found myself torn in similar manner. Admitting to a bit of fear at the thought of what the Communists might do to the hated Americans, I still felt like China was *home*. I loved it here and did not want to leave.

November came, and with Arthur home for the weekend, the folks came to a decision. For all concerned, they must leave Chinkiang. When they could reach Shanghai and meet with the mission secretary for Asia, Dr. Cauthen, they could plan further. Each of the missionaries reached a similar conclusion, as did the Yangchow missionaries. Several would plan to leave a week from Monday, the rest to follow in a few days. Aunt Grace determined that she would first help expedite our departure, then leave shortly after we did. She and Mama and Dad shipped as much to Shanghai as they could and planned to take just a couple of suitcases each, because train travel in China was already far more crowded than usual — and that was saying a lot.

That meant I had a week to say goodbye to Chinkiang, to tell Penny I loved having her for a friend, to say goodbye to Aiteh and other friends, and to decide what to do with Lady. I remembered how exciting it had been to go to the bird pet shop and pick out those two lovebirds. Now I had the sad duty of taking Lady back to the shop and bidding her farewell. The shopkeeper was so kind. He could tell my heart was hurting and kept reassuring me that he would personally keep Lady and take extra good care of her. I left the little shop with tears dripping down my cheeks. I never could bear to get another bird after her.

With the exception of the man on the steps that earlier Christmas morning, no memory is more vividly etched on my mind than the train trip from Chinkiang to Shanghai in November 1948. We left our house before seven in the morning, holding reservations for the first-class train due to depart at 8:30. We had heard tales of the wild crowds on trains in recent months, but felt that holding reservations would make it fairly easy to travel. How wrong can you be? One thing I had learned in our travel experiences was that you wanted, at all costs, to travel on a first-class train. If you were desperate to depart and there were no more seats, get a second-class ticket — but don't expect to have a comfortable or clean trip. There certainly won't be a little doily on the back of your seat. We had packed carefully, for each of us could just take two pieces of luggage — one of mine being the footlocker still holding the two tiny yellow balloons. With so little air in them, the little balloons didn't take up much space now. Several of the Yangchow missionaries met us on the station platform. There were Ruby Wheat and Marie Conner. Both had come out on the ocean liner with us in 1946 as rookie missionaries, and now they felt like old veterans. Thelma Williams, a nurse at Yangchow Hospital, was also leaving. My eyes got a little wide when I saw her pile of luggage. She clearly had more than two pieces, and one of the many was a big trunk.

The station master, a friend of Dad's, came to the platform area to greet us and see if he could help. Chinkiang was quite a terminus for trains, with several sets of tracks and a couple of walkovers and overpasses that hung above the tracks themselves. As I looked around the familiar station, I gave a little gulp and wondered if I would ever see it again. It felt like there was a lump in my throat, and somehow, I couldn't swallow it. When 8:30 arrived, there was no train. About thirty minutes later, here it came, and as it slowed to a stop, we saw with dismay that every car was jam-packed. People were sitting on top of the train, each one of them in harm's way. There was no way our group could board the train, no matter how many reservations we held. Reservations were worthless.

No matter, the station master assured us, "There is a second-class train due shortly. You can take it." Art and I looked at each other dubiously but said nothing. What good would it do? The next train belatedly arrived, and it was the same situation as before, with massive overcrowding and no way to board. Now the station master shook his head and gave us the only alternative he could think of. There was a third-class train sitting over on a far track — due to leave at 10:30. It was primitive, but we could be assured of having a seat. So, here went the some dozen or more of us to the far track, where we boarded the only train with room for us to sit. The seats were straight, wooden benches, with wobbly-looking luggage racks above. Along with the missionaries on this trip were Pastor Djang (Jang) and his whole family, so Aiteh and I were traveling to Shanghai together. Pastor Djang was the new president of Kiangsu Province Baptist Convention, so he had been asked to move to Shanghai while he could. The problem was, the train was soon so crowded that once we took our seats, there was no way to move around. Making the best of a bad situation, we got a seat and struggled to get all the luggage in. Wouldn't you know, Thelma Williams' big old trunk would certainly not go on the luggage rack above, so (me being the youngest member of the entourage) it fell my lot to ride the many hours to Shanghai with my feet on Miss Thelma's trunk. Glaring at it didn't help.

Things did not improve. It was clear that there had not been much cleaning done since the last occupants of the railroad car had departed, but it wasn't as bad as the condition of the bathroom at the end of the car. In typical Chinese style, it was a hole in the floor, and you had to learn how to manage. Nonetheless, by afternoon, that was a moot point, for people were standing in the bathroom so there was no way it could be used. One can readily imagine the problems that created for the next several hours. The train, due to depart at 10:30, was full of people by 10:00. And still it sat. And sat. It did not move — no reason given. Finally, at 5:30 in the evening, we had sent a message to Aunt Grace, and she came to the station with food for everyone. I can't remember food ever tasting better. Everyone's nerves were on edge, and all sorts of rumors began circulating: *The Communists have already reached Nanjing. The train will not be allowed to leave. We will all be captured.* On and on went the rumors. About 8 p.m., all was dark, and suddenly an authoritative voice called out: "Attention! Attention!" Everyone was quiet, and the voice spoke again: "I need a seat." The voice did not *get* a seat. Nonetheless, Chinese soldiers who were fleeing the Communists commandeered every rail car in our train, with the exception of ours. Thanks to the good graces of the station master, the foreigners were allowed to remain on board.

At 10 that fateful night, the train, at long last, left the station and slowly made its way to Shanghai. In Dan Yang, it stopped briefly, and no matter that there was no room, several soldiers got on and laid down in the overhead luggage racks. As if that were not bad enough, one of them got sick and repeatedly threw up. It's not surprising that I still have nightmares about that trip. At 8:30 the next morning, our third-class train limped into Shanghai terminal, and a dozen weary Americans tried to get enough blood circulating in their legs again to disembark. I remember gazing resentfully at Miss Williams' big trunk, yet learned some fifty years later that her trunk was an important part of that final trip. (But that's a story for another day.)

Mama said in later years that she feared that terrible trip would scar her children forever. We weren't exactly scarred, but neither did we ever forget it. I also learned a lesson in appreciation for the privileges that are mine. Those are unearned privileges.

Aunt Grace soon joined us in Shanghai, having also endured a nightmare of a trip, although not quite as lengthy as ours. Decades later, I read the letter Mama had written to Sumter right after we reached Shanghai. All she said about the trip was, "Travel now is such that words can't describe it." That has to be a masterpiece of understatement. All of us stayed at Rue La Fayette, the large house that had belonged to Willie Kelly. Miss Kelly had left it to the mission, and it was used by many a missionary who needed a place to stay for a day, a month, or for years. There were two large houses on the compound, and, in late 1948, both were full of missionaries. There weren't many children but lots of older missionaries. We realized afresh that Shanghai was truly a mixture of Chinese citizens with scores of other nationalities. Aunt Fay was right: It didn't seem like the China we knew.

I so clearly remember the little woman who sat each day at the gate of the Rue La Fayette house, her hand outstretched, begging for money to feed her children. She usually had at least two little ones with her wearing ragged clothes and no shoes on their feet. I began to notice each day that she was picking something off her toddlers. She would pick at some object, look at it, crack it with her teeth, and give it to the little ones. Curious, I asked Mama what was going on. Mama's eyes looked sad as she explained, "She's picking lice off the children, cracking them open, and feeding them to the toddlers." There came another lump in my throat. It persisted in staying stuck there.

That was a most unusual Thanksgiving and Christmas. Many missionaries evacuated, and most of those remaining were trying to arrange passage back to America. Dad and Mama spent a lot of time discussing what they should do and what kind of plans they could make in the face of such a precarious situation. In consultation with the mission office, they determined to get passage on the *USS General Breckinridge*, due to leave the first of the new year. Once more, it was going to mean another goodbye. The lump in my throat began to feel permanent. This time, when I looked at the yellow balloons, I found a tiny bit of air left in one. I wept because now we were returning to American air — but this time, China would have to travel in my heart.

Grace Wells, Lucy Smith and Alice Hall examine mission documents, Shanghai, 1948

Bob, age 7   *Bob, age 20*

TWENTY-ONE

AMERICA

This was the first (and last) Christmas we ever spent with about fifty missionaries. They were from various parts of China — all in a state of flux, all seeking to know the best thing to do in the face of war and danger. I naturally caught the general atmosphere of apprehension and uncertainty. Aunt Grace hoped to go back to her work in Chinkiang, but increasingly it looked like returning would not be a safe option. She and my parents knew that the presence of missionaries in a city as relatively small as Chinkiang would likely put our Chinese Christian friends in harm's way. Therefore, Aunt Grace reluctantly closed her promising, new mission out-station so recently opened in Dan Yang, and, along with the rest of us, departed for Shanghai — leaving behind everything except a few suitcases. Soldiers were already trying to occupy our Chinkiang houses. Thankfully, the four of us were able once again to have Christmas with Aunt Grace. Shanghai American School was still open, and Art attended classes right up until Christmas Eve. It turned out to be the last time he would ever see his school.

My parents spent hours, days, weeks discussing options and praying for clarity in what direction to go. Dad did not feel it wise to leave the family and go alone to some pioneer mission point in Asia — not with the world in such flux and turmoil. By Christmas, he and Mama reached the decision to return to the US, regroup, and seek what God had in mind for us next. The night before we left Shanghai, I checked my footlocker one more time. There lay my Chinese chop — my identity in this land. I knew chops were not used in America; I would need to carve my own identity there. Then I pulled out the last remaining yellow balloon, cradled it in my hands, and cried over something quite different. This time I was *leaving* China. There were no balloons with Chinese air to take to America. This time, I must hold China and its memories close in my heart, for they were part of me. With childlike faith, I simply prayed, "Lord, someday let me come back." Tucked into a special corner of my heart were memories of the man on the steps, and I prayed to never forget that man nor the prompting of God on my heart that long-ago Christmas morning.

Dad booked passage for the four of us on the SS *Breckinridge,* a converted troop transport ship manned by a US Naval crew. On New Year's Day 1949, we sailed for the US. I felt an aching hurt for Aiteh and my Chinese friends. Not only was I leaving them behind, but *they* did not have the option to leave. The Communists were coming closer, but where could they go for safety? We held American passports, but they had no recourse but to trust in God alone. Not for the first time I pondered the fact that life isn't fair. Why were we so blessed? I did not find a ready answer. Our whole family stood on the deck of the *Breckinridge,* and with heavy hearts, watched China grow smaller in the distance. I was just a child but realized this was Dad and Mama's life work. How their hearts must be grieving.

A voyage on the Pacific no longer seemed strange, and it brought back that now-familiar sense of vastness and open space. Standing on the deck and gazing out over infinite miles of ocean, I felt unbound and free. Was there land anywhere? Nothing but water was visible. At the same time, I felt helpless. We were at the mercy of the sea. Somehow, between the past and the present, I felt a bit like in-between myself — neither here nor there. I thought of my lovebird, Lady, and my friends all left behind. The lump in my throat was pretty tightly lodged, yet I didn't know how to get rid of it. Swallowing didn't help. Maybe time would, but that was a bleak thought.

Two weeks later, I was happily surprised to discover that the sight of the Golden Gate Bridge, as we sailed into San Francisco harbor, brought a welcoming glow to my heart. Maybe I just had to reconcile the conflicting emotions churning around inside and love two different homes. Dad and Mama had talked at length about initial plans upon returning to America. My grandparents were now in Coweta, where Aunt Mellie and Uncle Victor lived. Grandmama Hall was not quite seventy but was already suffering from advanced rheumatoid arthritis. At the same time, Granddaddy Hall was nearly completely blind. Several years earlier, Dad had purchased a little piece of land near Aunt Mellie's house, and my grandparents lived in a small house nearby. Consequently, Dad and Mama decided to temporarily settle in Coweta and build a small house on this property so they could help take care of their parents. We wept tears of joy upon seeing those dear faces. Those tears were mixed with shock, however, at how their health had deteriorated so rapidly. Grandmama was in constant pain, and Granddaddy's blindness tore at my heart as he tried to get from place to place on his own. Dad was able to temporarily rent the small house right next to our grandparents' place until our house could be built.

Our first trip to our South Carolina family was a mix of the known and the new. Those loved faces were still dearly beloved, but they were in a new setting. My grandparents were well into their eighties, and both were very frail. Consequently, along with Aunt Edith and Aunt Rhett, they had moved into town in Sumter to be near medical help. Still, Aunt Edith's flapjacks (pancakes) had not changed one bit, nor had Aunt Rhett's amazing pound cake. I watched her make it, one egg at a time, with 300 stirs of the batter after each egg. There was no pound cake in the world to ever match it for lightness. The warmth of family love was like a blanket of security to Art and me, and helped us over the trauma of adjusting.

One of our main topics of conversation during visits to South Carolina revolved around Aunt Grace, who was still in Shanghai. Mama and Dad understood, even more than could the rest of the family, the precarious situation in which she lived. Her letters were fairly frequent, although she was cautious in what she said. All mail sent directly from Shanghai was censored by the Communists. Occasionally, Aunt Grace could send a letter to Hong Kong by someone traveling there, and she could speak more frankly in correspondence mailed that way. Miraculously, the handful of missionaries still in Shanghai were able to work fairly normally. In the face of citywide unrest, multitudes of refugees constantly pouring into China's largest city, and the imminent threat of the Communist takeover, people were understandably greatly distressed.

That angst offered new opportunities for Christians to present the hope found only in Christ, and Aunt Grace wrote in nearly every letter about large crowds in services, new young people in her Bible classes, and scores of young adults coming to faith in Christ. The women's missionary societies flourished and seized countless opportunities to share the gospel message. Meanwhile, Americans were warned to keep a suitcase packed and some cash on hand, because Shanghai could fall at any time. In nearly every letter, Aunt Grace would say, "We have learned to live one day at a time." In April 1949, she wrote, "No one knows what the next few days will bring, but things do not look good for the future." She commented in typical Grace fashion, "I don't believe I am in any real danger — except to my nerves with the uncertainty!"

The Communists crossed the Yangtze River in April, and the few missionaries still in Shanghai knew that it was now just a matter of time. Fighting was raging within miles of the city, but still no battles in Shanghai itself. On May 23, 1949, Aunt Grace wrote, "The fighting Saturday night sounded like it was right at the civilian airport." Two days later, Shanghai was taken under Communist control. Miraculously, the foreign community was not harmed, but there were mass executions of politically incorrect people who were unfortunate enough to fall into enemy hands. In a letter mailed from Hong Kong June 4, she wrote, "We have been 'liberated' now more than a week, and it is hard to believe how normally we seem to be living since then." All the family heaved sighs of relief but remained on tenterhooks, wondering what might happen next to their dear one who could well be in harm's way. For two more long years, we waited weekly for news from Aunt Grace and prayed earnestly for her safety under daunting and menacing conditions.

Meanwhile, I certainly felt like we were safe enough back in America, but it still seemed a foreign country to me. Other than our family nearby, I tended to consider myself a stranger in a strange land. At least I could run over to see my grandparents every day, and it brightened them up to have young faces around. Granddaddy had an endearing little habit of speech that I have never heard anyone else use, even all these years later. He never used the word *forget*. He always said, "I disremember." Much later, I looked it up in the dictionary and discovered it was an old colloquialism from the South. Grandmama had an old Domestic Grand treadle sewing machine she had gotten from Montgomery Ward decades earlier. On days when she felt like getting up, Grandmama would instruct me in how to sew. She was a better teacher than I was a student, but other than gnashing my teeth over trying to fill the bobbin, I managed fairly well. Nonetheless, it quickly became apparent to Grandmama (and to me) that I was not destined to be a tailor.

Adjusting to a treadle sewing machine, however, came much more easily than adjusting to school in America. Challenges were thrown in my face there every day. Thank God for Aunt Mellie. She was the sixth-grade geography teacher at Coweta's small elementary school. Mellie Place was a take-charge kind of teacher with a kind heart, and she proved to be my buffer in this unfamiliar new setting. She became my anchor in a perplexing world. I came from a classroom of one, taught by experts at home since 1946, and now I was one of many in a classroom full of strangers. Furthermore, young girls just approaching their teen years are not particularly noted for kindness or inclusivity, and I was the outsider. Since our home schooling had been so accelerated, I was a year younger than the other sixth-graders. That didn't help anything. My mind told me I just looked *different*. It is hard to describe. Clearly, I was an occidental like my classmates, but on the inside, I felt different. In my imagination, the other students were thinking, *She's not like us.* My clothes felt odd as well.

In Chinkiang, I always wore dresses. That's what girls did. Here in America, many of the girls wore jeans and looked at my clothes a little strangely. (It seems ironic now, from the perspective of many decades, for it has been many years since I've even worn a dress!) Nonetheless, I was eleven, and I wanted to belong. People in China had stared at me because I was a *"yang gweidz"* (foreign devil). Here, I was a fellow American, but I thought my classmates still stared because I was just different. It took many months and a good bit of pain to overcome this feeling of being odd and not quite good enough.

Our Coweta church was a big help and became a second home. Rev. Silas Ulysses Butts was our beloved pastor. His nickname was Cal, and Pastor Cal was wonderful at making you feel like you belonged. I don't know that I ever had a good opportunity to tell him thank you for being so kind to the strangers in his midst. Best of all, I was now a GA among other GAs, learning together. I loved our meetings each week and thrived on doing Forward Steps. To this day I can quote the GA pledge and sing our hymn. (Even now, as I work with GAs in a new millennium and find the words of the pledge have changed, the heart intent of GAs has not altered.)

And there was Barbara. Barbara Morgan was God's gift to a lonely young girl who felt different. She was the quintessential "girl next door" and helped me over many a hump. Matter-of-fact, consistently kind and a lot of fun, Barbara was my blessing. My first birthday back in America is a fond memory. I woke up that morning feeling a bit melancholy as I recalled celebrating the year before in Chinkiang. Barbara asked me to come to her house that afternoon to play, and, lo and behold, I arrived to discover she had arranged a surprise birthday party. It's a wonder I didn't break down and cry over her thoughtfulness.

Dad did a lot of deputation and speaking in churches, and Mama did a good bit as well. Simultaneously, Dad joined the US Army reserves as a chaplain and was able to minister in that work as well. After about a year, our little house was completed, and we moved in. It was just about a block from our grandparents' place, and I regularly went every day to see how they were doing. By this time, Grandmama was completely bedridden, her body painfully crippled by arthritis. Granddaddy was now totally blind. Aunt Mellie got innovative and strung up a wire in the small backyard, attaching it to sturdy objects. Every morning and evening, Granddaddy held on to the wire and walked endless miles for exercise. Since their house was located between ours and downtown Coweta, just a few blocks away, I also stopped to see them on my way to run errands.

So many of my Coweta memories are wrapped around First Baptist Church and the love and normalcy it provided for all of us. In the 1950s, Baptist churches had a two-week revival every summer, and all of us looked forward to it. I vividly recall the last night of the meeting our second year back in America. Uncle Victor regularly went to services with Aunt Mellie and felt like part of the church, but I knew he wasn't. Aunt Mellie had been praying for her husband for all the years of their marriage, for he had never professed faith in Christ. Dad and Mama joined her in this prayer, asking that Victor realize that being "good" was not a ticket to salvation. That last night as the invitation was given, I noticed Mama quietly step forward just two rows and gently tap Uncle Victor on the shoulder. She simply whispered, "Victor?" Immediately, he took a deep breath, stepped out, and walked determinedly to the altar. There was massive rejoicing in the little sanctuary that night, along with a lot of tears. From that point on, and for the rest of his life, Uncle Victor was a staunch and faithful part of the fellowship.

The echoes of Chinkiang never stopped resonating in my heart, but I learned to accept reality and deal with the present. We lived in Coweta about three years, and several of us who were classmates had a "gang of four" who were GAs and students together. We visited in each other's homes and had frequent slumber parties. Summer camp at Heart O' the Hills Baptist retreat was a high point, reminding me of the sense of call my heart had experienced the morning I met the man on the steps.

I slowly grew accustomed to school in a classroom setting and tried to remain aware and sensitive to those around me who might feel different or left out. I knew how it felt. It was fun to go to the only drugstore in town after school, sit on a stool at the counter, drink Pepsi and eat potato chips. It was not hot, roasted chestnuts and *shau bing* bread, but it was tasty nonetheless. The best part was sharing it with friends. At the same time, I recognized that all these adjustments were harder for Arthur than for me. He had at least three points of difficulty: his age, his small stature, and being a year ahead in school. All these things made him particularly vulnerable. Art was brilliant and couldn't seem to *help* making top grades. The guys in high school nicknamed him "Archie Einstein," and I actually recall Art on occasion trying to make a B in order to avoid teasing.

From 1949 until 1951, we were all deeply concerned about Aunt Grace, and hung on to every letter from her. She was thankful that for most of those years her presence was a blessing and support to Chinese Christian leaders. Shanghai had an international flavor and was a large enough city that working in this setting did not present the dangers missionaries would have faced in rural China. However, the tone of my aunt's letters gradually altered, and we realized things were getting tighter. When the mission office moved to Hong Kong, Aunt Grace was one of only a handful of missionaries left in Shanghai. She, therefore, did a lot of what needed to be done at the former mission office and helped Chinese leadership to work as quietly and effectively as possible. By the end of 1950, there were only three missionaries left, and Aunt Grace realized her days there must be numbered. She was determined to present no extra burden to the Chinese Christians, and, increasingly, that seemed likely to happen. In March 1950, she took a train to Hong Kong and had great difficulty getting through customs and across the border. When we received a telegram stating her safe arrival in Hong Kong, it felt like celebration day to all the family. Our tears were tears of relief.

When I look at the positives and negatives of life for MKs (missionary kids), there are certainly plenty of negatives. A constant need to make adjustments is one of them. Frequently, however, that which is a negative is also a positive — for life is *full* of adjustments, whether sought or not. Learning to adjust is a big plus, and I have called on that experience many times and been grateful for those early challenges. I recall an older friend once reminding me, "A teabag isn't worth much until it's been in some hot water." That thought frequently continues to pop into mind.

Becoming a teenager probably feels like plenty of hot water, for it has multiple challenges. I often felt like those tumultuous teen years were something that had to be navigated in order to finally reach adulthood. I realized Dad certainly had his own set of challenges, needing to travel so frequently with deputation work and spending time away as an Army reserve chaplain. He longed for a steady place to preach and put down roots. My parents had always felt called to missions in China, but that door appeared permanently closed. They had no choice but to regroup and move forward. Long years later, I recognized some of the depth of sadness Dad and Mama experienced over not being able to return to China. It never ceased to be their call.

Dad was called as pastor of First Baptist Church, Kinta, Oklahoma, and here it came again — another move. Art had just matriculated at Oklahoma State University as an engineering student, so the shift was not quite as traumatic for him this time around. Working hard at not feeling sorry for myself, I intentionally wore a smile and prepared for change again. To my surprise, it wasn't as jarring this time around. Kinta High School was small, and it appeared that the "preacher's daughter" would be accepted and assimilated into the school. Maybe experience had taught me a little, and I tried to remind myself that I personally needed to make an effort to think about how other people were feeling. We had only been in Kinta a short time when news came that Grandmama's frail body had failed. This was the first time death had been part of our close-knit family, and through our tears we rejoiced that she was no longer in great pain.

Kinta was typical small-town America and seemed highly provincial to me — but then, most of my new classmates had never traveled farther than Tulsa or Oklahoma City, so what should I expect? School seemed easy, and there was plenty of time to take piano lessons and play on the basketball team. (I was a guard and generally fouled out pretty early.) On the piano, I was speedy but not very accurate. Nonetheless, music was a joy and an outlet. The folks had bought a little spinet piano the year we returned to America, and I loved being able to play and occasionally lose myself in music. Joining the school choir was also fun, and I discovered that dating was as well, although not all the time. With teenaged girls, there was always some drama going on. That might have been good practice for the future, because I learned that such drama frequently takes place with adults as well. Furthermore, some adults seem perpetually stuck in their teen years.

Summer 1953 proved to be the start of a new period in my life, although at the time I had no clue. That June, a summer missionary with the Home Mission Board (now North American Mission Board) came to northeastern Oklahoma to work for ten weeks. Bob Hunt began his summer ministry by speaking at an associational youth rally held in our Kinta church. From that point on, for both the visiting summer missionary and the pastor's daughter, life was never quite the same.

Bob and Rosalie
the week they first met

Rosalie at 13　　　　　　*Rosalie at OBU*

TWENTY-TWO

COLLEGE DAYS

A whole summer stretched ahead for our Baptist youth, and we discussed what vacation activities would be fun. When the associational youth rally met at our little church in June, we learned about Kiamichi Baptist Assembly and its special youth week. The information came from the rally's guest speaker, a Home Mission Board summer missionary who was leading youth ministries in our area of Oklahoma for the summer. I was pretty impressed with this good-looking, dark-haired, articulate college senior who would be directing our association at Kiamichi. I, therefore, made an immediate mental note to tell Dad and Mama I wanted to be part of the group going to summer assembly. Bob Hunt was a senior ministerial student at Howard College (now Samford University) in Alabama, and, furthermore, he was a missions volunteer. I had met very few young people in our years back in America who shared the same life goal I had.

　　Kiamichi youth week was in July, and I was excited — for our association would have its own cabin, and Mr. Hunt would be leading the cabin devotions each evening. I was a bit disillusioned upon arrival at camp to learn that there are pretty strict rules for HMB summer missionaries. Specifically — they are not allowed to date during their ten weeks. In the back of my mind, I had pictured a bit of special time to get to know this older man (he was nineteen, I was fifteen) and his missions aspirations. Nonetheless, in spite of that dating policy, we seemed to hit it off quite well. He had such soulful dark eyes, and they seemed so intent and interested. After all, there was no rule that said you could not confer. Mr. Hunt and I had a good number of conferences during that special week. I remember getting home from Kiamichi and Mama asking, "Well, how was youth camp?" My response must have caught her by surprise, for I drew a deep breath and gave a happy sigh, "Oh, Mama, I'm practically engaged!" I still give an inward grin all these years later, remembering that naïve fifteen-year-old girl. Bob of the soulful brown eyes had told me goodbye with the words, "I'll write you." After a few months, however, with no letter forthcoming, I decided that a letter wasn't going to happen. Nonetheless, the thought lingered in my mind.

I did not forget. Life went on, but every time I fell "in and out of like" in the ensuing teen years, the memory of those deep and intense brown eyes remained in my mind. Our time in Kinta was short-lived, for Dad and Mama were soon asked to lead a promising new mission church in Coffeyville, Kansas. Here it came: a new year, and another move. Practice doesn't make perfect, but it does lend perspective, and I was already looking ahead to college anyway. Edgewood Baptist Church in Coffeyville was a happy challenge for my parents, and they loved the people, finding special joy in inspiring them to grow in missions concern. Both my parents were gifted in personal evangelism, and their way of loving and reaching people set a sterling example for me.

Art was a junior at Oklahoma State and got home only for holidays. As a junior, I went from a tiny high school to a very large one in Coffeyville. With my mind already thinking about Oklahoma Baptist University, I simply looked on this move as a temporary one, so it didn't seem too hard. Friendships were quickly formed at church, and I began teaching a children's class and loved the new challenge. We were thousands of miles from China, but memories of the man on the steps still remained seared into my heart. I never doubted God's call on my life, although I found few young people who seemed to understand what I was talking about.

With Dad and Mama involved and busy at the church and with school during the year, summers were the only time we could go to South Carolina. Those times were always the highlights of each summer. We were only able to see Aunt Grace during one vacation time, because in 1952 she was sent to Indonesia to begin a publication ministry. Several China missionaries had gone to Indonesia to initiate work in that untouched field, and Aunt Grace joined them as the first single woman to pioneer there. At age fifty-five, Aunt Grace had to re-invent herself and adapt to a new country, new language, and new kind of work. She lived up to her name and did it with true grace. Southern Baptist missions work first began among the many Chinese of Indonesia, but within a few years, Baptists were also ministering to the Indonesian people. Indonesia is the largest Muslim nation on earth and a major challenge. Within short years, Baptists had put down strong roots and had a thriving seminary and hospital. Aunt Grace began the Baptist publication ministry and was later joined by my China favorite missionary "aunt," Fay Taylor.

Aunt Mamie retired from teaching in Columbia, and she and Aunt Rhett devoted themselves to caring for my grandparents and beloved Great Aunt Edith. She was in quite good health, but Grandmama had severe diabetes and lost a leg to it. However, she never lost that gentle smile, and it is as vivid in my memory now as it was six decades ago. I can never remember one time hearing her complain, and with her physical problems, that had to be a major achievement. She and Granddaddy were singularly devoted to each other and although not strong himself, he tenderly cared for her.

My semester at Coffeyville High School passed surprisingly quickly, and I wrote Oklahoma Baptist University (Dad's alma mater) about the possibility of early enrollment. With a good record and the credits already earned, I learned that I could enter provisionally, and if I ever wanted to get a high school diploma, I could transfer five credit hours back. Well, there appeared no need of a high school diploma if I was planning to get a college degree. (To this day, I am a high school dropout.) At the tender age of sixteen, I matriculated as a freshman at OBU. Oddly enough, I had met another summer missionary the previous year who knew Bob Hunt. I learned that he was now a student at New Orleans Seminary. My freshman year in college, I was shocked to get a Christmas card from him. No letter, just a promise to write later! I muttered to myself, *"It's already later, and I've heard that before!"*

Retrospect tells me I was very young to be in college, but at the time I thought it was exciting. I "majored" in music for about two weeks and right away saw I was out of my musical league. Switching to a major in speech was a good move, and it felt like my niche. I was inspired by Mrs. Opal Craig, an extraordinary teacher who invested energy and time in helping me develop. Math was never my strong suit, and right away I learned that if a student took twenty hours of foreign language, he or she would not be required to take a math course. Consequently, there followed ten hours of Latin and ten hours of French — and I enjoyed both, daily giving thanks for no math classes. I joined a local Baptist church in Shawnee and went by bus with fellow OBU students each Sunday. I have clear memories of the first day in Sunday School. The enrollment form asked for "Age," and I wrote "16." The secretary took up the forms and remarked, "Oh, you need to be in the Intermediate Department, not in here." I stared her down and firmly replied, "I am a college freshman, and I wish to remain in the college department." I remained.

A pure pleasure at OBU was having Katherine Timberlake as a piano professor. She was infinitely patient with a music student who had way too many poor musical habits but a willing heart. I loved to hear her tell anecdotes about her nephew, Van Cliburn, who that year, at the tender age of twenty, debuted at Carnegie Hall. I lived in a small dorm near the middle of the campus and immediately joined the Life Service Band, where I found a group of like-minded students who felt led to a career in missions. It was refreshing, because, with the exception of the dark-eyed Mr. Hunt, I had no other acquaintances with such similar goals.

That summer in Coffeyville, I got a job as a telephone operator and actually enjoyed the routine. In fact, I kept the job and transferred to Coffeyville Junior College for my sophomore year. Finding no organization on campus for Christian students, I was able to persuade Mama to sponsor a Baptist Student Union there. This junior college was mostly commuting students, so we met at break period each week. Mama had been a campus minister nearly three decades earlier but found that new times demanded a new approach. A number of students were regular participants, and it proved a bonding experience. My telephone job was back in the old days when operators sat in a crowded workspace, each on a high stool, and plugged connecting cords into the right numbers. Hundreds of times a day I would say, "Number, please," and plug them up. Admittedly, the repetition got a bit much, but it kept me awake and alert. Furthermore, it was a good feeling to get a paycheck. That summer I applied for summer missions with our state convention. Baptists' summer missions programs had impressed me ever since meeting the elusive Mr. Hunt a few years earlier. (It still rankled a bit to remember the Christmas card with the "write you later" that had ended up being a Christmas card two years later.)

The spring of 1955, our association had a School of Missions (now called Global Missions Conference.) In the 1950s, missionary guests were invited to stay in homes and taken to out to eat by members who enjoyed visiting with them individually. It was a special delight to invite a single missionary from China to be my lunch guest at a nice restaurant in Coffeyville on my day off from work. Miss Addie Cox was a tiny little lady who made a really big impression. She was seventy-five, but with the youthful outlook of a young adult. I grinned inwardly as I watched her take her silverware at the restaurant table and use her napkin to carefully wipe off each piece. That is exactly what we had always done in China. I loved hearing her tell stories of her many years of work in North China, and a couple of her hair-raising encounters with Communist soldiers and how she had rejoiced in being able to witness to them. Her bright eyes sparkled with joy as she recounted some of what God had done during those final dangerous years when she had been the only missionary left in her station.

Then she took a turn and began asking me questions. What did I plan to do with my life? I gladly took the opportunity to tell her about home in China, the man on the steps, and God's call to my heart. Then she looked at me expectantly and asked, "Are you in love, engaged, or soon to be married?" I had to tell her no — that hadn't happened yet. She looked quite crestfallen and sighed, "Oh, dear, I was hoping you were in love. You see, I live with my sister, Pat, and she adores a romance." (Upon inquiry, I learned that Miss Pat was eighty-five, ten years old than Miss Addie!) I certainly didn't want to disappoint Miss Addie, so I explained, "No, I'm not in love, but let me tell you about a young man who is my ideal of what I would like in a husband." I proceeded to tell her about the summer I was fifteen and met a summer missionary from her home state of Alabama. She seemed most interested and asked me numerous questions about this young Mr. Hunt. I explained that a friend had told me the previous year that Mr. Hunt was now a student at New Orleans Seminary. I thought no more about this conversation — but Miss Addie didn't forget it, as I was soon to find out.

Summer brought a rich experience as a summer missionary with the Kansas-Nebraska Convention. I loved the Vacation Bible Schools; summer camps; and the fresh, pioneer feel of ministry in those states. It felt especially new and challenging in Nebraska. All the summer missionaries in the area came to the state assembly in August, and it was the high point of fellowship. Lo and behold, there was one Home Mission Board summer missionary from Alabama there, and I remember thinking, *Déjà vu!* Oddly enough, during that week at the assembly, I received a letter from Miss Addie Cox. Curious, I quickly opened it to read, "I have written Mr. Bob Hunt at New Orleans Seminary and told him I met a young woman who remembered him from several years ago. However," she continued, "I didn't give him your name and address yet and will wait until you give me permission to do so." I sat there with the letter in my hand and a silly grin on my face. *Miss Addie,* I thought to myself, *you rascal!* I carefully folded the letter, tucked it away, and waited several months, because I was dating another young man at the time.

A big blow came to our family that year with the deaths of both Grandmama and Granddaddy Wells. Grandmama Ann died first, and Granddaddy Henry just quietly faded away after she was gone. They had literally been inseparable, but they only remained apart a matter of weeks. The year must have been an especially sad one for Mama because she had seldom been able to spend much time in South Carolina.

It was back to OBU for my junior year. I found it particularly enjoyable because most of the classes were in my major and minor fields. Not surprisingly, my closest friends were students who were also missions volunteers. Marie Morgan was a special friend. She was our school nurse, and we became prayer partners that year. Her serious boyfriend was Will J. Roberts, and I had the fun of being maid of honor at their wedding. Will J. and Marie ended up faithfully serving many years with the Foreign Mission Board in Kenya and Tanzania. (On a visit Bob and I made to Kenya about thirty years later, we had a glad reunion at their home.)

There were many friends at OBU, with a good number of them sharing similar life goals, but no young man about whom I was serious. When I broke up with my current beau that September, I decided to write Miss Addie and give her permission to send Bob my name and address. I always give an inward grin when recalling Miss Cox's PS to that first letter. It read, "If Mr. Hunt has any bad habits such as smoking, I would not recommend him as a nice boyfriend." About two weeks later, I received the first letter from Bob. To be honest, after awaiting a letter for three years, I was a bit apprehensive about opening and reading its contents. Taking a deep breath, I opened the letter and quickly read that Bob had reservations to attend the first-ever Student World Missions Conference to be held in Nashville in late December. He was wondering if I might be planning to attend. Great timing. I was already registered for that same conference and felt a little thrill of excitement. Plans had been made months earlier with Baptist student friends in Kansas, and I was now more eager than ever to attend the gathering.

In addition to my excitement about seeing Bob Hunt after three and a half years, I was anticipating meeting with more than a thousand young adults with whom I shared similar life objectives. One of the main speakers was none other than G. Kearnie Keegan, who had been my dad's friend in seminary and helped send him to China. Dr. Keegan was now director of the Baptist Student Ministries for the convention. Not only was he a dynamic speaker, Keegan also sang beautifully and began the conference with a challenging poem he had written. I was so impressed that I memorized it that very weekend:

> Why are you here?
> Are you more qualified than those you left behind?
> Are you more capable than they?
> Why are YOU here? Why? Why?
> Could it be that God has work for you to do?
> Work that no one else but you can do —
> Once you see the need and hear the cry of humankind.
> While you are here, your ears can be unstopped,
> Your eyes can see the world in stark reality,
> And you will know how much you do or do not care.
> But, if through carelessness, or faulty purpose on your part,
> You fail to heed the call of God,
> The cry of lost humanity,
> Satan laughs,
> Our Savior weeps.
> This hour, this day, your life has been in vain.

Bob and I saw each other that opening night — the first time in three-and-a-half years — and, yes, the spark was definitely there. I recall thinking to myself, *Miss Addie and her sister, Pat, are probably going to be very pleased.* The days, meetings, conferences, and a lot of time together seemed to fly by. At the end of the meeting, I wrote a quick note home, asking Mama if she possibly remembered what I had said three years earlier when coming home from Kiamichi. She did. I wrote her back at once, saying "Mama, that statement might actually come true."

Bob and Rosalie the summer of their engagement

TWENTY-THREE

SCENT OF ORANGE BLOSSOMS

Bob Hunt went from sending a letter every three years to writing me approximately every three days. The whole world seemed a bit brighter that spring semester at OBU, even with snow on the ground and gray skies above. I wasn't sure I was in love, but I was certainly in serious like. A number of friends commented on the new bounce in my step and were curious as to the reason for it. That semester I pursued my major studies with a new sense of purpose. Both my speech courses and those in psychology, my minor, took on new meaning. No question but that the most challenging course was a senior-level study of Abnormal Psychology. Our professor was on the staff of the state mental institution in Oklahoma City and warned our class that we were likely to catch "Intern's Disease" — fearing that we had caught one mental illness after another. He was so right. It was easy to find your own thoughts tending in weird directions, and I was ever after mindful of the "little bit of abnormal" in all of us. Of particular interest was the time we spent with the professor at the state institution observing him in clinicals. It was sometimes frightening to see how thin a line there was between being perfectly normal and mentally ill. Those experiences caused me to look at the passage in 2 Timothy 1 in a whole new light: "For God hath not given us a spirit of fear, but of power and love and a sound mind."

Oklahoma's Baptist Student Union was very active, and they had a terrific summer missions program. Two of the job locations that summer were for assignments outside of Oklahoma: Alaska and Hawaii. Yes! Hawaii! I applied that very week and waited and prayed. Word came in early spring that I was selected for Hawaii. I could scarcely take it in — home to Hawaii for the first time since my birth there. Mama and Dad were especially happy to hear the news, for Hawaii held special memories for them. By this time, Art had graduated from Oklahoma State and was now an officer in the US Navy, so Mama and Dad had an empty nest.

New Orleans Seminary was hosting a Student Missions Rally right before spring break, and Bob asked me to come, explaining that I was invited to stay with a missions volunteer couple who were his special friends. This meant I would be visiting New Orleans for the first time in memory, because when all of us went with Dad to New Orleans Baptist Hospital in 1941, I was just three years old. This trip to New Orleans was one more memorable weekend. Seeing the sights, visiting the French Quarter, and having square doughnuts (beignets) at Café du Monde became part of those memories. The missionaries and other speakers at the conference were challenging, and I relished the opportunity to take part in something so inspiring. New Orleans was abloom with spring — azaleas everywhere, and the moonlight over Lake Pontchartrain was as romantic as my eighteen-year-old heart could wish. Bob and I didn't make an official commitment to each other during those days, but there was no doubt in either of our minds. I look back and think of the comparative speed of all of this and repeat the phrase I've heard all these years: God takes care of fools, preachers, and children. I was at least two of the three, and He does take care.

Ever so quickly, it was summer — and with just one year left at OBU, I was off for Hawaii and summer missions. It did not disappoint. Mama and Dad took such pleasure in me being able to have this experience, and they were surprised at the number of people I met who remembered them from nineteen years earlier. I was asked to sing at Wahiawa Church (where Dad had been pastor) at a Sunday morning service and gave an inward groan — just wishing it had been an invitation to *speak* rather than sing! The congregation was gracious, however, and I made it through. Pastor Kong and his family took me out to lunch, and that was a special treat. This was Rev. Dan Kong, who had been a little junior boy when Dad and Mama were there in 1938. Also at Wahiawa church was Sue Saito, the state WMU director. She had been a teenager in the church during my parents' time there. I felt such an affinity for the people and the ministry and have cherished rich memories of working both at Pali View Church and Baptist Academy and Academy Church. Helping with Bible schools and summer camps were a terrific learning experience.

Somehow in the midst of all of this, Bob and I kept up a steady correspondence, both writing several times a week. I've saved his letters, and they bring a smile to my face each time I look at them and remember a young couple with stars in their eyes and believing the world well lost for love. Bob was busy on his church field in Janice, Mississippi, but we both managed to find time to make tentative plans for seeing each other again. I received a quick education about his little church in Mississippi through our summer letters. He served as their pastor (weekends only during the school terms and full-time in the summers). We decided that the quickest way to use our few weeks' break before school was for Bob to meet my plane in Dallas on August 13. We would then drive to Coffeyville, Kansas, together. It would be his first time to meet Dad and Mama. Then we would drive to Alabama, and I would meet his parents. My main recollection of Bob meeting my plane was our mutual excitement. Neither of us knew very much about patience. (Time has not seemed to help that issue.) Going down old Interstate 75, Bob pulled an engagement ring out of his pocket and thankfully there wasn't much traffic around. Between jet lag, excitement over being home again, and getting engaged, I have long remembered the week that followed. I'm sure Mama and Dad must have been thinking that all this was way too fast. Their only daughter had just had her nineteenth birthday, and here all these life-changing events were happening — getting married and finishing college within just a few months and then starting seminary, all within a single year.

I do recall a discussion I had with Dad. He reiterated, "Rosalie, you know I have always asked that you please finish college before you marry, and here you want to marry in December at Christmas break." He looked a bit apprehensive. Bob and I had actually talked about Dad's wish, and in our seasoned maturity decided we could do it all. I assured Dad that when the last semester of my senior year arrived, I would find a way to finish and keep my promise to graduate. With the sure knowledge that the world truly is "well lost for love," I figured we could come up with a way.

The following week, we drove to Alabama, and I met the Hunt family, although it was more like meeting a clan. It felt like half of Albertville, Alabama, was related to the Hunts. I was nearly overwhelmed by the number of uncles, aunts, and cousins. It was mind-boggling when Bob's mother told me she had 144 first cousins. My math couldn't count that high. The Hunts were a warm and welcoming group, and I was thrilled that they seemed to accept me at face value. It is likely this was due to their love and respect for Bob, their "preacher boy." I was happy to bask in his reflected glory.

Bob and I did find a way to honor Dad's request. The wedding date was set for December 27. We decided that after our honeymoon (which would last a whole weekend — neither of us had money), I would go back to OBU and finish the semester. Those were the days when colleges required students to return from Christmas holidays and have late January finals. Next, I would proceed to New Orleans. Upon returning to OBU's campus, I immediately visited the registrar's office. With a little coercion and a lot of planning, it was determined that I could take courses for my final semester of college work at New Orleans Seminary and transfer the credits to my OBU transcript. *Voilà!* I could keep my promise to Dad, *and* we could go ahead with wedding plans!

Dad and Mama had just moved to Wichita, Kansas, to pastor a church there, and I had no ties in that church or city. On the other hand, Bob had spent all his life in Albertville, Alabama, and his family had been in the same church all his life. We decided to have the wedding service in his home church in Albertville. However, that meant that at Christmastime, Dad could not leave his duties to come perform the ceremony. In retrospect, I wish we had gone ahead and just had a small wedding in Wichita anyway. But then, youth is headstrong and wise decisions do not always win out. I have regretted that in later years. Mama did come to the wedding, and I don't think I would have gone on with the plans had she said she could not come. I also later reflected that this was just one of a number of ill-planned choices made through the years. I frequently shake my head over that immature young person who often conceived and followed through with hasty plans before there was time to think them through.

Meanwhile, there was a fall semester following the wonderful Hawaii experience, and I had grand ideas of learning to cook along with all the classwork those fall months. With that in mind, I moved from the main women's dormitory on campus to Shawnee Apartments, where you could have a room in conjunction with a kitchen. However, it did not automatically follow that learning how to cook was built into the apartment contract. That was not part of the deal, but I did try. One glaring attempt with a cake is still vivid in my mind. That thing took a lot of time and effort and was an abysmal failure. I looked at my roommate, she looked at me, and I just shrugged in defeat. To make it worse, I slipped out to take it to the nearby residence where the neighbors had some chickens in their backyard. Maybe this cake would work for chicken feed. I recall eagerly watching the reaction of the hens and little pullets. They came, they tried, and they rejected — not exactly uplifting.

However, one providential advantage of Shawnee Apartments soon became apparent. Esther Lo, a Chinese student coming from Indonesia, had just matriculated to OBU and lived in the apartment complex. She and her two friends, sisters Dorcas and Dorothy Yau, came as college juniors. Esther and I bonded immediately. My Chinese was really rusty by this time, but Esther and I talked rapidly to each other in a mixture of Chinese and English, seeming to instinctively know what the other one meant with little or no explanation. She was highly amused at my predilection for *jyáng yóu* (the two of us referred to soy sauce by its Mandarin name). Esther frequently reminded me, "You need to name your first baby Jyáng Yóu." (Our firstborn daughter is relieved I didn't follow through on that thought.) Esther's background was fascinating. Her grandmother lived in North China and was led to Christ by Lottie Moon, then raised her children in the faith, deeply grounding them in biblical truths. Esther actually was able to come to America to school because of grateful parents whose two daughters were led to Christ by their friend Esther. In gratitude for her influence on their lives, the Yaus financed both daughters and Esther to study abroad. The three of them were terrific cooks, and we enjoyed some wonderful, *real* Chinese food. The biggest serendipity of that final semester, however, was having Esther for my prayer partner. Simply listening to her pray gave my heart a spiritual boost. It was clear that she and the Lord had a long-standing relationship, and her depth of faith gave me life lessons in what trust is all about. *(See Appendix for Esther Lo Wu's remarkable story.)* I didn't learn to cook that semester, but I gained a lifelong friend and inspiration named Esther.

Dad had a super-fun cousin about his own age who lived not too far from Shawnee and OBU, and I enjoyed several weekends there. In addition to all her other talents, Larita Moses was a tremendous seamstress, and she offered to make my wedding dress. Was ever a nineteen-year-old more fortunate? Since we planned for the wedding to be two days after Christmas, I decided to use velvet. The wedding gown was white velvet, and the bridesmaids wore red and green velvet. It's safe to say the wedding was a bit unusual and was certainly seasonal. Several of my OBU friends and Bob's sister and sister-in-law were bridesmaids, and Rev. J.O. Colley, Bob's beloved pastor from his high school years, came to the wedding to give the bride away and assist the pastor, Rev. Richard Crowe, in conducting the ceremony.

We had one guest at our wedding that meant something very special to both of us. Clarabel Isdell had lived in the house on Main Street in Albertville when a baby boy was born to the family next door. That baby was Bob Hunt, and Miss Clarabel, a recent college graduate, was a very early friend of his, doting on the new little baby in the neighborhood. A few years later, Clarabel was appointed for mission service in China, and lived next door to the Harold Halls. Clarabel was one of the well-wishers who threw rice on us as we left the church. She could scarcely take in the coincidence of having lived next door to both the bride and the groom, on opposite sides of the world no less. Furthermore, it was Miss Addie Cox, the one who played Cupid for us, who had been the greatest influence on Clarabel in her call to missions.

A week or so after our honeymoon, we both got a good chuckle out of the column in the local paper about "Hunt-Hall ceremony held at First Baptist." The society editor had written, "Following a wedding trip to points south, the new couple will reside in New Orleans." Our wedding trip consisted of a whole weekend driving along the Gulf Coast and spending our first Sunday as a couple at First Baptist Church, Montgomery. From there, Bob left to go in one direction, and I in the other. There were three weeks left in the semester, and the new bride had the romantic experience of studying late each night, taking her semester finals, and packing up the apartment in twenty-one days. Again, hindsight is forever 20/20, and this was a case in point.

Nevertheless, at the end of his semester, Bob drove to Oklahoma and got everything loaded up quite quickly. Off we went to seminary in New Orleans to begin a new period of our lives. My roommate, plus dear Esther and other friends, saw us off — and again I remembered the phrase "the world well lost for love." I also recalled having heard Dad remark a number of times during my teen years, "You can't live on love." Little did I realize all that I needed to learn, not just about people but about life and how to go about it. Sometimes the lessons were hard-earned; other times, they proved a great blessing.

The first order of business was to get in classes so I could transfer credits back for graduation. There was really not much "moving in" to do, for Bob had an efficiency apartment that is difficult to describe. Just picture an area about fifteen-by-fifteen feet (generously speaking), containing a bedroom, closet, bath, and efficiency kitchen. The minuscule size of the kitchen was an appropriate match for the minuscule size of my cooking skills. We could only get into the kitchen one at a time. Our bed was a Murphy bed that pulled down out of the wall. We had to move our two chairs in order to pull it down. The dining table was a card table set up near the kitchen "closet," as we called it. I always smile when remembering those endless tuna/noodle casseroles; and for variation, chopped wieners in ketchup casseroles; and about once a week, a hamburger from Schwagman's supermarket. That store was huge, but cheaper than any other grocery, and you could get hamburger meat (remember, this is January 1958) for twenty-five cents a pound. A good half of it was fat, of course. Our first "company" were Nelle Davidson, seminary librarian, and Helen Emory Falls, our missions professor. Bob worked during the week in the library, and kind Nelle found employment for me there as well. We had a couple of folding chairs, so the four of us ate at the card table. I don't recall the menu, and that is probably just as well. Whatever it was, the guests were gracious about the meal.

I was especially excited the first weekend of my arrival in New Orleans. This would be my first chance to go to Bob's church field in Janice, Mississippi. Some 120 miles from New Orleans, Janice is located thirty miles below Hattiesburg. The rest of the world had passed by the little hamlet about fifty years earlier. Actually, you would pass Janice by and not know you had been through town if you blinked at the wrong time. Janice was mainly one general store with a service station, Janice Baptist Church (pastor, Bob Hunt), and not far away a county school, Class 1A.

I was a little startled that first Sunday at church to sense a bit of antipathy. I wasn't expecting that; after all, these people didn't know me, and I had been anticipating encountering good old Southern hospitality. I learned the reason for the "atmosphere" from the couple that became dear friends of ours, Ruth and Preston Stoddard. To us, they were Maw and Paw Stoddard, although they were probably only in their late thirties or early forties. Preston, from Meridian, was principal of the school, and they had four active children. Bob had been having most of his weekend meals with the hospitable Stoddards, and considering my underdeveloped cooking skills, I was happy to keep up the practice. When I sounded puzzled about the somewhat tepid welcome I had sensed, Maw Stoddard laughed and explained that there were a number of mamas in the church who had designs on their single preacher and now here he goes and marries a foreigner. Well, I could understand that — and, yes, I knew about being a foreigner.

Nonetheless, that atmosphere didn't last long, and I soon felt a part of this tiny community and took its problems and needs to heart. The young people adored Brother Bob, and I could certainly understand that as well. The church rented as a "parsonage" a tiny little old rundown house that had once been part of a small farm. All that remained was the rather derelict little four-room cottage, with its brown faux shingle siding peeling in places, and a run-down little weatherboard barn a number of yards away. My main memory is of how *cold* the house was. The only heating was a fireplace, where you toasted on the front and the rest of you froze. When we got up in the mornings, it was bitterly cold, so here was a new challenge. Furthermore, the plumbing broke our first weekend there and was never repaired. We giggled a lot over one of our wedding gifts. It was a three-quart cooking pot that we aptly renamed the "pee-pot"; it saved a lot of nocturnal trips to the barn in freezing weather.

Did I ever have a lot to learn about life and living and growing up, both at Janice and at the seminary! Some of it was painful, some delightful — and some, lessons I had never thought to experience. All of it turned into great preparation for the joys and trials we would come across a world away in years to come.

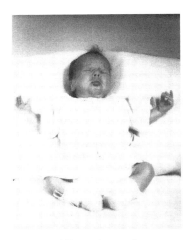

Alice at 1 month

TWENTY-FOUR

NEWLYWEDS GENERATION TWO

At only nineteen, there was so much I needed to learn about life and how to negotiate it. I also discovered that the opportunity to get to know my husband came *after* the wedding. We had so little time actually together before we married that it was important to get acquainted. Doubtless, much of what he discovered about his new bride was a shock, although he already had a good idea about my family and missions background. That had been the initial mutual tie that sparked our friendship in the beginning. Going back and forth on weekends to the church field provided a tailor-made opportunity to finally become acquainted. Bob would regale me with stories from his growing up years and what everyday life was like on Sand Mountain. I was fascinated with stories about all the relatives scattered in the area. My upbringing wasn't exactly typical, whereas his was fairly traditional for life in the southern United States in the mid-1900s.

Bob grew up on a dairy farm, on land that had belonged to his

Grandfather Hunt and adjoined his grandparents' farm. His hands were unusually strong, for they were accustomed to milking cows at 4:30 every morning and 3:30 every afternoon. Bob once said he asked his father, "Daddy, why can't we train these old cows to just give milk one time a day? It would save us a lot of work." I asked him how old he was when he began milking. After a bit of thought, he replied, "When I started walking!" He then amended that to explain it was actually about the time he was ten that he began milking twice a day with his dad, Carl Hunt. He learned what hard work was early on. However, when Bob was in high school, Bang's disease got in the herd, and they could no longer sell milk, marking the end of Hunt Dairy Farm.

Bob's brother, Joe, two years his senior, joined the US Air Force after graduating from high school and met his future wife, Catherine, in Mobile, Alabama. They married in 1952, and Catherine told me years later that she was a city girl who came to Sand Mountain knowing nothing about the country and dairy farms. Joe got a big chuckle out of her honest query, "Besides your milk cows, do you also have bull cows?" I don't think Joe ever let her forget that question.

Prior to running a dairy farm, Bob's father had owned and worked in the White Castle (not part of the chain) in downtown Albertville. Not surprisingly, his best-selling item was hamburgers. Homemade pies were not far behind. His mother, Ora, worked in a clothing store in Albertville, raised three children, taught Sunday School, sang in the choir, was active in WMU, baked wonderful cakes (including beautiful wedding cakes) to supplement their income, and kept everyone and everything running smoothly. After the dairy business had to be abandoned, Bob's father went into construction work and thrived. Nowhere in the Hunt family was the word *lazy* applicable.

Bob and Joe had a younger sister, Druscilla, who was born when Bob was eight. However, their father came from a family of seven children and their mother was one of ten. I found it both delightful and slightly overwhelming to now be part of such a large family. My new in-laws met when they were both students at Snead Seminary in Boaz, a Methodist high school founded in 1898. They were graciously accepting of me, and I didn't long feel a stranger in their home. The amount of work my new mother-in-law could turn out in a single day was astonishing. Bob grinned when he told me about her prowess in the cotton fields each summer. (I remember in my high school years trying to pick cotton on one single occasion and quickly realizing that if I had to do this for a living, I would starve.) Ora Hunt could out-pick practically anyone in her large family. She normally picked 300 pounds in a day, and Bob remembers summer days working alongside her in the fields and hearing her tell her children, "Come on, pick a little faster." I never discovered anything my mother-in-law could not do well. Ora was a remarkable woman. Moreover, she was one who exhibited a deep-found faith that propelled her actions.

One day when in a talkative mood, Ora told me about Bob's birth, and how he barely survived. I found it chilling to hear. All her babies had been born at home, and a doctor came to deliver them. With Bob, she was in labor for two days, and he was called a "blue baby," for he was born with the umbilical cord wrapped around his neck. God had plans for him, however, and Bob fought through — showing the same determination he later exhibited in tasks and challenges set before him overseas in years to come. Close calls were fairly common in the Hunt family, for his dad Carl was also born at home and arrived about eight weeks early. Carl was so tiny his mother could put him in a shoebox for a number of weeks. Mama Hunt (Bob's grandmother, who lived to be 97) loved to tell about his birth and informed me, "I could fit Carl in a coffee can!" It sounded like I had married into sturdy stock.

Bob's family had been faithful members of Albertville First Baptist Church since before his birth. He was enrolled in Cradle Roll when he was a week old, and we still have his certificate framed and hanging on the wall. Lots of our family tales revolve around church experiences, but just as many memories seem to be about food. Bob often talked about delivering milk when he was a boy. He, Joe, and their father delivered milk to numerous customers, and on the way home would often stop and get a dozen doughnuts. Bob wore a reminiscent smile when recalling all the milk and doughnuts he had consumed as a boy.

He also has vivid memories of the "deviled egg incident," as he calls it. One evening, the family had company, and his mother made a big platter of deviled eggs. Like all her cooking, the eggs were delicious. One of the dinner guests ate, and then ate some more. He finally reached for the last egg on the platter and declared, "These are so good. I don't know how many I've eaten." Eight-year-old Bob piped up: "You ate eight!" The look his mama gave him did not bode well for what would happen after the company left. I loved the story, and asked him, "Now, how old did you say you were?" Bob looked pained when he replied, "Old enough to speak my mind but not wise enough to know when *not* to." I cannot count the number of times we have told the tale of the eggs when someone brings up the subject of healthy appetites.

It always prompts a grin to remember another experience in our travels to the church field that first year of marriage. The Thursday before our first weekend trip, Bob got a paycheck from his work in the library and very happily handed me three crisp dollar bills, saying, "I want you to have some money in your wallet in case you need it. I think this will be a good plan for each week." Sounded like a plan to me, and I gladly tucked the three dollars into my purse. It was less than twenty-four hours later that we stopped to get gas for the trip to Mississippi. Bob pumped gas, then walked back to the car and rather sheepishly inquired, "Could I borrow back that three dollars?" That was the end of weekly allowances.

With several hours driving time each way, I discovered in the course of those weekend travel discussions that pastoring a small country church consisted of a lot more than preaching twice on Sunday, visiting the sick, and visiting regularly in the homes of church members and prospects. I knew about that kind of work but didn't know farming might be a sideline. The first summer of Bob's pastorate there, a particular need to finance a project arose, and church members discussed how to raise the needed funds. One generous old farmer told the congregation he would donate an acre of land to be planted in cotton for the church, the members to do the work on it, and all profits to go to this project. Everyone happily agreed, but they were not quite as happy to do the work. Raising cotton is more than planting the seeds, as Bob came to know all too well — and raising a crop extended over a period of five or six months. It ended up with Bob doing the majority of the work, mostly with help from a few of the youth. His clearest memories of that challenging money-raiser were how that pesky cotton refused to produce a bumper crop, and how those cotton bolls pricked your fingers when you harvested the crop. It further solidified Bob's conviction that he was indeed called to preach and not to plow.

I got to know some of the town's characters in the few months we remained there, most of whom were in the church. The wealthiest family in town owned the only store and pretty well controlled what went on in Janice. I was shocked to learn the plight of the scores of tenant farmers who came in weekly to the little store to buy staples and get a little gas. Living from crop to crop, most had to charge their staples and canned goods and pay when the crops came in. Those charged purchases had high interest placed on them. Furthermore, the farmers were charged *tax* on the gas, which of course already had tax figured into the price. I recall hearing of an angry confrontation in which a tenant farmer asked in dismay, "Are you even a Christian?" The owner's wife drew up in indignation, declaring, "Of course I am. I teach a Sunday School class!" I found it impossible to forget that definition of a Christian and sadly realized such business practices went on regularly and were tolerated by people who felt they did not have an option.

Bob did not cater to any local edicts, and yet was universally respected by the little community. There was one farm family that has stuck in my memory all these years — the Hegwoods. Ma Hegwood, as we called her, was part Indian, and, consequently, was looked down upon in the community. Pa Hegwood had built up his defenses through the years, and the elderly couple for the most part lived a solitary life, quietly going their own way and living mostly to themselves. Upon first arriving in Janice, Bob visited the Hegwoods and found them extremely defensive. Old Pa Hegwood declared, "You didn't have to come!" Bob answered at once, "I know I didn't. I came because I wanted to." He refused to be rebuffed, returning again and yet again, simply and quietly loving them and making

them feel accepted. In turn, the couple finally opened up and recipro-
cated his friendship. The entire little town was shocked when they first
saw the Hegwoods walk into the church to hear the sermon. This elderly
couple also gladly welcomed me, and I still remember Ma Hegwood's jars
of canned steak. I had never heard of nor tasted canned steak before, and
never have again since those months in Janice. It was delicious, meltingly
tender meat canned with gravy. We frequently sat around their table. When
any problem in the community arose, Pa Hegwood would remind Bob,
"Just button your coat up to the top, son, and don't let the trouble come in."

Preston and Ruth Stoddard were our friends and mainstays in Janice,
and going to their home for a couple of meals every weekend was something
I looked forward to the entire semester. In fact, it was Preston Stoddard
who later recommended Bob to the pulpit committee of his home church
in the Hebron community, just out of Meridian, Mississippi. (It would
be our next home.) It was also one weekend at the Stoddards when I was
nauseated two days in a row and quickly figured out why. I'm sure Mama
and Dad must have rolled their eyes and shook their heads when they
received the letter saying they were going to be grandparents. Mama, who
had given birth to me after her thirty-eighth birthday, was thinking, *My
child. My nineteen-year-old child is going to have a child.* This was clearly
another of life's adventure's in which I received on-the-job experience,
because I absolutely didn't have a clue about being a mother. After all, I was
just now a novice-in-training on how to be a *wife.*

We had been married for only a few months when I learned a bit more
about the letter Miss Addie wrote to Bob back when I was a college junior. I
was mortified that she had taken artistic liberty with my characterization of
the "young man who was my ideal of what I would like in a husband," and
interpreted that in her letter to Bob as, "This young lady describes you as
her Prince Charming." You can believe that I heard that definition repeated
many times as Bob would pass on the story about "how she chased me until
I got tired of running." In later years, people would say, "How did you and
Bob meet?" My usual reply was, "Do you want to hear Bob's story or the
true story?"

I did absorb a few lessons quite quickly. One of them was what *not* to do. Lesson one: Do not critique your new husband's sermons. There I was, fresh from a speech major where each week in class Dr. Craig would have her students make all types of speeches, and then she and the class would critique them. It wasn't always fun but was a great learning experience. I was so proud of Bob when I heard him preach the first time. He asked me that afternoon, "Honey, how did I do?" I naïvely thought he really wanted to know, so I proceeded to show my knowledge — and, beginning with a particularly good comment about his excellent communication, next went down the little list where I had jotted down suggestions. I saw the look in his eyes. Believe me, I learned in a hurry. That specific mistake was nevermore repeated, and we remained married.

Trips back and forth between seminary and Janice were a thing to be endured by early spring, because I became nauseated when riding in a car. Thankfully, that only lasted a few months, and we both decided I would live through it. In the earliest class each morning, I frequently would have to run out of the room and throw up, but the professor was surprisingly tolerant. I loved the classes: Missions, Old Testament prophets and platform leadership. By this point, Bob was in his final semester and more than ready to finish and get that degree.

In April, we received an invitation from Hebron Baptist Church, located in the Vimville community about nine miles from Meridian, to come preach "in view of a call." I thought this was really exciting, and it felt like this was our first joint adventure. In looking back these many decades later, I am sure some of the parishioners took one look at us and wondered if they were robbing the cradle. We met scores of people that day, and I clearly recall the conversation of the Irby brothers during the offertory. Descended from charter members of Hebron, Ezra and Zery were both very elderly and extremely hard of hearing. They sat together near the back of the sanctuary, and as the offertory music was played, Zery leaned over and said to his brother in a voice that his deaf brother could hear, as could the rest of the congregation, "Ezry, did they say his name is HURT?" I tried really hard not to smile. Nonetheless, the young minister must have seemed acceptable, because the vote was taken that night and it was unanimous.

Hebron proved a lasting blessing in our lives, and we formed friendships there that have lasted a lifetime. Bob became their first full-time pastor, and Hebron was his first full-time church. The church family knew from the beginning that we were aimed in the direction of international missions, so our tenure in a pastorate would not be long. The Stoddards moved back to the Vimville community from Janice about the same time, and that helped make our move to Meridian in April an easy transition. Hebron was a whole different atmosphere and culture from lower Mississippi, and I had more life lessons to learn. One clear impression entered my mind those decades ago and has solidified through the years that have followed: Language, customs, ideas all vary from place to place and time period to time period, but basic human nature does not change.

Hebron took us right in and made us part of the church family, and we both looked forward to finishing seminary and moving full-time to the field. In May, I returned to OBU for graduation. Nausea was still a frequent problem, and I wondered how to deal with it at the graduation ceremony in an auditorium without air-conditioning and wearing a heavy, black robe. Thankfully, I took along some dried apricots and nibbled on them to keep the nausea at bay, especially when walking across the stage. I recall thinking that our unborn child would be graduating from college even before being born. Within days, it was back to New Orleans and Bob's graduation, then on to our new church field and preparing for baby. In the 1950s, gender reveal parties had not even been thought of, so we would wait along with all our family and a new church family to see if the first little Hunt would be a boy or a girl.

Alice with Ho Se Mo and Ho Shien Sun
in Wichita, Kansas, 1960

TWENTY-FIVE

THE FAMILY GROWS

Hindsight is a marvelous thing that provides perfect clarity. I mistakenly assumed that the average church would be as loving and accepting and enthusiastic as Hebron Baptist Church. Alas, time told a different story, but we loved our year and a half with wonderful, caring, serving people who illustrated the concept of living out your faith. Most of the families in the congregation had ancestors who had belonged to Hebron, and the majority came from families who had been charter members. There was amazingly little bickering, and we saw none of the factions that are the bane of many a church. Above all, we loved their missions zeal and concern. They were always ready to do a bit more.

Hebron's Woman's Missionary Society was a model of stability and missions involvement, and they nurtured me as I drew on their wisdom and common sense. One of their many ministries was quilting to help the community. A group would gather each week, visit, and make quilts on order as well as many for the needy. All of the quilting proceeds went each year to the Lottie Moon Christmas Offering. However, Hebron had no missions organizations for children when we arrived, but they happily agreed with plans to organize two GA groups, choosing a leader for each auxiliary, with me assisting both groups. At the end of the first year, when we had a GA recognition service, the entire congregation was impressed with what the girls had learned and done. Bob and I were touched to realize that every girl in Hebron's congregation became a part of Girls Auxiliary.

Bob and I visited in every home, and, in each, were invited to return for a meal. Hebron really pampered us. That certainly didn't help my sketchy cooking skills, but Bob was happily well-fed. There was one clan that became especially close friends — the Smiths. Old Brother Albert Smith, as we called him, was a long-time deacon and particularly noted for his propensity for speaking out, even in the middle of a service. His family loved telling us the tale of the Sunday morning years earlier when a rather crusty guest preacher had publicly scolded the congregation by declaring, "The devil just gets in you people!" Brother Albert spoke up immediately, "The devil can get in the preacher, too!" The visiting minister was none too pleased.

It was with the two younger Smith families that we developed a close and abiding friendship. Ginnie and Ralph Smith and Ouida and Billy Smith took turns inviting us to Sunday dinner. We were quickly spoiled. I do not recall preparing one Sunday meal the entire time we lived in the Vimville community. I can still taste Virginia Smith's tender, crispy teacakes and Ouida Smith's orange-pineapple sherbet.

Bob and I were interested in getting as much of a variety of experiences as we could, feeling it would help us on the field one day soon. We visited in homes, which gave us frequent opportunities to share the gospel with individuals. We worked in Bible schools, which didn't seem like work at all. Then, teaching youth in Sunday School helped me learn more than the students. Additionally, there was an active Lauderdale associational WMU organization, and I gleaned many practical ideas from those older women.

Bob and I both enjoyed going into the city of Meridian. It was a large, bustling, friendly town about ten miles from our home. However, there was one discordant note that niggled at my mind and brought an uncomfortable pang to the heart. Not long after we arrived, I went to Meridian one morning with an older woman from the church. On the road into town was a small wooden structure over on the right. As we were passing, I asked in curiosity, "What is that building?" It appeared sadly alone and weather-beaten, and was about the size of a very small cottage. It looked like it had never seen a coat of paint. My friend casually replied, "Oh, that's the black school." Puzzled, I naively asked, "Why don't they go to the Vimville school?" My new friend looked blankly at me and said, "Oh, we've never done that. Schools are segregated. We go to ours — they go to theirs." I was struck silent. You would think I would have been more cognizant of the realities of 1958, but in all the rush of school and staying busy, the depth of the problem had never struck this Oklahoma girl. Of course, I had heard of Brown vs. Board of Education, but had not encountered the reality of things as they were in this part of the country. I finally summoned up a few words and looked at her with honest dismay, "But why?" Now she looked surprised and frowned a little, "It has always been that way." That answer did not satisfy me.

Disturbed, I talked to Bob about it that evening, for this whole idea and concept was most troubling. He and I, of course, had grown up in very different environments — he on the Sand Mountain area of north Alabama and I a world away in China, where I was one of those in the minority and had a fairly good take on what it felt like to be an outsider. Bob was surprisingly untouched by prejudice. I did not realize how rare that was until years later when we lived in his home area and saw the lingering effects of prejudice there. Meanwhile, at Hebron, we had a great core of faithful members who were regular on Wednesday nights at Bible study and prayer meeting. About this same time, one of the deacons asked Bob in one of our Bible study periods, "Pastor, what does the Bible have to say about race and prejudice?" I did not realize until much later what an unusual question that was to hear voiced in the South in the mid-1950s. Bob promised the deacon he would do some investigation on that, and we would have a Bible study centered on the issue of race in the near future. Writing the Christian Life Commission of the Southern Baptist Convention, Bob asked for material and brochures they might have that addressed the question.

In a matter of weeks, we had a Bible study, plus a question-and-answer period on the topic. Considering what a hot button issue it was, we had an extraordinarily congenial session. Bob gave out material from the Christian Life Commission that dealt with the issue, and a good number of members took their material home to read more thoroughly. The discussion was very measured, although it was obvious there was a clear difference of opinion. I spoke briefly about what it felt like to be "outside of the norm," explaining that it was difficult for me to understand racial prejudice. Bob led a study of the Scriptures related to the topic, and people seemed keenly interested. A number of members genuinely wanted to understand the origins of prejudice, and what gap there might be between what they had seen (or been told) all their lives and what God's Word really said. After a week or so, we heard no further questions, but over a year later, the issue very certainly came up again. The whole subject, nonetheless, prompted me to do some self-examination. *In what ways was I prejudiced?* Too many. It's always easy to note another person's flaws. *What about my own?* (This ended up being a lifetime of self-examination. Prejudice takes so many guises. Sometimes it really hurts to "know thyself.")

By late summer 1958, you would have thought the whole church family was expecting a new baby in their own homes, from the interest and thoughtfulness of the membership about the new little Hunt who was to arrive in December. They showered us with baby gifts, and each gift made our impending arrival just that much more anticipated. Gratefully, the nausea had subsided, but there was another challenge or so. For some quirky reason, October arrived, and I began to itch all over, especially at night. I know Bob must have found it disconcerting to wake up in the middle of the night to find me sitting up in bed with a hard-bristle brush, scratching my back. I also became unusually skittish. We lived in a neat little house the church had rented as a parsonage for their first full-time pastor. There were no other houses close by, however, and it was a bit isolated. When the itching woke me up, I began hearing sounds. On one particular night, around midnight, I needed to go to the bathroom (which was just next to our bedroom) but could hear a noise outside the window. I stopped scratching with the brush in order to listen intently. There came the sound again, just like the loud hissing of a cat. We didn't have a cat. After the third hiss, I grabbed Bob in the middle of his stomach and whispered loudly, "Bob, wake up, there's something out there."

It took him a moment to rouse, and I pleaded with him, "I've got to go to the bathroom, and you have got to help me." (I had no sense of logic by this point. Go figure.) I know my voice was agitated, and he was really puzzled by this time, "But what can I do?" I could read the question in his voice. "Stand guard," I replied. "Stand guard for what?" he was really confused now. "Get your rifle and stand guard. There's something out there, and it sounds like a wildcat or maybe a bobcat! I'm scared to get up by myself." Bleary-eyed and stumbling, Bob found his old rifle from boyhood hunting days and obligingly came to stand guard. I insisted he *had* to be able to hear that wildcat. By the next morning, Bob found it funny and enjoyed repeating the wildcat story. That was more than six decades ago, but I have never lived down the bobcat incident, for such creatures had not been seen in those parts for many years.

Living in a small, tight-knit community meant that my ears were bombarded with all sorts of birthing "war stories." Some of them I just shrugged off, but others were a bit jarring. I remember dear Mrs. Eula Carlisle, small and up in years but still very spry and a super cook. Mrs. Eula delighted in reminding me that her son, Harold (now a deacon at Hebron), weighed a whopping fifteen pounds when he was born. Just the thought gave me heart palpitations.

Late in October, Bob and I were able to make a quick trip to Alabama to visit his parents, driving through the night so as to have more than just one day to visit. About 2 a.m. that foggy morning, we were driving along a particularly curvy Alabama road when Bob missed a curve, and we went careening off of the road. The car was finally stopped by a railroad track with our car sprawled across the tracks. I appeared to be in one piece, but the baby, who had been very active for several weeks, now did not move. Bob was petrified that the baby was hurt. He quickly hiked out of the spot and found a country house not too far away. Arousing the owner, he soon returned with an old man bearing a lantern. The farmer politely inquired if I was injured. Seeing that I seemed in one piece and coherent, he said, "Well, only problem is — a train usually comes along every morning 'bout this time." At this point, all I could do was scramble out of the car and ask the farmer to take us to the small hospital in the nearby town to check on the baby's condition. A frightening two hours followed, with no movement on baby's part. We were both brought to happy tears when the little one finally decided to tap on the wall to let us know all was well.

Like all expectant first-time mothers, a day seemed like at least a week. By November, I was more than ready for our baby to arrive, and so was Bob. Our obstetrician was in Meridian, and we were looking at a due date near Christmas. That meant we had another two months to go. However, the newest Hunt was so eager to arrive that it happened before Thanksgiving. Going into early labor on the morning of November 19, I somehow needed a whole day to accomplish the task. This was in the days before husbands were routinely allowed in the delivery room, although Bob did stay by my side as long as he was permitted to. However, the nerve-wracking hours stretched on, and in the early evening a young doctor from the church came by the hospital and kindly took Bob out for a steak dinner. I have never quite let Bob live that down. He did return in time for the arrival of Alice Esther Hunt, all five pounds and eight ounces of her. She was a tiny thing, but with beautiful little cheeks just like a chipmunk's. Had she weighed one ounce less, doctors would have treated her as a preemie. That one important ounce meant we were able to hold her and keep her near. The whole church celebrated, as did our parents when we called with the news. Of course, Mama got emotional when we told her that her first grandchild was named Alice Esther.

Alice's first Sunday at church was four days after her birth, and she quietly lay in her infant seat next to the piano as I played for the services. Everybody in the congregation felt like she was *their* baby and treated her accordingly. We never lacked for a babysitter or someone to rock and love on our little one.

In our next communication with the Foreign Mission Board, we reported on the new family member and how our plans were still on target for service in Asia. We realized, of course, that the board required a certain amount of practical experience prior to appointment. Furthermore, we had to keep in mind that the earliest age the board accepted for career appointment was twenty-four, and I had a good bit of time remaining before reaching that mark. Meanwhile, in addition to several church responsibilities, I was able to gain firsthand experience giving piano lessons, instructing several young children in the congregation who wanted to learn to play. It was a salutary lesson in patience for me; however, I don't know what kind of help the children really got. Lynda Smith of the Smith clan was a quick learner, and she actually made her teacher look good. In years to come, she left her early fledgling piano teacher far behind.

Bob and I often talked about what kind of mission service might best suit our skills and interests. Whatever it was, evangelism was the main aim. Bob had felt for some time that working with students was where he was most at home. He had a knack for relating to young people and bonded with them quickly. I often watched him interacting with high school and college students and recognized in that interaction a natural gift. He just instinctively loved young people, and they could sense his acceptance of them just as they were. When we talked of where to go and what type of ministry would be most effective, both of us knew that Asia was tugging at our hearts. To be honest, I never seriously thought about any other part of the world, and long before Bob and I ever met, the Orient had been foremost in his mind as well. Nevertheless, a particular type of work was something we needed to think through. Teaching would be needed wherever we went, and Bob was torn between preaching and working with students. We looked at various scenarios where he could hopefully do both.

The Foreign Mission Board suggested that it would be helpful to get some practical experience working directly with students to see if that was a fit. Possibly that would help our minds and hearts settle on a specific area of ministry. This sounded like a plan, so we prayed together for God to provide clarity and an opening. Happily, both were not long in coming. Within a few months we were contacted by Baptist leaders in the northern part of Mississippi. They had heard of Bob's interest in students. There was a brand-new growing and thriving junior college in Booneville, and they were looking for a campus minister. Would Bob be interested? Yes.

Nevertheless, even with the possibility of this timely opportunity in the field of his interest and skills, we felt a real sense of loss at the thought of leaving Hebron and our wonderful friends. Despite having known from the beginning that we would only be there temporarily, we suffered separation pangs at leaving the Hebron community. We felt like a part of us was left behind because they had become so dear. By that point, we were getting a picture of how painful goodbyes were going to become in our lives. There would be no way to escape them.

The most difficult part for the church family was saying goodbye to "their baby." We were leaving the Smiths, Camps, Carlisles, Stoddards, Irbys, Butlers, and Rasberrys, among others — all of them dear to us. Alice was not quite nine months old when she got her first taste of goodbyes. Although still too young to understand, it would soon be a common occurrence for her, although that did not make it easy for either the child or the parents. (Time proved that on every furlough, we had a great reunion with the Hebron family, and the ties still linger.) Here we were, once more headed into a new experience and the next step on the road to appointment.

Alice, age 3

TWENTY-SIX

A STEP CLOSER

Here it came again — the mixture of sad and happy. Goodbyes to Hebron friends were wrenching. At the same time, welcomes to the new adventure were exciting. Bob was walking into a new position with no guidebook to follow — just instructions to try what he thought might work. Northeast Junior College was several years old but had never had a campus minister. There were six counties in north Mississippi that made up the school's board, and the college already had several thousand students. Knowing Bob's instant rapport with young people and their love for him made me feel this was going to be a perfect fit. It was — and he thrived on being with the students on campus, having lunch with them each day at the student center, and beginning Bible studies as well as relating them to our local church.

Alice was about eight months old when we moved to Booneville, and we stayed busy keeping up with her pace. Of course, we were convinced she was the smartest baby that had ever been born. Her first words were the predictable "Da Da," but when she really wanted something, she would call out "Ma Ma." She had a lively attachment to her pacifier, and her mother, of all people, could relate to that — having "kept" her own thumb as a built-in pacifier for eight years. We allowed the pacifier to remain until Alice began speaking in phrases and could say, "Paci — I need it." Paci accidentally disappeared, and I figured that was a lot easier than a thumb.

First Baptist Church Booneville became our new church home. Loving history as I had since the early years in China, the church and community both appealed to me. First Baptist was founded right after the Civil War and just ten miles away was Brice's Crossroads battlefield. It wouldn't be long before I was teaching American history at the local high school and would be hearing some interesting versions of "The War," as it was called, and the reasons for it. As I had already come to realize in our frequent moves from one place to another, each town had its own special flavor. Booneville certainly did, and we met some wonderful new friends who remained special friends through the years to come. Six decades ago, America had more provincialism and regionalism than it now does — probably because in the 1950s, there was not as much mobility in society. Most of the folk in Booneville had been there all of their lives and did not know anything else. It behooved us to adjust and learn the needs of people in our new home, develop friendships, and put down roots.

Before we had been in Booneville many weeks, a completely unexpected incident began one evening when our doorbell rang. We opened the door to find the pastor of our new church standing there looking extremely anxious. A scholarly man, he was clearly more at ease in a classroom than in one-on-one relationships with members of his congregation. We quickly invited him in and asked him to have a seat and make himself comfortable. He immediately began wringing his hands and haltingly told his story. Apparently, a member of the White Citizens Council in Booneville had an acquaintance who belonged to the citizens council in Meridian. We nodded politely but were puzzled as to what this had to do with us. We personally certainly knew nothing about the group, either in Meridian or in Booneville. In fact, we were unaware there was a local council. Our only knowledge of the organization was the obvious fact that it was racist and not something with which we wished to be associated.

Our pastor sounded disturbed as he described the situation. It developed that a man in Meridian who was in the White Citizens Council of that city had visited in the home of his uncle in Hebron community, saw the brochure from the Christian Life Commission about "The Bible and Race," and asked his uncle, "Where did you get this?" His uncle explained that his pastor had given him the material one Wednesday night in prayer meeting when they were having a Bible study about race. The nephew asked if he could borrow the brochure and, of course, was given permission. The brochure was then discussed at the next council meeting, and the members "wanted that pastor investigated." The long and short of it was that the Meridian council notified the Booneville council that a preacher had just moved to Booneville who was "going to promote integration in their schools."

Our new pastor was so distraught that he had brought along some medicine to give to Bob, saying, "Here's a sleeping pill. Maybe it will help you get some rest tonight." Bob and I both looked taken aback as he continued, "I'm afraid you are going to have a cross burned on your lawn, and I just don't know what to do." Bob tried to calm his anxiety, assuring him we would talk this over with friends in the church, and please don't worry — we would certainly be able to sleep that night. (We did, but wondered if our pastor got any sleep himself.) As quickly as possible, Bob gathered together some deacon friends and explained the circumstances. Immediately, a man in the group volunteered to investigate. He was a well-to-do businessman with many connections in Mississippi and, having appointments in Meridian that same week, volunteered to check the matter out and calm the troubled waters. Thinking ahead, the Booneville man took along a tape recorder (this was before the days of cell phones and instant videos) and visited several leaders in the Hebron church, asking them about the now-infamous "integration prayer meeting." Deacon after deacon gave the same answer: "We did a Bible study on the topic of race, and we learned what the Scripture said." Bob and I had a good laugh when the Booneville businessman reported one old deacon as saying, "Why, no, we didn't talk about integration. We talked about the Bible. Now, that preacher's wife ain't always real friendly, but they aren't out preachin' integration." There was no cross-burning, but I will admit to checking out our front lawn every morning when we first got up.

My first love was missions involvement, so joining the Woman's Missionary Society was a logical first place to get involved at the Booneville church. I also offered to help with the children's missions organizations and, within weeks, found myself the leader of the older Girls' Auxiliary. In the 1950s, GAs were nine to sixteen years old, so I worked with the intermediate students. They were eager to work on Forward Steps (now known as GA Journey), and the girls were thrilled to have their first presentation service the following spring. The church also had a good number of senior high and college-age young women, partly because we had a junior college in Booneville. Leading Young Women's Auxiliary was a challenge in a different sort of way, because I was just about two or three years older than the girls. However, the YWAs quickly became my favorite group. I still remember one evening when we were meeting in a home, and I had to leave the room for a few minutes. I came back down the hall in time to hear them discussing "Mrs. Hunt," and one said to the others, "My goodness, I hope I'm that well-preserved when I'm that age!" (I was twenty-two years old.) The association had an active WMU organization, and for some reason and almost before I knew it, I was the associational director. It was pretty obvious that no one wanted the job and the responsibility of the office. Although I was young and green, they were happy to find young feet willing to take on the task. I learned a lot more from those older women than they ever did from me.

Since teaching overseas was what I was hoping to do, Bob and I realized that some practical experience in a formal classroom was important. Although I had a college degree, I did not have teaching certification. Providentially, Blue Mountain College, a small, well-established school for women, was located less than thirty miles away. I only needed a couple of courses to complete certification, so I enrolled and commuted three days a week. Blue Mountain was a Baptist school with small classes and a lot of individual attention. It was my first experience of traditional Baptist education in the Deep South. Blue Mountain College was founded shortly after the end of the Civil War by General Mark Lowrey. At the time I was there, their president was Dr. Lawrence Lowrey, grandson of the founder. There had been four presidents in its history, and all were Lowreys: father, son, then another son, and last, the grandson of the founder. I quickly realized the name Lowrey in Mississippi was synonymous with Baptist, and the beautiful little campus was a piece of history itself.

I remember just one thing from the course in education taught by Dr. Samuel Sargent, who seemed to me as if he himself had been there since Blue Mountain was founded. He was a tall, stately, white-haired gentleman who had likely given those same lectures for the past thirty or more years. My one memory? A maxim of Dr. Sargent's — with which he began nearly every class: "Be not the first by whom the new is tried, nor yet the last to put the old aside." And through the years I have occasionally found use for that phrase — although I did not always follow its instruction. However, I needed to resolve one sticky problem at Blue Mountain before I could obtain the proper teaching credentials — practice teaching. My major field was speech, and the local high school did not offer such a course. The solution to the problem was actually a delightful one. I was allowed to practice teach with the Blue Mountain speech classes, which proved to be an ideal experience for preparing to teach at the same level overseas. Mid-term, one of the speech teachers developed a health problem, and it turned into a blessing for them to have someone to step in and teach her classes.

In retrospect, I wonder how we had all the energy that allowed us to maintain the pace we did. It's exhausting now even to think about those schedules, but to a young couple in their early twenties, it felt natural. There was a pastor and his wife of another Baptist church in town who had fallen in love with Alice. Evelyn Grubbs, the pastor's wife, agreed to add "babysitter" to her resume and keep Alice on the days I traveled to

Blue Mountain. Alice quickly learned to call her "Me Maw." (Late in 1961, when we were appointed as missionaries and left Booneville, Me Maw cried, and so did Alice.) Alice was talking, crawling, and pulling up on furniture with impressive speed, but she seemed hesitant to walk. It wasn't until she had a head to toe physical, as required by the mission board prior to appointment, that we discovered the reason. She had severe astigmatism in her eyes, and the world appeared distorted and blurry to her. She was quickly fitted with tiny little glasses, and her world blossomed — she could finally see it clearly. We felt guilty that we had not known, but it certainly didn't stunt her then nor in the future.

Bob thrived at working with college students and usually had lunch with several of them, or sometimes individually with a student who had a special need. I cooked only one meal a day, for he ate at the student center, and, depending on the day and need, would often have a hamburger with one group and then a little later, with another. I learned to never serve burgers at home. Baptist churches in the six area associations sponsored the new campus ministry, and Bob did a lot of weekend visiting with churches in the area. When summer came, he was invited repeatedly to hold revivals in various churches. That first summer, he had ten revivals and was appreciative of the fact that he could re-use many of the same sermons because each audience was different.

Having completed teacher certification, the next step was to find a job. I interviewed with the high schools both in Booneville and in nearby Baldwin. At the time, neither school offered a foreign language course, and both were eager to begin one. Baldwin wanted to offer French, and they and I were green enough to think that my ten hours of college French would be adequate preparation to teach. To this day, I can remember just one clear moment of that job interview. Taking Alice with us, we met with the principal, who worked at making friends with our little toddler. The principal jovially took her on his lap and engaged her in conversation. However, Alice was totally focused on just one thing. The man had a large and protruding brown mole on one cheek, and Alice was fascinated by it — continually trying to pull the mole to see if it would come off. The poor man kept pulling his face back, and the interaction developed into a tug of war. I wanted the floor to open up and swallow us. It was a shock a few days later to actually receive an offer to teach there, so I figured the principal must be desperate. Nonetheless, Booneville High School also offered me a job teaching Latin, American history, and speech (my favorite). I chose Booneville for three reasons: It was closer, I could teach my favorite subject, and the principal didn't have a mole.

Teaching high school juniors and seniors when just twenty-two years old myself presented some unique challenges. I was a little surprised to find myself enjoying all three subjects and watching the students respond and learn to build new skills. It was just like teaching Sunday School in one very important way: I acquired more knowledge than the students. Having three preparations for three different subjects each day was time-con-suming but a helpful learning tool for organizing and time management. Sure enough, the speech class was particularly enjoyable. I could finally put into action some of the things I had been studying for several years. This time, it was part of my job to do critiques, so I worked at wording them in positive ways. Since Latin and speech were elective courses, those classes were mostly made up of students who *wanted* to be there. American history was required, but I loved the subject so much that some of the students actually realized that history could be fascinating. It was here that I learned all-new reasons (to me) for America's Civil War. One boy's uncle was a super defender of the "glorious Old South" and kept on fighting the war. To him and to his nephew, it was the "War of Northern Aggression." The young nephew was convinced that the war was fought "because the North was jealous of the South." I quickly realized it was best to simply discuss the lessons we could learn from history and move on to something else; otherwise, we would have had a daily skirmish in class.

Both Bob's parents and mine tried to visit when they could. It was a long drive from Oklahoma for my dad and mama, and Bob's father seldom had more than two or three days he could get away. The visits were doubly precious because we realized that soon these visits would not be possible, even with a long drive. Dad and Mama realized what was coming more keenly than did Bob's parents, and even more than we did. The pain of separation was not new to them. Dad and Mama had experienced it when *they* went overseas, and now they had a new look at separation, because their *children* would be leaving. Alice had a marvelous time with all the attention from doting grandparents, and I tried to store up in memory the treasure of those days together to pull out and enjoy later, when the only visits possible would be in memory.

We were looking toward appointment in another year or so; therefore, we began the process of filling out preliminary forms and getting started on writing the required autobiography. I began with a flourish, thinking this would be a simple matter, and that it was likely to be a short account. After all, there were only twenty-two years that needed to be covered. Think again. Long is always easier than short, and this task took a good bit of soul-searching.

For the first time ever, we would be in the same place two straight Christmases. Considering the number of moves we made during our first three years of marriage, this was an accomplishment. In the weeks prior to Christmas, Mama and Dad were able to make the drive to Mississippi and stay for an entire week, and Alice loved all the attention. The following week, we drove to Alabama so Alice could enjoy time with her Hunt grandparents as well. She now had a new cousin, for Bob's brother and his wife had a little son named Wayne. They had been married a number of years and had not been able to have children. Wayne was a tiny baby when they adopted him, and we all fell in love with the adorable little fellow.

Now a new wrinkle entered the picture. While in Alabama, my suspicions were confirmed: There was another little Hunt on the way. Immediately, we began calculating how this might impact the appointment procedure. In fact, it proved to be ideal, for it appeared we might actually be ready for appointment by the end of the following year. Nonetheless, there was one nagging little detail over which we had no control, something we could not change at will. It might require some divine intervention.

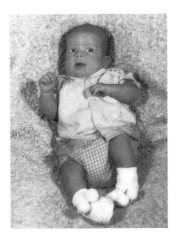

Jody at 6 weeks

TWENTY-SEVEN

An Unfolding Future

Time was not ours to control. I was just twenty-two, and the minimum age for appointment was twenty-four. We wrote of our concerns to the Foreign Mission Board's area personnel consultant, and after several weeks he replied — first reiterating Board policy, but then adding that the personnel committee would look into the protocol. The fact that I had grown up as an MK in China might be an influencing factor, he noted. That wasn't exactly reason for great hope, but it made us think it just *might* be possible to leave for the field prior to my twenty-fourth birthday.

Meanwhile, I was about to gain some new experience in a couple of areas that had not previously crossed our paths. First Baptist Church Booneville had a very accomplished organist who had served for a number of years. The lovely old pipe organ was about as old as the sanctuary itself, and we loved hearing the great hymns of faith that Mrs. Nabors played each Sunday. However, shortly after our move to Booneville, the organist was in a horrific car accident that nearly severed one of her feet; she would need several surgeries and rehab. That meant there was no one to play the organ, so I suddenly became organist by default. A talented young musician who had grown up in the church came to visit his parents for a week and graciously took time to give me a three-day crash course in how to play a pipe organ. That first Sunday my feet were shaking as badly as my fingers, but we made it through. If organs could "talk," that one would likely have admonished me, "Young lady, just settle down and let me do the work."

Thankfully, morning sickness was more manageable with this baby — and that was fortunate because, for some unknown reason, I was asked to be the young adult on the pastor search committee when Booneville's current pastor left to take a teaching position in Texas. As with the organ, I knew nothing about pulpit search committees other than they often opened themselves up to a lot of criticism if they didn't "make a good pick." Would you believe, we traveled to a number of places and listened to many sermons — but ended up in Kentucky, literally in Hatfield and McCoy country, where, just the week prior to our visit, there had been a shoot-out on Main Street. After a period of time, all the committee, with the exception of this young adult, concurred that the Kentucky preacher was the right choice. This choice really did not seem to be a "fit," in my thinking. I finally bowed to pressure and agreed to agree. That turned out to be a mistake, but I learned a bit in the process about when to compromise and when to stand firm. Thankfully, the new choice soon moved on and there was more than one prayer of gratitude offered.

Both the GAs and YWAs and my high school students were excited about our soon-to-arrive baby, and with the nausea in abatement, teaching was no problem. This was in the days when expectant mothers wore maternity clothes rather than their regular wardrobes. It was not "the thing" to show a pronounced baby bump, so I dressed according to current style, wearing a loose top that modestly covered baby and me. As the spring progressed, so did baby. One of Booneville high school's "characters" was Nob Peek, a fifth-year senior. Nob was a terrific football player who had used up his four years of high school eligibility but still didn't have quite enough credits to graduate. The football team gladly welcomed him as unofficial coach, and it seemed like he spent a lot of time roaming the halls of BHS. Nob was certainly not fashion-conscious, and always went around with his shirt tail out, never mind that the school had a strict dress code that decreed no untucked shirts and shoes required at all times. The code didn't bother Nob.

One morning in April, Nob strolled down the hall and stopped at my classroom door to listen to a bit of American history. Used to his drop-in visits, I didn't pay much attention until he interrupted our history class to comment, "Miz Hunt, look at you — and I thought the school dress code says no untucked shirts." Of course, he got the giggles and sniggers he expected from the students, but, for once, I thought of a likely retort right on cue. Fixing him with a school-teacherly look and an eagle eye over the top of my spectacles that inspected his own clothing, I responded, "Nob Peek, if *your* shirt tail is out for the same reason *mine* is, we better find you an obstetrician." The class loved it, and I never had any more sass from Nob after that.

First period every morning was Latin, and it became an established routine that on the last school day of each month, our principal, Mr. Tudor, would go to each classroom to deliver that teacher's salary for the month. This became a time game for my first period Latin students. Mr. Tudor would deliver my salary check about 8:15 or 8:20; it never varied. Then, at approximately 8:25, more steps could be heard coming down the hall. Bob was coming to pick up my check. The students vied with each other to see who could first hear "Brother Bob," as he was called, coming to get the check. Bob always entered Latin class to find the whole room smiling at the veracity of their private wagers and predictions.

I had mixed emotions when school ended the last week of May. The year had been a terrific educational experience, and realizing we would likely be leaving the country within the next year, it was apparent I wouldn't be walking those halls anymore. The future was exciting, but I loved those kids and would sorely miss them. Meanwhile, I was still playing the organ at church and learning to get along with the ancient pipes. This was in the days when trios were popular, and I was part of our church's women's ensemble. The minister of music's wife, a deacon's wife, and I made up the trio, and we frequently sang for services. Coincidentally, all three of us were expecting a baby that fall. In August, we were singing for a service when we noticed smiles on first one face and then another in the audience. Then, in the midst of the special, it dawned on me why so many were grinning. For some reason I can't recall, we had chosen to sing "How Long Must We Wait?" Thankfully, the three of us finished the last verse before losing control of our own faces.

Bob and I spent a good number of hours looking at information from the Foreign Mission Board related to requests for student work in Asia. There were several, but our eyes kept returning to the request from Taiwan. There were several women serving in student work there, but no men. The lure that also drew us to Taiwan was its proximity to mainland China. In fact, Taiwan was known as the Republic of China, and mainland China had the title People's Republic of China. Taiwan felt like China to us, and that spoke to our hearts. In talks with the personnel consultant, we learned that the Board, in light of my past experience of overseas missions firsthand, would move forward with the appointment procedure now since I had recently turned twenty-three. This was exciting. (Naturally, in not many more years, getting older wouldn't be all that exciting.)

Before going any further in the appointment process, however, we awaited the arrival of baby. Of course in 1961, we did not know if we were expecting a boy or a girl. Our obstetrician was in Tupelo and used the excellent regional hospital there. Tupelo was about thirty minutes from Booneville and quite convenient. However, during the last week of September, there was an outbreak of hepatitis in north Mississippi. This time around, just like prior to Alice's birth, not only was the terrible itching back, but my skin turned yellow and even my eyeballs took on the same sallow hue. Dr. Bourland, our obstetrician, was quite concerned and decided we needed to get this baby born. Consequently, I checked into the hospital, the doctor did a quick procedure, and baby number two, thankfully, didn't wait a long time but was born before eight that evening. The amniotic fluid was bright yellow — but this little fellow's skin was pink with no hint of sallow. The doctor never figured it out, because I tested negative for hepatitis. And now there was a daughter and a son, and our cup of joy was really running over. Jody was slightly over seven pounds, strong and healthy and with lungs that worked really well.

Both sets of grandparents were elated, and in about two weeks, my parents were able to come from Oklahoma and have precious days with their only grandson. Realizing how rare such opportunities were going to be, we all made each moment count. The following week, Bob's parents came, and it looked like Granddaddy Joseph Carl could not bear to put Jody down. He would just sit and hold him for long periods of time, content simply to look down into the sleeping face of his grandson who bore his name, Joseph. In fact, both grandfathers' names were now the baby's as well, Joseph Harold Hunt. This tiny baby was not much longer than his name, for he also had a third name, after a dear friend from Corinth, Mississippi — Delbert Forsyth. Delbert had lost his battle with heart trouble just months earlier. On Jody's birth certificate it reads Joseph Harold Delbert Hunt. Time would prove that Alice and Jody would be my parents' only grandchildren, and they were loved unconditionally on both sides of the family.

Often during the night when giving Jody his bottle, I would sit quietly rocking him in the little vintage Victorian rocking chair in which Bob's mother had rocked her three babies. Lightweight and armless, its soothing motion had lulled little ones to sleep many a time. I often daydreamed about sitting and rocking our little ones in this chair half a world away and remembering how all of us were part of the cycle of life and of living out God's plan for each one. Taking that small rocker to Taiwan with us was like taking a tangible piece of "home."

Bob and I were now actively engaged in the appointment process and submitted our autobiographies to the Foreign Mission Board personnel department. These gave a view of our lives, education, and our accounts of God's direction. It took a lot of soul-searching and introspection but made us even more conscious of the sense of call we both had experienced. That was also the time when it first began to dawn on me that God does not just call us "one time" but that we would have repeated experiences of understanding His will and direction. Within a month, it was time for a complete physical and a professional psychological evaluation. The Foreign Mission Board asked that we have these done at New Orleans Baptist Hospital. The psychiatrist was also in New Orleans. The medical exams were, thankfully, quite routine. However, the psychological evaluation was the first such testing either of us had experienced and was certainly an eye opener. Of course, there were multiple forms and questions. Thanks to a minor in psychology, I was just conversant enough with psychological terminology to know what I *didn't* know.

At the final consultation with the psychiatrist, he handed me the evaluation report based on the multiple tests and went over the chart with me. I saw one particular spot on the graph that looked very skewed in the lower direction. Puzzled, I asked him what this was. He gave a little smile, replying, "There are several questions thrown in that monitor the honesty of the patient's answers." My eyes must have looked questioning, for he continued, "For example, one question states: My table manners at home are just as good as they are out in public." The little smile still on his face, he explained, "Anyone who answers 'yes' on that is obviously lying." My face turned red, and I pled guilty. Thankfully, that one question didn't sink me beyond reproach, for both of us were cleared psychologically. I still remember that incident, however, and often "check" my own reasoning to see if it meets the honesty test.

Appointment week in Richmond was a high moment. Nearly sixty years later, I cannot remember a lot of details. I do recall earnest conferences with Board staff about needs for student workers in various parts of Asia. Several countries were appealing, but none spoke to our hearts as did Taiwan. As part of the final process, we met with the East Asia committee, and those members quizzed us thoroughly on our calls, doctrine, and goals for the coming years. We were asked to give our testimonies, and as I was telling about the man on the steps, one member of the committee began to weep. I seriously wondered if I would be able to keep my own composure.

Most of that week is a blur after many years. It is largely a memory of special hours of inspiration and commitment. One staff member after another asked about Mama and Dad, and Dr. Cauthen felt like one of his own MKs was coming for appointment. I recall an FMB staff member entering the conference room where we missionary candidates were gathered, and asking, "Which one of you is Alice Wells Hall's daughter?" It was Rachel Newton Dickson, who had sailed on the ship with Mama to China in 1929, now an emeritus missionary working on staff. My parents could not be there for the appointment, but this marked a time of fulfillment for them, with their daughter going even as they had gone. (Just short weeks ago, I came across a copy of what I said at the service. One sentence of that testimony made me smile: "In 1947 in Chinkiang, China, my brother Art and I were discussing what we wanted to be when we grew up. I told him, 'I'm going to be a missionary.' Art quickly chimed in, 'And I'm going to be a millionaire and support you.'")

That moment of the culmination of those dreams of so many years was nearly like an out-of-body experience. Dr. Baker James Cauthen, president of the Foreign Mission Board, concluded the service with a charge to the ten new missionaries. Dr. Cauthen told about Alice Wells and Harold Hall going to China, meeting there and marrying. He spoke of those years in China and our family ties, and of feeling like we were his own children speaking at this service. I sat there with my mind transported back to memories of a nine-year-old child, realizing that God's call is bound neither by age nor geography.

Orientation for the field during the early 1960s was eight days at Gulfshores Baptist Assembly. We met with a number of couples and single missionaries headed to several fields on different continents. Orientations are much longer now, but, in 1962, we were "pushed out of the nest" in just slightly over a week! I recall group meetings where couples shared their calls and goals, of wonderful fellowship over meals, and short periods of recreation. Most vividly, however, I remember the messages of Dr. Cauthen. Listening to the FMB's president was another trip down memory lane, as I remembered a little eight-year-old girl at the dinner table in the Cauthen home in Shanghai on Christmas Day 1946. One statement of his has stuck just like Velcro in our memories for sixty years. Dr. Cauthen looked at each one of the assembled young adults preparing to spread out across the globe and quietly reminded us, "Do not ever forget. Take your clutter in your hands — not in your hearts."

Jody was only a few months old during the days and weeks of shopping, preparing materials, packing as compactly as possible, and traveling to say final goodbyes. We spent several weeks with my parents who were now in Wichita, Kansas, and then made Bob's parents' home headquarters for packing and preparing, using every little nook and cranny of space possible in the crates in which we shipped household goods. I tried to "guess ahead" about birthday and Christmas presents for the little ones, and clothing sizes as well. We didn't know how much we would be able to purchase in Taiwan. Now, of course, it is very different, with a lot of things available in many countries.

One clear impression remains with me from those weeks of preparation for departure. Bob's father would sit for hours on end just holding Jody and playing with him, or simply gazing into his sleeping face. It was as if he was storing up treasures to remember for the coming five years when he could not be with the children. On the other hand, my parents did have an inkling of the pain of separation by a literal ocean and a number of years. It was something new for Bob's parents and a difficult reality with which to grapple.

Naturally, Jody was blissfully ignorant of all the movement and impending change going on around him as he ate, slept, and charmed his family every day with smiles and coos. His pediatrician had discovered Jody had mild adduction in both of his feet. This condition is commonly known as pigeon-toes, and the doctor felt like it could be quickly remedied while he was tiny. Therefore, he was fitted with little shoes that looked like we had put the wrong shoe on the wrong foot when he wore them. Time and again, when we spoke in churches those months prior to leaving for Taiwan, we would leave Jody in the church nursery — and later come to pick him up, only to find the nursery workers had switched his shoes from one foot to the other. Sure enough, he only needed to wear those stiff little corrective shoes a few months, and his feet grew normally. When we would take them off to give him a bath, a blissful look would come across his face at having those heavy old shoes removed. (Jody ended up winning the 100-yard dash in his ninth-grade track meet, running on perfectly straight feet.)

We were shocked at the number of times people would ask us in honest perplexity, "Are you going to take your children *with* you?" At first, we were astounded that anyone would think otherwise, but over time, it became apparent that many people thought it dangerous or foolhardy to take children to some foreign land. I finally began explaining to people how happy I was that my parents *had* kept me with them and allowed me the privilege of being part of their ministry.

Alice was old enough to be aware of the impending changes swirling around her. For the most part, she enjoyed the excitement. I recall one time, when we had done something special for her, something only adults could have done, she commented, "Say, what if everybody in the world were kids at the same time, and we didn't have any grownups to take care of us. Boy, that would be a mess, wouldn't it?" (I have often reflected that most of the adults in the world can also make a mess of things on their own, grown up or not.)

By this time, Bob and I were looking ahead with that all-too-familiar mixture of feelings — excitement at our impending arrival in Taiwan, meeting people yet unknown but loved already, all mixed with the angst of goodbyes. We flew from Birmingham to Wichita on March 5, 1962, carrying in our hearts the memory of the looks on Carl and Ora Hunt's faces — stoic but resigned, rejoicing for us, but sorrowing in thinking of the five years of separation. We swallowed the lumps in our throats several times as we got the children settled in for their first of a lifetime of airplane flights. That night we landed in Wichita and spent three weeks with Ho Shien Sun and Ho Se Mo. Our children always called my parents by their Chinese names. (In time, they were known by these names by all of our larger family.) Dad and Mama loved every moment of our time together, and all of us soaked up family and America and memories to last for five long years. They knew what to expect, of course, because they had experienced this before, except going in the other direction. They handled it with grace, and that made it easier for us.

Boarding the flight in Wichita while handling a three-year-old and a not-quite-six-month-old baby was enough of a challenge and distraction to hold back some of the tears of that goodbye. For me, this time in San Francisco was different indeed from sailing out under the Golden Gate Bridge in 1946. A whole new life of missions involvement was stretching ahead, and we had no way of knowing just what to expect. We only knew the One on whom we depended. The depth of our faith was sure to be challenged over and over again. At this point we could simply envision and trust. The night before we flew overseas, the lingering fragrance of a special conversation with Mama lodged in my thoughts. It was when Mama reminded me of the message of her favorite lines from Longfellow, "Rosalie, print on your mind, 'Lives of great men all remind us, we should make our lives sublime, and — departing — leave behind us footprints in the sands of time.'" The clearest memory of all then flooded my heart with resolve, as I saw before my eyes the outstretched hands of the man kneeling on the steps. We were actually being handed the opportunity to fulfill the call of that Christmas morning. Guided by God's grace, we were on our way to share the gift that never ends — God's unspeakable gift.

AFTERWORD

This afterword is not actually an epilogue, but, rather, a preview of the sequel to this volume. My original intent was to write in one volume an account of the lives of two generations in a missionary family. It didn't turn out to be quite that straightforward, for the story spanned nearly a century and a quarter and would not conveniently fit in one volume. Work on the rest of the story has already begun — as I weave a way through a wealth of memories and materials, including literally thousands of letters that flew across the ocean between 1962 and 2020.

What began with ministry in Taiwan in 1962 evolved through the years to include work in eight different countries of Asia, each with its own unique flavor and challenges. Some moves were planned ahead; others occurred because of world conditions. The journey took us from Taiwan back to America, then to Hong Kong, followed by mainland China. The Philippines came next, before church planting in Australia, then stints of itinerant ministry in Singapore, Malaysia, India, and ultimately back to the Philippines.

The sequel will move through periods of several world crises — both man-made and natural — and will be influenced by the vicissitudes of several world powers. It encompasses more than two generations, just as the work of missionaries in scores of countries continues in new ways — as old avenues of ministry often close, and we as a denomination seek new approaches to never-changing heart and spirit needs.

Each letter, each memory stirs emotions ranging from joy to uncertainty, from determination to sadness, from grief to elation. No moments were more beautiful than reunions in China after more than thirty-five years of being unable to reconnect with Chinese friends in that beloved country. I hope the totality of the journey will evoke a sense of coming full circle, from the day Aunt Grace arrived in China, to my parents' investment of their lives there — and, ultimately, until I was able to return and renew the bonds the previous generation forged so many years earlier. Those moments of reunions exceeded my fondest hopes. Plan to come along on this journey into the lives and needs of people half a world away, friends with whom we were privileged to minister. It is a journey of legacy.

Esther and Sammie Wu with the Hunts

ESTHER'S STORY

Esther Lo was one of the first residents to welcome me to Shawnee Apartments my senior year at Oklahoma Baptist University. The grandiose idea of "mastering the art of cooking" prompted this move to apartment living in September 1957. I was newly engaged, with a wedding date set for December 27. That didn't provide a wide window for developing culinary skills prior to marriage, but young love is ever optimistic. In years to come, I realized that the main learning that went on during that semester at OBU was gifted me through the life of a beautiful soul. Esther's friendship became one of God's lasting gifts to a young student with so much to learn.

Because of our "China connection," Esther and I bonded at once. The highlight of that final semester of OBU was Esther Lo as my prayer partner. Our friendship has lasted these more than sixty years, no matter that half a country often lay between us — and, frequently, half a world. In an indirect way, it was Esther's deep faith and commitment to Christ that made her own college education a reality and allowed her to get an education in

America. I found her life story a testimony to God's miraculous working in a life. It is truly a "once upon a time" tale.

In the early 1930s, two young Chinese women met when both matriculated as students at a well-known seminary in north China. Lo Su Wen had come from far away in Fujian Province in southeast China. On the other hand, Chii Shiu Tsen had grown up in north China. Her parents were from Shan Dung Province, and Shiu Tsen's mother had come to know and trust Christ through the influence of Lottie Moon. Her mother, in turn, then raised Shiu Tsen and her siblings to know about God's love. And, as God planned it, following seminary graduation Shiu Tsen went with her friend Lo Su Wen to serve in Quanzhou, Fujian Province. Both young women became involved in evangelistic ministries in that area. "Bible women" was the name frequently given to those women who felt God's call to share the gospel, and these two were both called and gifted in what they did in reaching women throughout the area. Shortly after arriving in Quanzhou, however, Shiu Tsen met her dear friend's brother, Lo Han, and the two fell in love and married in 1933. The Lo family, just as the Chii family in north China, were second-generation believers — something quite rare at that time in China. All of the seven children in the Lo family were educators as well as believers, and Chii Shiu Tsen was warmly welcomed into the Lo family. Lu Su Wen rejoiced that her dearest friend was now also her sister-in-law.

Meanwhile, Lo Su Wen continued her church ministries, and Shiu Tsen, her beloved new sister-in-law, gave birth the next year to a healthy baby girl. Lo Han, the baby's father, chose as her name Ping Ren, which means "Equal Responsibility." To him, it was a declaration of the value of their firstborn, a little girl born in a land where the birth of boys was considered most important. With this auspicious choice of names, Lo Han declared that this precious little girl was equally valuable in God's eyes, and the young couple forthwith dedicated her to God's service and keeping. Unexpectedly, however, when baby Esther was only eleven months old, she contracted a severe case of whooping cough. Her mother immediately took her to the hospital and remained at her side the entire time, nursing her back to health. While at the hospital, however, Esther's young mother contracted typhoid fever and died just days later. Esther, not even a year old, was now motherless. Lo Su Wen was away in itinerant ministry when her sister-in-law's death occurred — and she was devastated to return only to find her best friend dead and already buried, her little niece motherless. That very day, Su Wen vowed that this precious child would be as her own child and she would dedicate her to God's service.

Within a short time, Esther's father and his other brothers and sisters were all asked to go to Indonesia to establish schools there for the large Chinese population. Su Wen felt she should remain in her ministry in Fujian Province and wanted to keep her niece with her, raising her as her own daughter. Lo Han, the bereaved father, left for Indonesia, not realizing that war would soon tear Asia apart and make it impossible for him to see his only child again for many years. Lo Han never remarried. Meanwhile, Su Wen remained in her church ministry in Fujian. Esther's grandparents, who felt too old to adjust to another world, likewise remained in China. Unknown to any of them, a deadly menace was soon to come — Japan invaded the country, and the following years were filled with uncertainty and the constant threat of peril, with frequent bombing and families torn apart by war and death.

Su Wen dedicated her life not only to her Christian ministry, but also unstintingly poured her love into the little girl who had truly become like her daughter. Young Esther's grandparents doted on this one precious child who became especially dear to them. The elder Lo was a long-time deacon in their church and Esther's grandmother a leader among the women. At a very young age, Esther came to faith in Christ, and, in later years, her aunt-mother often reminded her of how the people in their city came to identify Lo Ping Ren as the little girl who always encouraged her young friends and anyone who would listen to just trust Jesus and He would change their lives.

Esther's mother, as she came to call her aunt, kept life as normal as possible for her child during war conditions. Japan controlled large areas of China by 1937, and bombing raids became all too frequent. Esther and her young friends attended school as much as possible, and Sunday School and church were every bit as important in her young life as was school. The young ones were taught how to run to the safest place during air raids, and, if possible, get to a bomb shelter. A life-changing moment occurred in Esther's life when she was just a little girl. Japanese bombings became more and more common, and late one morning as she and several of her little friends were returning home after Sunday School, the ominous sound of air-raid warnings shattered the silence of the quiet Sunday morning air. Frantically, the young children looked around for a safe place. The nearest sturdy-looking structure was, of all things, a Buddhist temple, complete with large open foyer area containing a giant bell suspended in a tower. Just beyond was the temple, a substantial building. The children raced to the foyer and called to the worshippers kneeling before the altar in the temple — pleading for permission to come in for shelter. These children from Christian homes had never before entered a temple, but they desperately needed protection.

However, the worshippers at the altar recognized the children as Christian and called out in alarm: "Oh, no, no — you are Christian. You will bring us bad luck!" The frightened children then pleaded, "Please, please, may we stay out here in the foyer area then?" Granted permission, the frightened children put their arms around each other and huddled together on the ground, trembling and praying as the sound of bombing grew closer and closer.

Without warning, there was a giant "thud" — and sudden and total darkness. Too frightened for words, the children simply prayed. Muffled explosions could be faintly heard. Esther only recalled crying out to God to help them — weeping and pleading for protection. At long last, and as if from a far distance, came the sound of receding bombers. Then absolute silence. The children were in total darkness and totally puzzled. In the strange, pitch-black darkness, they began reaching out with their small hands, feeling for what might be in front of them. Their hands touched metal. Metal? Iron? Slowly the truth dawned — they had been completely covered by the giant bell hanging in the temple foyer. Not a child had been touched. God had provided a bomb shelter for His little ones.

Then came a new realization. This was a giant bell — it weighed tons. They were trapped. The children began yelling, calling out for help. After what seemed like a small eternity, voices could be heard calling,"Hello! Hello! We hear sounds. Anyone there?" The frantic children chorused, "Yes! We are here! Under the bell! Look under the bell!" Muffled sounds could be heard, and within minutes, people were using a giant metal pole like a crowbar to dislodge the giant bell so the children could emerge. All the onlookers were in awe. Here were the Christian children from the town — unharmed. And as the children stared around in wide-eyed amazement, they saw all around them the rubble of what had been the Buddhist temple. Everything was in ruins. Not one of the worshippers had survived. That moment lived forever in the heart of Esther Lo, as she saw the literal evidence of God's protection on her life. Esther recognized with absolute certainty that God had a purpose for sparing her, and she vowed to both find and fulfill that purpose.

At long last, Esther and her mother (as she called Su Wen) were able to go to Indonesia in answer to the call of a church there who asked Lo Su Wen to join their staff. This meant that after fourteen years, Esther would finally be reunited with her father. The next years of her life, through high school and then attending a seminary, were spent in Indonesia. Esther was the only Christian among the 3,000 students in her high school, and she quickly earned the nickname, "Hallelujah Lo." She grinned about the name when telling her story, for it ended up being a term of love and respect from her fellow students. Esther, young as she was, influenced many lives with her radiant testimony, including that of the Yau sisters. Dorothy and Dorcas were the daughters of a wealthy rubber plantation manager. Much to the dismay of Mr. Yau and his wife, the two daughters insisted on going to China for college. Of course, China was under Communist control, and the Yaus feared that if their daughters went to university there, they would come under the influence of Communist doctrine and end up losing their precious freedom. Mrs. Yau knew Esther Lo and appreciated her influence on the youth of their city. She talked at length with Esther, earnestly asking that she "talk some sense" into their daughters. Esther not only became good friends with Dorothy and Dorcas, but in the process, led them to faith in Christ. And with their newfound faith, their desire to receive an education in a Communist country faded — and Dorothy and Dorcas determined instead to go to America for their higher education. In deep gratitude for this change of heart, Mr. and Mrs. Yau not only financed their daughters' education, but also sent Esther as well. All three girls completed their education in Baptist institutions in the United States. In 1955, the three friends matriculated at Southwest Baptist College in Bolivar, Missouri, and in 1957, transferred to OBU. And that became my great blessing.

As we talked about our childhood and our families, Esther happily told me about Sammy Wu. Back in China days, when Esther had been in elementary school, one of her pals had been young Samuel (Sammy) Wu. He, too, came from a Christian family, and they loved playing together. Esther later moved to Indonesia, but after several years a mutual classmate put the two in touch with each other again, and their correspondence began. Before Esther finished college, God provided a way for Samuel to come to America to complete his education as well. Their correspondence got serious, and romance blossomed. Esther and Sammy married and moved to Atlanta, where Sammy did his medical internship. His residency took them to Texas, and both attended Southwestern Seminary. Four years later, Esther received a doctorate in religious education, and Sammy acquired not only a medical degree but also an MPH (Master of Public Health) from UC Berkeley and a Doctor of Public Health from Johns Hopkins.

God has used Esther and Sammy in countless ways and on several continents in the ensuing years — healing, preaching, teaching and raising three amazing daughters. Rebecca, the oldest, did a concert tour of Europe and Israel at the age of eight, playing the piano for entranced audiences. She is an educationist in St. Louis, teaching gifted children and giving piano lessons. She has taught Sunday School for thirty years. Elizabeth, the second daughter, is a federal attorney in Richmond, Virginia, and leads colleagues in a weekly Bible study group. Sarah, the youngest, is a CFO in Winston-Salem, North Carolina, and very active in church ministry. Esther and Sammy rejoice that all three girls have married fine Christian men.

One of this remarkable couple's greatest joys has been to return to both China and Indonesia a number of times to teach and preach, as well as renew friendships with family and others there. Both of them have powerful testimonies, whether speaking in Chinese or in English. Who would have thought that a motherless little baby born in a country torn by war (and saved by a bell!) would have ended up impacting hundreds of lives, and spreading sunshine wherever she found herself? Even in a new millennium and six decades after college days, I still smile inwardly when remembering the move that was supposed to lead to good cooking. Instead, it led to a lifelong friendship — God's gift that keeps on giving.